A ROSE CROIX ORATORY

ROSICRUCIAN REFLECTIONS AND RESOURCES

FROM A KNIGHT OF THE EAGLE AND PELICAN

C.R. DUNNING, JR.

A Rose Croix Oratory:
Rosicrucian Reflections and Resources from a Knight of the Eagle and Pelican

Published By:

Stone Guild Publishing
P.O. Box 250167
Plano, TX 75025-0167
http://www.stoneguildpublishing.com/

First Paperback Edition Published 2023

ISBN-13 978-1-60532-077-9
ISBN- 1-60532-077-3

10 9 8 7 6 5 4 3 2 1

THIS WORK IS DEDICATED TO
DIVINE LOVE

"Who is this who appears like the dawn,
beautiful as the moon, bright as the sun,
awesome as an army with banners?"
Song of Songs 6:10 ISV

"Love the Lord your God with all your heart, all your soul,
all your strength, and all your mind. Also, love your
neighbor as you love yourself."
Luke 10:27 NCV

"So these three things continue forever: faith, hope, and love.
And the greatest of these is love."
1 Corinthians 13:13 NCV

"God is love. Those who live in love live in God,
and God lives in them."
1 John 4:16 NCV

ACKNOWLEDGMENTS

First, special recognition is owed to my late teacher, mentor, and dear friend John F. Miller, III, Ph.D., who died while this book was being written. His influence is most evident in Chapter 3, which he read a few months before his death. John was very pleased with it, and even passed it along to some of his other friends and former students. It means a great deal to me that we shared that meeting of hearts and minds as one of our last interactions.

Another mentor and dear friend who influenced this work was Jim Tresner, Ph.D., 33° G.C.. We shared a special love for the Rose Croix Degree and had many wonderful conversations about its symbolism and philosophy. He too has passed from this world, but it wasn't hard for me to hear his voice as I wrote.

This book also significantly benefits from the invaluable contributions to Rosicrucian historical scholarship made by Christopher McIntosh, Tobias Churton, Susanna Âkerman, and Frances Yates. The work of Arturo de Hoyos in the literature of Scottish Rite Freemasonry has also been of great assistance.

Thanks go to the Fort Worth Valley of the Scottish Rite for providing a meaningful experience of initiation into the 18th Degree, which is still memorable to me after more than 30 years. Special acknowledgment is owed to the Guthrie Valley, which has done so much to welcome and support my efforts to provide contemplative experience and esoteric education in Masonry.

For spiritual, philosophical, and fraternal camaraderie and encouragement to serve others through contemplative advocacy, facilitation, and consultancy, I am indebted to the brothers of the Academy of Reflection and the Masonic Legacy Society, as well as my closest companions in Rosicrucianism and esoteric Christianity. I am truly grateful to M∴A∴, R∴D∴, A∴S∴, C∴R∴, and T∴A∴ for welcoming me into the systems of Rosicrucianism or Christian esotericism they have each represented.

Sincere appreciation, affection, and thanks are extended to Lisa and Kevin Main of Stone Guild Publishing for their dear friendship and their generous support in editing and publishing this text.

I am grateful to my friend, Greg Kaminsky, for agreeing to write the foreword for this book. His work as an author and podcaster extraordinaire has been instructive and stimulating for me and many others.

Warmest thanks, admiration, and respect go to T∴F∴S∴ for being a constant source of inspiration and care in my explorations and expressions of Light, Life, and Love.

I am indebted to my departed dear parents for raising me in a Christian home where our spirituality valued love, community, and Nature. Much admiration and respect go to my beloved sisters and their consistent dedication to family and Christ.

Finally, this book and so many other things would not be possible without the kindness, understanding, support, and dear partnership of my wonderful spouse, Susan. Thanks, babe.

TABLE OF CONTENTS

Illustrations	11
Foreword by Greg Kaminsky	15
Preface	19
Part One: Foundations	25
Introduction	27
Chapter 1: A Cornerstone	31
Chapter 2: The Rosenkreuz and the Rose Croix	59
Chapter 3: The Masonic Ethos	83
Part Two: Reflections	105
Introduction	107
Chapter 4: Psychospiritual Chivalry	111
Chapter 5: From the Cubic Stone to the Mystic Rose	117
Chapter 6: The Alchemical Mystery of the Rose Croix	137
Part Three: Resources	159
Introduction	161
Chapter 7: Cabala	165
Chapter 8: Magia	215
Chapter 9: Chymia	253
Chapter 10: Service	307
Afterword	329
Appendix	343
Glossary	351
About the Author	365

ILLUSTRATIONS

Important Note: This text is illustrated with many symbolic images, most notably the emblems from the gifted Lutheran theologian, Daniel Cramer. The original collection of Cramer's emblems, *The True Society of Jesus and the Rosy Cross* (1617), was reprinted and expanded in later editions and other works, including *Emblamata Sacra* (1624), *Emblematum Sacrorum* (1627), and *Octaginta Emblemata Moralia Nova* (1630). It is very important to understand that his emblems, as well as those from various other sources, have been taken out of their original contexts. In fact, the numbers on Cramer's emblems have been removed for their use in this volume. Thus, the provided or implied interpretations of many images do not necessarily reflect the original intentions, even when agreeing with other scholars and practitioners. Some persons may understandably regard this practice as disrespectful or inappropriate, but it is hoped that this use of the images prompts further attention to them and their sources.

Outside Cover: *A Rose Croix Oratory*, Ryan Flynn, 2022.

Inside Cover: *Tracing Board for Princes of the Rose-Croix*, artist unknown, c. 1820.

Dedication: *Emblem from Knight Rose Croix*, Chapter 18, *Morals and Dogma of the Ancient and Accepted Scottish Rite*, Albert Pike, artist unknown, c. 1860.

Part One Frontispiece: *Superaedificor*, from *The True Society of Jesus and the Rosy Cross*, Daniel Cramer, 1617.

Chapter 1 Heading: *Mollesco*, Cramer.

Chapter 2 Heading: *Radicabor*, Cramer.

Page 77: *Retort and Pelican*, artist unknown.

Chapter 3 Heading: *Amo*, Cramer.

Page 93: *Unity of Divine Attributes*, C.R. Dunning, Jr., 2020

Page 100: *Mystic Ladder of Kadosh*, artist unknown, c. 1860

Part Two Frontispiece: *Illuminor*, Cramer.

Chapter 4 Heading: *Nec Citra Nec Ultra*, Cramer.

Chapter 5 Heading: *Emigrandum*, Cramer.

Page 123: *Fuxi and Nuwa*, artist unknown, c. mid-8th century.

Page 124: *Rebis*, from *Azoth of the Philosophers*, by Basil Valentine, 1613.

Page 125: *Masonic ourobouros*, from *Hermes Trismegistus, Old and True Natural Path* OR: *The Secret of How to Prepare The Great Universal Tincture Without Glassware, For Humans And Metals, by a True Freemason*, Adam Friedrich Böhme, 1782.

Page 127: *Azoth*, from *Theatrum Chymicum*, Stolzius von Stolzemburg, 1614.

Page 129: *Tree of Life with Lightning Flash and Planetary Correspondences*, Dunning, 2019.

Page 130: *Sefirot on a Human Silhouette*, Dunning, 2020.

Page 131: *Man with Spiral of Planets*, from *Theosophia Practica*, Johann Gichtel, 1696.

Page 133: *The Cubic Stone and Mystic Rose,* Dunning, 2020.

Page 135: *Rose Cross Lamen*, Hermetic Order of the Golden Dawn, c. late 19th century.

Page 135: *Dat Rosa Mel Apibus*, from *Summum Bonum*, Robert Fludd, 1629.

Chapter 6 Heading: *Revivisco*, Cramer.

Page 139: *Cross of the Hermetic Masons, from Knight of the Sun*, Chapter 27, *Morals & Dogma*, Pike, adapted from *Dogme et rituel de la haute magie*, by Elphas Levi, 1861.

Page 140: *Cross of the Four Elements*, Dunning, 2021.

Page 141: *Fire and Water Axis*, Dunning.

Page 142: *Air and Earth Axis,* Dunning.

Part Three Frontispiece: *Qui Sitit, Bibet*, Cramer.

Chapter 7 Heading: *Ex Fructibus*, Cramer.

Page 168: *Ancient Etz Chaim*, from *Portae Lucis* (1516), attributed to Johannn Reuchlin.

Page 169: *Tree of Life with Furniture of the Tabernacle*, from *Oedipus Aegyptiacus*, Athanasius Kircher, c. 1652-1654.

Page 171: *Tree of Life with Three Pillars*, Dunning.

Page 172: *Lightning Flash of Creation*, Dunning.

Page 174: *Tree of Life with Abyss and Veils*, Dunning.

Page 189: *Four Worlds*, Dunning.

Page 190: *Four Worlds Concentric*, Dunning.

Page 205: (1) *The Luther Seal*, attributed to Lazarus Spengler, 1530. (2) *Andrea Coat of Arms*, Jakob Andreae, c. 1550. (3) *Cross Within Wreath of Four Roses*, from the frontispiece of *Speculum Sophicum Rhodostauroticum*, Theophilus Schweighardt Constantiens, 1616.

Page 206: (1) *Dat Rosa Mel Apibus*, Fludd. (2) *Monas Heiroglyphica*, from *Monas Hieroglyphica*, John Dee, 1564.

Page 211: (1) *The Rose Croix Jewel*, unknown. (2) *The Cubic Stone and Mystic Rose*, Dunning.

Chapter 8 Heading: *Fidens Non Videns*, Cramer.

Page 233: *Drawing the Sign of the Rose+Cross*, Dunning.

Page 238: *Chaplet*, Dunning.

Page 242: *Supernal Triad*, Dunning.

Chapter 9 Heading: *Probor*, Cramer.

Page 264: *Staff of Aesclepius*, unknown.

Page 270: *Rosary*, Dunning.

Page 275: *Tetragrammaton*, Dunning.

Page 276: *Silhouettes with Sefirot and Tetragrammaton*, Dunning.

Page 277: (1) *Christus tetractys*, from *Libri Apologetici*, Jacob Boehme, 1730. (2) *Silhouette with Pentagrammaton*, Dunning.

Chapter 10 Heading: *Mellifico*, Cramer.

Page 309: *Compassion Compass*, Dunning.

Page 326: *Fidelis Sum, and Cresco*, Cramer.

Afterword Frontispiece: *The Fall of the Tower of Babel*, Cornelis Anthonisz, 1547.

FOREWORD

BY GREG KAMINSKY

Author of Celestial Intelligences: Angelology, Cabala, and Gnosis: Giovanni Pico della Mirandola's Quest for the Perennial Philosophy

The book you hold in your hands is actually much more than just a book. It is the result of a labor of love – one man's quest to become better than he was, involving a lifetime of work, including years spent learning from some of the greatest teachers. Yet, this book is even more than the result of extraordinary effort, it is also the result of divine grace descending in response to his effort to learn and grow.

I have known Chuck Dunning for almost five years and been following his work for even longer. During this time, I have been regularly impressed with his warmth, fraternal spirit, compassion, tenderheartedness, intelligence, knowledge, and wisdom. Of all the Freemasons that I've met and known over the years, few have the level of dedication, accomplishment, and capability to do what Chuck has displayed. That is why I am such a devoted follower of his work, a reader of his books, and why I was thrilled when he asked me to write the foreword to this volume.

Rosicrucianism has always held a very special place in my heart. Perhaps it was the mysterious origins of the tradition, or the manner in which they gathered together various strands of esotericism to syncretize them into an authentic spiritual path, or the way that members never professed themselves to be one, or that their purpose was to heal the sick at no charge, or their desire to reform society at every level, or perhaps the combination of all of these motives that led me to study the Rosicrucian writings and practice their methods. But more likely than not, it was the emphasis on love as the basis for life and the pursuit of wisdom that won me over. Regardless, I was hooked and never really let it go. I find the Rosicrucian philosophy and tradition to be sublime, inspirational, and something I feel drawn to as a way of being and knowing. That is why I spent so much time and effort devoted to learning about and understanding what it meant to be a Rosicrucian, how this tradition spread from Europe to the New World, how Jewish Kabbalah came to be adopted by Christians, and how Rosicrucians employed alchemy as a means for healing and spiritual growth.

Along with my devotion to the Rosicrucian tradition, there were several books that guided my way and both informed and inspired my studies. Paul Foster Case's *The True and Invisible Rosicrucian Order* was the first, followed by the *D.O.M.A.* manuscript published by Manly P. Hall, and more recently by Michael Martin's edition of the *Fama Fraternitatis*, with commentary that interprets the documents in a more mature manner. But until now, I had never encountered a book that informed and inspired in such a way that the path was clear, accessible, and traversable.

Yes, Brother Chuck Dunning's book is primarily concerned with Rosicrucianism within a Masonic context. However, even if one is not a Freemason, the concepts and exercises provided within are certainly valuable and practicable. But if one is a Mason and interested in following this path, you could not ask for a more thorough, well-considered, thoughtful, and inspiring guide than this.

Brother Chuck's absolutely beautiful, sublime, and pointedly accurate devotional poetry is a very fitting accompaniment and demonstrates accomplishment of the authentic understanding of this spiritual path. These odes are stunning in their clarity. From my perspective, this clarity and ability to express it is only gained by one who actually lives the words.

The inclusion of the emblems of Daniel Cramer is such a special touch and a reminder of the origins and ultimate meaning of the Rosicrucian tradition. Accompanying each chapter is a sacred emblem whose contemplation is a doorway. They are some of the most supremely sublime symbols I have ever seen, and it is a blessing for them to grace this book.

I cannot actually imagine a better gathering of author and subject than Chuck Dunning and Masonic Rosicrucianism. As I mentioned, since the time I met him, Chuck has demonstrated the accomplishment of virtue, the embodiment of fraternalism and love for humanity, a keen intellect, and devotion to and knowledge of the traditions of Freemasonry and Rosicrucianism beyond anyone I know. For him to author this text and share it with us is a huge blessing. He honors the origins of the Rosicrucian tradition, its philosophy, the teachings on Cabala, alchemy, magic, and its integration with Freemasonry, particularly within the Scottish Rite. Even his insights into the creation of a Christian Cabala that borrowed from the Jewish tradition, a thorny issue at best, is mature, well-considered, and kind. Finally, Brother Chuck graces us with his words on service and most importantly, love as the basis and result of this spiritual path. It would be accurate to say that while reading this book, I was moved between respect for the impeccable communication of knowledge and feelings of heartfelt emotion when encountering sublime poetry and the underlying intentions beneath the words.

Chuck Dunning is a true and worthy guide. This book is an authentic presentation of the Rosicrucian philosophy, from its inception in the seventeenth century to its modern expressions. The inclusion of his personal experiences, reflections, insights, and devotional verses, along with the sublime symbolic artwork, ensures that this book is one that you can depend on as you traverse the path. It is accurate, well-considered, intentionally crafted to aid you on your journey, and if you follow its teachings as methods to practice, you will not go astray.

I have tried my best, but I find that my words may not be a worthy foreword to this sublime text written by Brother Chuck. His wisdom, understanding, knowledge, and ability to communicate it both effectively and with tenderheartedness often leaves me speechless. His words seemingly anticipated all my protestations, arguments, and criticisms and masterfully addressed them as they arose. The demonstration of the mastery of the information, combined with skillful employment of it in a practical sense, is extraordinary. So, please forgive me if my words can only point out the nature of Brother Chuck's, and I trust that you will understand what I mean as you progress through the book.

Finally, it is crucial that you understand that the Rosicrucian philosophy presented herein is not truth. It is method. Meaning that if one practices and accomplishes the methods described within, then one may know truth. Because, if practiced over years, the results of these methods inculcate a way of being that allows one to know exactly what the Rosicrucian masters of old knew.

The true meaning of life is found within service in love, and we must devote ourselves to our labors and prayers with diligence and become the human beings we were always meant to be. This text is a wonderful aid to guide our steps along the way to becoming that. I want to thank Brother Chuck for the opportunity to read this book and introduce it to you. And I want to thank you for reading this and, hopefully, following the precepts laid out here, so that you too can one day know the truth of the Rosy Cross.

Sincerely & fraternally, with Love,

Greg Kaminsky
March 30, 2022

PREFACE

Dear Reader,

If the image of a rose and cross conjoined provokes a feeling of mystery, if it suggests something precious and noble, if it persistently calls you to gaze upon its beauty and inhale its mythic fragrance, then I greet you as a kindred spirit. If you have already been moved to investigate Rosicrucianism, then I also welcome you as a fellow aspirant.

At the start, I want you to know that the aim of this book is not to inform you about all things Rosicrucian. Rosicrucianism is incredibly diverse, with various authorities offering significantly different, even conflicting, beliefs, symbolism, and practices. In fact, some points in this book will probably draw sharp disagreement from persons pursuing different Rosicrucian paths. This book does not offer a comprehensive and detailed exposition of Rosicrucian history, symbolism, philosophy, or practice; there are better scholars offering works of that sort. Rather, my primary goal is to offer ways to engage a particular flavor of Rosicrucianism through the work of ritual, the exercise of virtue, and related internal activities. In effect, this book is a course in such Rosicrucian inner work for those who either do not want to join an organization or take correspondence courses, or for those who are looking for something different from their other Rosicrucian involvements. It is laid out to sequentially guide one through these phases: (1) setting cornerstones for your own ongoing development of a historical and theoretical understanding of Rosicrucianism; (2) entering into practical applications with methods that are grounded in appreciation for the material world, while also open to inspiration from beyond it; (3) diving deeper into contemplation of certain symbolic keys within the Rosicrucian movement, and by doing so, allowing them to accelerate corresponding processes in the psyche; and (4) conducting experiments designed to directly engage the most transformative possibilities of the Great Work.

This kind of work is not about merely "getting it" intellectually. It is not enough to become familiar with its concepts, learn how the practices are done, and have a theoretical understanding of the kinds of experiences and changes they are meant to facilitate. One must devotedly and repeatedly practice these things, allowing them to unfold meanings and developments in the soul that are deeper and more life-changing than the intellect alone can ever produce. For anyone relatively inexperienced with inner work of this sort, ***the sequence of readings and exercises in this book should be strictly followed***. They are a carefully structured and integrated set with an appendix and glossary to assist one's progress. Skipping steps or taking them out of order can be seriously problematic. At the very least, it would dilute the potency of one's efforts. At the worst, it risks psychospiritual imbalance that could prove damaging to oneself and relationships with others. Persons who have significant experience with similar systems of inner work may be better prepared to adapt various elements as they see fit. Even so, those with hard-won wisdom also understand the benefits of starting any system at the beginning and working through it as designed.

The perspectives and methods offered here are ones I have been privately taught or personally developed during my own long history with the Rosicrucian tradition. It will also be apparent that I am writing from the perspective of a Christian esotericist. Such a Christian is one whose experience, understanding, and expression of the religion has been significantly influenced by studies and practices in various currents of theosophical, mystical, or gnostic wisdom. In my case, and for many others on Rosicrucian paths, such wisdom traditions include Cabala, Neoplatonism, Hermeticism, and alchemy, as well as Christianity's own more orthodox forms of mysticism.[1] The history of Rosicrucianism shows that its founders regarded themselves as devout Christians who had benefitted from such studies and practice, following in the footsteps of Renaissance luminaries like Marcilio Ficino, Pico Della Mirandolla, Theophrastis von Hohenheim, and Giordano Bruno. Even so, I want to make it very clear that I do not think it is necessary to identify as Christian in order to walk a Rosicrucian path. Familiarity and comfort with Christian symbolism and concepts is important, but I have personally known people of other religions, and some claiming no particular religion, who have found great value in Rosicrucianism. I think the tradition likewise benefits from their presence.

You have seen that I am using *Rose Croix* instead of *Rosae Crucis*, *Rose Cross*, or *Rosy Cross* in the title. The main reason for doing so is to draw attention to the Knight Rose Croix Degree of Freemasonry, also called *Knight of the Eagle and Pelican*, which has been a very important part of my Rosicrucian journey. We deal with that degree in greater detail further along in the book, but for now I assert that there are meaningful connections between it and Rosicrucianism in both symbolism and philosophy. Any Freemason who values the Rose Croix Degree or is a member of the Masonic Societas Rosicruciana should find something of interest in this book, and hopefully something of practical use in transforming one's own life and having positive effects

---

1. Note that in this book the term *Cabala* refers to the theosophical systems beginning with the Jewish Kabbalah and maintaining a close symbolic relationship with it while developing significantly different theological and practical aspects. The spelling with a *C* is used herein because that is how it was spelled in the first of the Rosicrucian manifestos.

on the world, as both Rosicrucianism and Freemasonry call us to do. All that being said, I am not writing this book exclusively for Freemasons, members of Rosicrucian organizations, or Christian esotericists such as Martinists, and I warmly welcome the interest of persons with no involvement in any of these traditions.

An oratory is a chapel or space set aside for meditation and prayer; its name comes from the Latin *ora*, for "prayer." Along with words like *sanctum*, *lodge*, and *temple*, the term *oratory* is commonly used among people identifying with Rosicrucianism to refer to one's private place of study, meditation, prayer, and ritual. I am using *oratory* in the title because the contents are drawn from the Rosicrucian activities that I have pursued in such a space in my own home.

In addition to prose, you will find poetry I have written for more symbolic, romantic, and inspirational expressions of insights received along the way. No claims are made about the artistic quality of those pieces, but they are sincere, based on real experience, and communicate some things better than ordinary prose. I am also including such works by others that have been especially meaningful to me. In my view, nearly all esoteric and mystical endeavors have inspirational and aesthetic aspects, and the way is incomplete without them.

According to the *Fama Fraternitatis*, anyone following a Rosicrucian path should profess nothing other than to serve the healing of others, and at no cost. My writing and other forms of service in both Rosicrucianism and Freemasonry are guided by that rule, and what would have been my royalties from this book are instead being contributed to a relevant philanthropy.

Finally, it is my conviction that no individual or organization speaks for all of the Rosicrucian movement or for Freemasonry. In Freemasonry, this limitation is especially true with regard to our individual religious perspectives, as I offer in this book. Everything here must therefore be taken as an account of my personal studies, experiences, and perspective. I encourage you to consult others, follow your own heart, exercise your own best judgment, conduct your own investigations, and develop your own understandings.

By the Cross and Rose,
C.R. "Chuck" Dunning, Jr.

PART ONE:
FOUNDATIONS

Introduction

The three chapters of this part are intended to lay the foundation for the rest of the book. The first chapter has two main objectives: (1) describing how I came to my own experience and understandings of things relevant to the Rose Croix Degree and Rosicrucianism, and (2) explaining the essential points of my understandings, since they guide the remainder of the book. The second chapter directly addresses the emergence of Rosicrucianism and its relationship to the Rose Croix Degree of Freemasonry. Because any Masonic expression of Rosicrucianism must always occur within the circumference of Masonic ethics, the third chapter clarifies the ethical nature of Freemasonry as I see it. Preparing the way for all those objectives, I offer the following poem for your contemplation.

The Untamed Unowned Rosy Cross

O Rose and Cross conjoined!
How deeply stirring is your simple splendid image!
Great awakener and blessed weaver of mystic dreams!
Beckoning, mesmerizing, metamorphic visage!
Divinely crafted talisman of the Supreme Mysteries!

Holy icon born from the ever-renewing womb of Nature,
Infused with the silent prayer of the All-Pervading Spirit!
Your transcendent voice calls out to those with hearts to hear,
Chanting the unutterable, unenculturated, timeless truths
Of Light, Life, and Love.

O seeker who has heard these heavenly hymns sung,
Look upon and listen to that blossoming cruciform revelation!
Open your quickened soul to its most essential vibration
Despite the cacophony of clanging cymbals and babbling tongues.

Be not deceived by the self-deluding hucksters
Posing as magi, adepti, perfecti, and wizards,
The self-serving hierarchies of haughty hierophants,
Moneychangers mimicking mystagogues,
Knowing in part yet pretending to the entirety,
Their inspirations clouded in the misty fog of sophistry.
Manufacturing metaphysical models in minutiae,
Drafting theologies and cosmologies ad nauseam,
They stack up abstracted sandcastles,
Clods of grainy words fantasized as grand temples,
Protecting fragile fictions rather than preserving sacred relics,
Inventing histories and supposed successions,
Gathering up patents, charters, and constitutions,
Proliferating parchment and paper playthings
As the proud purveyors of tawdry titles and trinkets.

Yet, in sympathy see that, like you, they too are spiritual moths,
Instinctively drawn to the bright enchanting flame
Of the untamed unowned Rosy Cross.
Entranced, we all flutter and dance together,
In varying awareness of that fire's two-edged offer,

Basking in the charity of its warm illumination,
But inherently threatened by the transformation
Awaiting those who would enter its burning center.
Igne Natura Renovatur Integra!

Chapter 1:
A Cornerstone

The symbolism of a cornerstone has long extended into popular culture from architecture and stonemasonry. It appears in several books of the Holy Bible, and in the New Testament, it is connected with Jesus Christ. Connections later came to be made with the Philosopher's Stone of alchemy, and the cornerstone is certainly important in Speculative Freemasonry. In general, people regard the cornerstone as symbolic of whatever is needed to ensure a true and enduring basis for some endeavor. It is in this sense that it is used in this chapter, which sets the stage for all that follows. Since a cornerstone has eight points, this chapter is arranged in eight sections: (1) a review of my relevant background and how it creates perspective in this book; (2) the ways I currently make sense of psychospiritual work; (3) what esoteric psychospiritual work entails; (4) how we can conceptualize what is happening behind the scenes of such work; (5) different mindsets on performance of the work; (6) the meaning of initiation; (7) consideration of whether or not it is good to have a teacher; and (8) addressing the pros and cons of group work.[2]

A Peculiar Perspective

At this point, I feel it is important to share some of my own background relevant to the Rosicrucian tradition. Everything in this book cannot help but reflect a perspective developed through decades of personal training and experience, and this sharing is meant to help readers more fully understand that view, which undoubtedly differs from, and on some points even contradicts, other expressions of Rosicrucianism. It is also my hope that readers find meaningful parallels with their own stories.

This perspective begins with the fact that I was born and raised in a devout Christian family that was very active in the Methodist church next door to our home in North Texas. I was baptized at the age of 14, and today I identify as a Christian esotericist. As a professional in mental health, my understanding of the human psyche includes awareness that I have been thoroughly conditioned to experience and comprehend things in Christian ways. While still in the womb, I was hearing the sounds of Christian music, and from the moment of birth, my awareness and understanding of everything in life was woven together with Christian words, concepts, and practices. Even the story of my birth has always emphasized that it happened mid-morning on

---

2. The term *psychospiritual* references both the psychological and the spiritual. While it can sometimes be useful to distinguish between the two, this term emphasizes their interconnectedness. In order to fully address either, we must include the other.

a Sunday, just before our church's worship service. With only minutes to spare, a red rosebud was placed on the altar to announce my birth to the congregation, as was the custom. Like the rest of my family, I grew into active participation and leadership in our church.

My relationship with mainstream religion has not always been rosy. I went through phases of rebellious conflict, as some children do. Even as adults, many people are understandably at odds with their childhood religious experience, and for a while that was true for me. I found that the faculty of reason permitted me to transcend some of that conditioning, but not all of it. There are unconscious parts of our being that conscious reason cannot penetrate, control, or purge. Eventually, I came to accept how powerfully moved I continue to be by the ideas, sights, sounds, and smells of Christianity. They tap into depths of my soul, into the innocent, childlike spirit within me, like nothing else can do. Thus, I chose to make a watchful, collaborative peace with my Christian identity rather than spend the rest of my life either in denial of it or at war with it.

With that acceptance came a sense of responsibility to engage in an ongoing development of more educated, seasoned, and integrated ways of being a Christian in my own somewhat unique relationship with God. Even as a young child I had an interest in world religions, no doubt sparked by my father's Masonic books, and that interest grew into comparative studies. I also had a precocious fascination with the workings of the mind and states of consciousness, in part because I began lucid dreaming at nine years of age. That fascination led into my career in mental health and higher education and, combined with religious studies, it drew me into the practice of contemplative methods to include dreamwork, active imagination, meditation, mindfulness, reflection, and dialogue. Furthermore, social responsibility was interwoven with Christian ethics in my upbringing, exemplified by my elder sisters' as well as my parents' involvements with church, school, and civic organizations. I followed in their footsteps and, as an adult, have grown increasingly sensitive to the interconnectedness and interdependence of the individual and society. Finally, I was instilled with a love of Nature at a very young age, which was due to my father being an outdoorsman, my mother growing beautiful beds of irises and daffodils each spring, and most of our vacations spent camping. Experiencing the Divine in Nature has therefore always been part of Christianity for me, and it has only deepened over time. Although my understanding of it is much different than in my childhood, an old hymn that can still move me to tears with its evocative lines is "This is My Father's World."

> This is my Father's world,
> And to my listening ears
> All nature sings, and round me rings
> The music of the spheres.
> This is my Father's world:
> I rest me in the thought
> Of rocks and trees, of skies and seas;
> His hand the wonders wrought.
>
> This is my Father's world,
> The birds their carols raise,
> The morning light, the lily white,
> Declare their maker's praise.
> This is my Father's world,
> He shines in all that's fair;
> In the rustling grass I hear Him pass;
> He speaks to me everywhere.

This is my Father's world.

O let me ne'er forget

That though the wrong seems oft so strong,

God is the ruler yet.

This is my Father's world:

Why should my heart be sad?

The Lord is King; let the heavens ring!

God reigns; let the earth be glad![3]

By my mid-20s, I had found genuine teachers in esoteric wisdom and practice, who helped me discover that all of these themes (the studies of religion and philosophy, the investigation of the mind, contemplative practice, social responsibility, the love of Nature, as well as a commitment to freedom of thought and conscience) were important aspects of both Masonry and Rosicrucianism. Both traditions encourage all of these things as parts of the *Great Work*, the process of self-transformation that aims at realizing union with God and serving that unity in the reformation of society. So, in 1988, I sought and received initiation into Masonry, which soon included the Rose Croix Degree, in which I immediately saw Rosicrucian themes and imagery. Through some of my Masonic brothers, I then connected with intiatic traditions of Christian esotericism outside of the Fraternity. In time, those connections led to initiations and active participation in Rosicrucianism through a number of different lineages.

The history you have just read informs what I offer in this book. As a Christian esotericist, my understanding of things like creation, the soul and its relationship with others and with the Creator, and the nature and role of Christ, have been significantly influenced by

---

3. These three stanzas are adapted from an originally longer poem written by the Presbyterian minister, Maltbie Davenport Babcock (August 3, 1858 – May 18, 1901). In 1915, it was set to music by his friend Frank L. Sheppard. *https://en.wikipedia.org/wiki/This_Is_My_Father's_World*

Neoplatonism, Cabala, Hermeticism, and studies in many other religions and philosophies. On some points, I significantly depart from today's mainstream Christianity, having more in common with various mystic and gnostic theologians and theosophers found throughout the religion's history.

An important point here is that readers should not expect this book to provide a worldview or interpretations of symbols that are entirely consistent with any of the previously named traditions, with any particular authority, or with the doctrines of any organization. In fact, it is not my intention to present a detailed, comprehensive, and carefully constructed exposition of Rosicrucianism as a whole. My aim is instead to provide reflections on various events, concepts, and values relevant to the overall Rosicrucian movement, and related practices I have found useful for gaining deeper experience and insight into the mysteries of our being. It will be necessary for readers to consult other sources to more fully explore and understand many things mentioned here. Readers are therefore trusted to regard this book as one among many tools that might be useful in their pursuits of the Great Work.

THE FRAMEWORK

Now I should summarize some of the theories, perspectives, and values that guide my approach to the Great Work, since they are constantly infused in the following chapters. I do not expect readers to agree with any of them, yet without them, much of the coherence in this book would be lost.

1. All things, even our own minds, remain mysterious to some extent. Indeed, the more we probe into the nature of things, the more mystery we often discover. This is a fact to be embraced with awe and joy rather than resisted in angst and despair. Such an embrace helps us remember that all our best concepts, especially about things beyond the veils of our senses, cannot avoid

being inaccurate and incomplete. We are thus enabled, if not compelled, to recognize and respect the fact that no single religion, philosophy, or political ideology, or any combination thereof, can be rightfully asserted to capture the whole and undisputable truth to which all must conform. Liberty of thought, conscience, and speech are not merely noble ideas, they are inherent realities of human nature that we are wise to nurture and uphold for all.

2. Regardless of their history and intent, the Rosicrucian manifestos created a myth that inspired many people to seek a more esoteric experience of Christianity under the sign of the Rose+Cross, and over time that myth has spoken to non-Christians as well. Over the last 400 years, such inspirations, quests, and experiences have in turn been expressed through an immense, diverse, and sometimes conflicting body of poetry, prose, visual art, drama, ritual, contemplative practices, and organizational designs. Rosicrucianism in a broader sense is therefore a *mythopoetic movement*. The term *mythopoetic* literally means the power of mythmaking. To regard Rosicrucianism as a mythopoetic movement is to recognize that the manifestos and the image of the Rose+Cross were, and still are, possessed by an intriguing and inspirational quality that connects people across the generations. This view also affirms that Rosicrucianism in its many forms moves people to reflect on the meanings of their lives, to wonder at the beauty and mystery of things, to dream and envision beautiful possibilities for themselves and the world, and to communicate those things to others. The Rosicrucian spirit is thus acknowledged as a liberating and expansive force that transforms lives and even entire societies in ways that cannot be precisely predicted, controlled, or systematized. In this context, other than the common roots of the Rosicrucian manifestos (1614-1616) and reverence for the Rose+Cross symbol, there is no litmus test or checklist of characteristics that finally determines what can or cannot be included within the movement.

3. *Panentheism* is the worldview that best describes the nature of existence. In short, it holds that what we call the Divine is present in every point of space and time, while also remaining unmanifest in some way. As the Apostle Paul preached to the Athenians, the "Unknown God" is nonetheless that in which "we live and move and have our being."[4]

4. The process of creation may be described as an emanation of the Divine Source, and thus the essence of all things is regarded as one with the Divine Source. This view of emanation is therefore non-dualist. Nature is divine, and its material aspects are the physical body of God and are revelatory of God. As recorded in the Gospel of Thomas, Jesus said, "Split a piece of wood: I am there. Lift a stone, and you will find me there."[5] Nature is therefore worthy of our reverence, protection, and intimate identification with it.

5. There is value in the Hermetic Axiom, *as above so below, and as below so above.*[6] It is perfectly congruent with the declaration in the *Book of Genesis* that humanity is created in the image of God.[7] It therefore makes sense that the spirit and soul within the human body naturally reflects metaphysical aspects of the Divine, or the Spirit and Soul of the Universe. The more familiar and insightful we become with the operations of the human soul, the more we understand *by analogy* the different aspects and functions of the Divine Soul working behind and through what we can perceive of Nature. "Know thyself and thou shalt know all the mysteries of the gods and the universe."[8] This point should not be interpreted as justification for ignoring the limitations of human consciousness, an extreme anthropocentrism, or for

---

4. Acts 17:22-28.
5. Gospel of Thomas, 77, Layton translation.
6. This axiom is paraphrased from the beginning of the *Emerald Tablet of Hermes Trismegistus.*
7. Genesis 1:26-27.
8. Traditionally attributed to Pythagoras.

projecting the limitations of human personality onto God.[9] All creatures partake in the Divine in their own ways, and thus all are also revelations of the Divine.

6. Because the human psyche is found in Nature and operates according to the laws of Nature, it too is inhabited by God. "The kingdom is within you and it is outside of you."[10] This must be true of all human beings, no matter who they are, what they believe, or how they live. In fact, one's union with the Divine may be realized through direct mystical experience. It is not only a matter of inference or faith, and it is not contingent upon adherence to any particular religion.

7. In exploring our oneness with Nature and the Divine, we become more aware that we are intimately interconnected with each other and all things. The old materialism that viewed physical entities as absolutely separate and discrete from each other has not held up. Among the many implications of this realization is that self, society, and the environment are not separate from each other, and that a virtuous care and concern for any of them necessitates virtuous care and concern for the others. There is no longer a *you* or a *me*, an *us* or *them*, a *this* or *that*, in any isolated sense. Our supposed separation from each other is an illusion, albeit a very powerful one that causes much suffering.

8. There is nothing more important than love. "God is love. Whoever lives in love, lives in God, and God in them."[11] In human terms, love is the desire for, experience of, and expression of the Divine. Since all things are united in God's presence, *everything* we do is in some way driven by love, an expression of love, and an experience of love, whether it be the love of God, Nature, truth, others, or

9. Anthropocentrism is the belief that, of all things in existence, human beings are the most important. At its worst extreme, it disregards care of the environment and the other beings inhabiting it with us.
10. Gospel of Thomas, 3, Blatz translation.
11. 1 John 4:17, NIV.

self. Even the things we regard as evil can be understood as twisted, distorted, often extremely one-sided manifestations of love. There is nothing more important than love, although there is also nothing more mysterious. Love, like all things Divine, is not only immediately present but also beyond our ability to fully conceptualize. We close these eight points by considering that love in various forms is at once the motivation for the Great Work, the means of the Great Work, and the effect of the Great Work – Love *is* the Great Work.

WHAT ACTIVITIES DOES THE GREAT WORK INCLUDE?

Taking the manifestos as our guide, it is fair to say that Rosicrucian psychospiritual work is aimed at the transformation of our character, the acquisition of mystical knowledge or gnosis, and the integration of our highest principles into every aspect of our lives for the benefit of others. Rather than merely thinking and talking about esoteric psychospirituality and metaphysics, it is actual experience that provides the fullest possible measure of realizing and manifesting these possibilities. While some aspects of such experience are outside our conscious awareness and control, we can maximize our potentials through the following ways of intentional effort:

1. Being consistently attentive to the present moment, both internally and externally. The popular term for this practice is *mindfulness*, and it has been described as thinking about what you are doing and doing what you are thinking about. There are times when it is wise to occupy ourselves with thoughts about some other place and time, but too often we distract ourselves from being more fully conscious, whole, and responsive in the immediate reality.

2. <u>Practicing nonjudgmental awareness.</u> The extent to which we experience and understand things as they truly are determines the extent to which we can interact with them as completely, fairly, and effectively as possible. We create many misunderstandings and illusions for ourselves and others with knee-jerk reactions, jumping to conclusions, and other habitual responses based on automatic assumptions. Often, we are attempting to categorize things as repetitions of previous experiences, or as elements of patterns we believe already exist. We do these things to try taking shortcuts through life. They are also the essential mechanisms of prejudice, which literally means a judgment about something or someone before a full examination and understanding can be developed.

3. <u>Developing empathy and compassion for other beings based on deeper awareness and acceptance of our own whole being.</u> Empathy is attentiveness and awareness in the emotional dimension of being, and compassion is empathy for the suffering of others and the desire and willingness to help ease it. This ongoing and ever evolving work is essential to recognizing and acting in congruence with the wonderful reality of our unity as well as the beautiful fact of our diversity. It involves integrating the heart and the mind in being more fully aware of ourselves, others, and our interconnectedness. This work is essential for the Rosicrucian aim of individual and collective healing and nurturing the bonds that facilitate true peace and harmony within ourselves and the world.

4. <u>Exercising virtue in our ordinary daily activities and relationships.</u> Virtue is consistently doing that which serves the good for oneself *and* others. To be as virtuous as possible, one needs to be as attentive and aware as possible to all aspects of our being, individually and socially. It therefore requires mindfulness, empathy, and compassion. Virtue is the devoted actualization of our most noble and loving ideas about truth, beauty, and goodness.

5. <u>Developing greater ability to fine tune and sustain concentration, including mental quietness and stillness.</u> In order to more fully engage all the other elements of this list, it is very helpful to improve our ability to focus the mind. By doing so, we are better able to penetrate deeper into particular ideas, symbols, or feelings, and more precisely see how they relate with other things. We also directly encounter how the mind and heart actually work. We become more aware of and skilled with their various energies and contents, including uncomfortable truths about ourselves that we might often deny or avoid, as well as admirable potentials that might otherwise remain hidden and untapped.

6. <u>Welcoming intuition, inspiration, and creativity directly into our conscious awareness.</u> All practical approaches to esoteric psychospirituality include entering into non-ordinary states of consciousness. Such shifts are made in order to more directly access psychospiritual energies and metaphysical sources of information, and to engage in ways of processing and applying them. This work can free one from many limitations typically placed on our own potentials and on other possibilities. It can lead to deeper insight as well as novel and innovative ways of facilitating beneficial change for ourselves and others.

7. <u>Performing ritual that affirms and reinforces the previous points.</u> Ritual helps anchor ideas deeper in our minds and integrate those ideas with other information. It also improves retention and recall of the information it contains. The symbolic aspects of ritual facilitate novel insights, and the actions of ritual often constitute rehearsal of accessing its information and applying it with helpful attitudes like confidence and optimism. Furthermore, ritual can assist with eliminating distractions, focusing the mind and heart, entering non-ordinary states of consciousness, and squelching some energies while amplifying and directing others toward desired ends.

Any comprehensive and well-integrated approach to esoteric psychospiritual work will address each of these seven points in some measure. Each person naturally finds some of them easier than others, but if psychospiritual work was always easy, then perhaps we would not call it *work* or use terms like *practice*. In any case, some progress in each area is possible for almost anyone with the will do so.

What is Really Happening in the Great Work?

This is a good place to consider how we conceptualize psychospiritual work like meditation, prayer, ritual, and creative imagination. Many of these activities are traditionally supposed to engage metaphysical forces and noncorporeal beings beyond oneself, such as archangels. There are three basic views relevant to this issue, which are here labeled the *psychological*, the *mechanistic metaphysical*, and the *divine*.

The psychological perspective holds that all of these psychospiritual activities are actually just tapping into different parts of our own individual psyches. This view does not necessarily deny there is value in the *idea* of metaphysical forces and noncorporeal beings apart from us, or even in behaving *as if* they have reality independent of our own minds. However, persons of the psychological view frame that value in terms of greater self-awareness and mental health in much the same way as is done with dreams and fantasies in therapy.

The mechanistic metaphysical stance acknowledges the psychological aspects and potentials of psychospiritual work, and also regards the psyche as being connected with parts of existence that are not limited to matter and energy as known by physics. However, this view considers concepts and images of noncorporeal beings as actually referencing impersonal metaphysical forces and dynamics. Work that is directed beyond ourselves is therefore about manipulating those metaphysical things in the same way ordinary technology manipulates matter and energy in the material world.

The divine view affirms that psychospiritual activities have both psychological and mechanistic metaphysical elements and effects, while also regarding noncorporeal beings as significantly more than figments of human imagination. It holds that we can interact with such beings in ways analogous to the ways we interact with creatures in the material world. The divine view best aligns with the panenthestic perspective of this book.

However one views such things, it is wise to keep in mind that conceptualizing the work is not as important as actually *doing* it. At the minimum, psychospiritual work can have significant psychological challenges and rewards, and so the psychological view is always a wise and useful frame of reference, even if we do not limit ourselves to it. In any case, it is important to engage in the work wholeheartedly, which may mean experimentally taking the *as-if* approach, momentarily suspending disbelief in order to perform activities that traditionally reference metaphysical forces and noncorporeal beings about which one has doubts.

Is the Great Work an Art or a Science?

Here again is found a threefold arrangement of practitioners – the *artists*, the *scientists*, and the *craftspeople*.

Psychospiritual work can be seen as predominantly artistic, and for those who hold this view, it relies more heavily on intuition, inspiration, and creativity than other faculties. Because these things enter awareness from outside the ordinary cognition that we consciously direct, persons who engage the work as an art tend to be less concerned with learning and applying detailed cosmologies, maps of consciousness, diagrams of metaphysical realms, or precise and multilayered hierarchies of noncorporeal beings. Likewise, they are not as strict in following exact formulas for their activities. Consistency of methods and results, verification of efficacy, and repeatability are not as important to the artists. Often, fully giving oneself to the experience, as it is happening, is of greater import than any effects it may later generate. Each instance of psychospiritual activity is more like that of drafting a sketch or poem than conducting an operation in a laboratory. In fact, actually producing physical works of art may be an important form of psychospiritual activity in itself. Artistic psychospiritual workers may also be more comfortable learning through their own exploration of psychospiritual methods. However, as with other arts, such efforts may still be guided by the general rules of a certain school, style, or tradition. Finally, artistic psychospiritual workers who take the previously noted divine perspective are also usually more open to and trusting of guidance and support from noncorporeal beings they regard as benign and closely connected to the reception and manifestation of intuition, inspiration, and creativity.

Scientifically minded practitioners can be genuinely convinced of the reality of metaphysical forces and noncorporal beings apart from themselves, yet in practice tend to think and act in ways more consistent with the mechanistic metaphysical approach. They are much more concerned with precision guided by logic and confirmation of results through repeatability, the observation of effects by other persons, and elimination of other plausible explanations for those results. Conscientiously following the rules of a tradition, a school, or system is esteemed when they have been tested over time and are judged to be valid because of the available evidence. Exacting attention to the smallest details of conceptual frameworks and methodology are usually given a very high priority. Such things are viewed in much the same way a laboratory worker views the significance of being diligently careful with measurements and using the proper tools and techniques. Scientific psychospiritual workers understandably place the highest regard on their own conscious control of most elements in a psychospiritual activity as vital to its effectiveness in generating specific outcomes. They can respond to intuition, inspiration, and innovation with especially cautious testing.

The craftspeople of psychospiritual endeavors combine elements of the artistic and scientific. They often find value in being part of a tradition with a long history of producing beautiful and useful artifacts, whether powerful ideas, fascinating images, actual objects, or changed lives. Thus, aligning with a tradition is an act of homage to its past, and is also a commitment to its continuing legacy as well as the individual's own learning and growth. That alignment well may include the language and structure of apprenticeship and mastery, as is done in paths like Freemasonry and shamanic traditions. Craftspeople thus respect the importance of faithfully learning and adhering to time-tested methods, while also recognizing that people must develop their own personal connections with the traditional tools and materials. Furthermore, those who have adequately proven themselves, through dedication to and demonstration of the traditional techniques and forms, may even be welcomed to bend or break the old rules when inspired or intuitively driven to develop new expressions of their craft's various dimensions. In the case of psychospiritual work, the tools and materials of the craft certainly include particular metaphysical forces and noncorporeal beings as they are historically presented within that craft.

All three orientations to the Great Work are found among people identifying with Rosicrucianism. Most organizations seem to employ a largely craft-like approach, with some leaning more toward the artistic and others toward the scientific. In any case, recognizing your own proclivities may help you maximize your natural talents while also suggesting possibilities for exploring untapped potentials.

THE MEANING OF INITIATION

The word *initiation* obviously speaks of a beginning, yet every beginning is itself the outcome of various factors and processes. It can therefore be more fitting to think of initiation as a turning point, one which is especially noteworthy for its power to provide access, direction, and focus to future factors and processes. With this understanding, initiation in Rosicrucianism and similar traditions is valued as an experience of transition into significant alignment with and commitment to the philosophy, symbolism, and practices of the given tradition. Such an initiation may or may not occur within the context of a ceremony. In fact, while the ceremony of joining a lineage or group may be called an initiation, it is not actually psychospiritually initiatic unless it is a watershed moment of change in the way the neophyte thinks and acts. That change may not necessarily produce immediately dramatic results, yet it is definite, and over time its significance can be further appreciated in hindsight. As anyone who has navigated with a magnetic compass knows, a small course change is not especially noticeable at first, but, when followed to a longer distance, it results in traveling through very different territory than would have been otherwise encountered.

Many people also believe that for an initiation to be valid in Rosicrucianism, it must include one or more of the following conditions:

- Delivery by an officially qualified initiator, one recognized as a legitimate inheritor and perpetuator of a lineage originating from a particular individual or group identified as a worthy Rosicrucian source

- Conducted in person with close physical proximity or actual contact occurring between the candidate and the initiator

- Adhering to certain ritual elements commonly used for all initiates of the lineage or group

- Invocation of Deity, perhaps also including particular spiritual beings such as angels or saints

- Metaphysical transmission of subtle energy in some particular form to the candidate from the initiator or group

- A sacred vow or oath to abide by the rules and customs of the lineage or group, typically including a commitment to maintain some degree of secrecy about teachings, symbolism, practices, and/or the identities of members

As important and potentially impactful as each of those conditions might be, even with all of them present and provided in the most optimal manner, a true initiation cannot occur without the candidate making an internal shift of interests, desires, and intentions. This is one reason for the customary probationary period required by many lineages or organizations, which, at least ideally, allows the candidate and the initiator or group time to clarify whether or not there is a promising resonance of spirit and aims. Some authorities further assert that the candidate's own internal process is of such importance that it makes self-initiation a suitable option for individuals who feel powerfully drawn to Rosicrucianism while unable or unwilling to connect with a specific teacher, lineage, or group.

Of great relevance to these matters is a statement in the *Confessio Fraternitatis*, the second of the original Rosicrucian manifestos, plainly stating that it is possible for someone to be "one of us" without even knowing it![12] This statement clarifies that becoming a Rosicrucian is essentially a matter of change in one's being rather than membership in a lineage or group. Paul Foster Case upheld this point when he declared, "The Rosicrucian Order ... is a state of mind. One *becomes* a Rosicrucian: one does not *join* the Rosicrucians."[13]

12. *Rosicrucian Trilogy: Modern Translations of the Three Founding Documents*, trans. Joscelyn Godwin, Christopher McIntosh, and Donate Pahnke McIntosh (Newburyport: Weiser, 2016), 46.
13. Paul Foster Case, *The True and Invisible Rosicrucian Order*, First Paper Edition [York Beach: Weiser, 1989], 5.

If you feel drawn to Rosicrucianism, then whether or not you join a particular lineage or organization is a choice you may freely make as part of your own journey. Similarly, you are at liberty to decide if you undergo any ceremonial event or events, whether self-administered or received from others. The following sections may also have relevance to such decisions for you.

SHOULD I HAVE A TEACHER?

This is one of the most common questions among people who are considering in-depth Rosicrucian studies and practice. The short answer is that you should at least regularly consult with someone you regard as a genuine mentor or role model, someone who inspires you to grow beyond who you are now, someone with the courage and insight to ask hard questions, someone who exemplifies the possibilities to which you feel drawn. Teachers may also offer initiation into an established lineage with inherited generations of initiatic and transformative insight to assist them in serving your psychospiritual growth.

In the modern world, with its rational concerns for egalitarianism and autonomy, the idea of a teacher in psychospiritual pursuits often seems an anathema. Indeed, some people with the experience and skill to be genuine guides in such matters reject the use of the term *teacher* as an artifice, even arrogant. To some extent these views are understandable, yet the title has value in communicating the simple fact that some people are qualified and positioned to help others learn useful information and skills. As mature adults, we can let go of the notion that *teacher* automatically places one on a pedestal of unquestioned authority and veneration.

Just think for a moment about any other field of interest where human beings are dealing with the refinement of unusual skills, a considerable amount of theoretical or historical knowledge, and performing actions that can have significant effects on a person's wellbeing. Examples include medicine, law, psychology, and engineering. If you wanted to become truly adept in one of these fields, would you just read some books and then try to wing it on your own? Or would you pursue a legitimate course of studies, involving the development of actual skills with the guidance and supervision of people more experienced and knowledgeable than you?

People often make the counterargument that psychospiritual matters are different, mostly because the main thing you are working with or learning about is yourself, and nobody can be an expert on you but you. This argument overlooks two facts: First, while each soul may be unique, we all have a huge amount in common with regard to *how* our souls function and change. Second, some people have made unusually sustained and intensive efforts to learn more about how souls function and change. Knowing *how* to effectively learn and work with the soul is a field of expertise that transcends individual cases. Good esoteric teachers have done their own work in that field and know how to help others do likewise.

One common fear people have is that an esoteric teacher might try to manipulate them, control them, or impose some set of beliefs or attitudes the person would not otherwise choose. While it is absolutely true that some beliefs and attitudes can rub off of anyone with whom we are close, a good esoteric teacher should let you know up front which (if any) attitudes and beliefs are expected of you. Furthermore, the best teachers are more interested in helping you have and conceptualize your own experiences for yourself, even if they are prescriptive about processes eliciting your experiences.

Another real concern is personality worship. Here we are talking about a student-teacher relationship in which the teacher has, perhaps unconsciously, an agenda to be adored, esteemed, identified with, and ultimately needed by the student, and/or the student is looking for someone to idolize, to give them "the answers," or rescue them from their fears. Because teachers are themselves human beings, it should be no surprise if some take a little pleasure in being valued by others.

That fact in itself is not unhealthy. A well-developed teacher practices awareness of such things and is conscientious about helping all parties maintain healthy attitudes and boundaries in their relationship.

What often most worries many people about the student-teacher relationship is authorizing someone to challenge them in one or more ways. Behind that concern might be a desire to avoid accountability for what one actually is or is not doing, or for the quality of one's efforts. It might be motivated by a fear of having one's vices, facades, and psychological shadow more fully seen and understood by another person (or even by oneself). Similarly, the more one sees esotericism and psychospiritual work as a means to escape from reality and into self-aggrandizing fantasy, then the less likely that person will want to be close to someone whose job includes helping to reveal such things. If what you really want is genuine transformation, then a real teacher will challenge you to more fully encounter the layers of illusions and truths within you, embrace psychospiritual death, and be reborn into something you cannot fully foresee. That is an inherently threatening prospect to our egos and personalities, and so it is no wonder that most people do not really want a teacher like that.

If you are still unsure about entering a student-teacher relationship, then you are advised to carefully consider everything that sounds undesirable or risky about it. Once you have identified your specific concerns, then ask yourself how you and a teacher might address those concerns in ways that are in your best interest. Your next step is to try to find someone who has walked the path you would walk, and then initiate that conversation. In any case, proceed in prayer and meditation for inner guidance with all these considerations. By doing so, you will be much better prepared to make wise decisions in this matter.

WHAT ABOUT JOINING A GROUP?

If you are interested in Rosicrucian psychospirituality, then it is smart to think carefully about whether or not to join a group and how to choose one. There are many such groups, and some overtly identify as Rosicrucian, while others only claim a philosophical resonance with Rosicrucianism. The latter include groups focused on Hermeticism, esoteric Christianity, alchemy, or related traditions like Freemasonry. The following paragraphs offer some points of consideration in the process of deciding if joining a group is a good idea for you.

POSSIBLE BENEFITS

While it is undeniably true that you must ultimately be carried forward by your own inspiration and will, it is also undeniably true that we are social beings. We have been wired by our evolution to maximize many of our potentials through engagement with other people. The ways and extent to which we are engaged can differ a great deal from one person to another, but we all do so in some way. As evidence of this, consider the examples of the Buddha and the Christ. Each did indeed retreat from society for some period of time, but eventually they came back and created communities to serve others. The fact of our psychological need for community may be understood as evidence of our intuition, or our deep psychospiritual knowledge, that we are all interconnected.

A strong benefit of groups is that they provide a common symbolism, structure, and process for doing the work of initiation and transformation. These elements serve as a foundation for interpersonal trust, mutual understanding, and a stabilizing sense of companionship when the work takes one into new, uncomfortable, and even rigorous psychospiritual territory. It also facilitates the development of elders who can offer much needed counsel and reassurance about the value of the work, even when the outcomes seem most uncertain.

When we come together in groups, there is a confluence of energies from which everyone draws, which can boost an individual member when personal energy runs low. This convergence can also produce synergy within the group, manifesting results that are greater than the mere sum of the parts. People can begin to see things in new ways that nobody could have predicted, and to develop innovative and deeper understandings more quickly than they would on their own.

Groups also provide us with more opportunities to have our thoughts and behaviors tested in an atmosphere of trust and good will. Strong groups develop an interpersonal intimacy that facilitates the sharing of deeper and more private issues connected with their work. There are opportunities to be candidly observed by others and get their feedback, and thus through their eyes we can see more of ourselves than we otherwise would.

POSSIBLE DRAWBACKS

Even though we are naturally drawn to community, we also instinctively know that we must develop into fully functioning individuals in order to give and get the most we can within our communities. However, for some people the effect of group membership is not so much about mutually supportive movement toward greater self-awareness and self-actualization. Instead, it becomes about gaining reinforcement for a false self that one has accepted from childhood conditioning or created in reaction to it. That false self may be constructed around the strokes and perks of being a heroic overachiever, or an acquiescent follower, angelic caretaker, mirthful entertainer, mysterious loner, distrustful rebel, or any number of other possibilities. In fact, most if not all the risks of group work connect with the problem of playing out roles that mask our more authentic being.

One such risk is groupthink, the tendency for people to increasingly conform their thinking to the norms of their group, and to do so without careful consideration, and with decreasing levels of awareness that this is happening. Submitting to groupthink is largely a strategy to avoid accepting responsibility for fully facing and answering various uncertainties, ambiguities, and paradoxes in life. In short, groupthink seemingly offers one the chance to reclaim the comfort of a beloved childhood blanket or stuffed companion. Yet that comfort is in actuality smothering, because the more groupthink takes hold, then the less freedom one has to be really alive as a whole, mature human being.

Similar to groupthink is a phenomenon in which the individual so completely identifies with the group that its changes are believed to be that person's own changes. If the group is happy and experiencing a sense of progress, then this individual feels happy and believes personal progress is being made, even if the person has not changed in any substantial way. If the group is unhappy and experiencing a sense of losing ground, then the individual feels unhappy and believes ground is being personally lost. This dynamic is illustrated by the enthusiasm trance of faith revivals in Protestant Christianity. The trance happens when people have been caught up in the emotions of the group mind and momentarily imagined themselves to be "on fire for the Lord," redeemed, born again, and sanctified! But after the music, preaching, and pageantry has ended, it is only a short matter of time before they are right back in their same old sinful ways of thinking and acting. No real transformation has occurred at all, only a moment of euphoria induced by a group mind rather than a drug, but nonetheless deluding and potentially addictive.

Another drawback to highlight for now is the amount of time, energy, and money that group membership can gobble up. Families can be destroyed and good jobs forsaken by the "dutiful soldier" who shows up early and stays late at every meeting, whether necessary or not, and who volunteers for every committee or chore. They usually get a lot of positive strokes and other rewards from the group's leadership and other members. They can even get the idea, if not the clear message, that these behaviors are all signs of psychospiritual progress, when the only progress that might be happening is toward the emotional storm that could, hopefully sooner rather than later, blast their tower of illusions back down to earth.

Be wary of groups that play the old secret society game of not letting people know anything about them until after joining, especially if that also requires taking oaths that are not explained in advance. The truth is that most teachings that were once regarded secret, and are sometimes still treated as such, are now available in books and online. Still, there can be noteworthy benefits to a structure of grades, courses, or degrees where some teachings and practices are reserved for people who have actually done the work of a previous level. In that respect, there is no difference from most of our ordinary educational systems. Rosicrucian-related groups with tiered curricula should be up front about why the progression exists, how it works and, at least in general terms, what it contains.

It is also wise to be cautious about any organization claiming to be *THE* Rosicrucian organization, or disallowing cross-membership in other organizations identifying as Rosicrucian, or otherwise intimating that they are the only legitimate Rosicrucians. Some leeway can be given for the perfectly human tendency for loyal affections toward one's own group, but as we have already seen, Rosicrucianism is definitely not essentially tied to lineages and organizations. Groups can have much to offer, but they can never *own* Rosicrucianism.

MAKING A CHOICE

Based on the previous considerations, here are some questions that could be helpful to anyone thinking about joining a group.

- What are the group's objectives and rationale for why it exists, and do those things match well with what you want?

- To what extent is this group known and respected by other similar groups or relevant authorities?

- How open is the group to you getting to know its leaders and other members, and speaking privately with them before joining?

- How authentically do the leaders actually live and exemplify the group's espoused values, virtues, and practices?

- What specific benefits, challenges, and drawbacks do its members report experiencing?

- How open, trusting, and comfortable do the members seem with each other?

- How much are members encouraged to relate their esoteric psychospiritual work and experiences to every other aspect of their lives?

- How much are members encouraged to respectfully question leaders and each other?

- How much time, energy, and money are required, expected, or preferred from members?

- How welcome are members to set and maintain their own limits on the amount of time, energy, and money they give to the group?

Another way of thinking about membership in an esoteric group may be helpful in making your choice, which is recognizing that it will be a relationship with some degree of intimacy and commitment. As is wise with any other relationship, think about how much you and the other persons are ready for that intimacy and commitment. Ask yourself about the extent to which the circumstances of your lives are conducive to the relationship being mutually beneficial and healthy.

Finally, give yourself abundant time in meditation and prayer to see what wells up from deep within you. This approach, combined with thoughtfulness about all the possible benefits and drawbacks of committing to such a relationship, will go a long way in helping you make a good decision.

CONCLUSION

Now you have examined the cornerstone set in place for the rest of this book. It has been lovingly crafted, but it is definitely not perfect. You are encouraged to continue crafting your own cornerstone and to judge what else from this book can contribute to your foundation and edifice in the Great Work of Rosicrucianism.

CHAPTER 2:
THE ROSENKREUZ AND THE ROSE CROIX

This chapter begins with a brief historical review of the Rosi-crucian movement. Along the way, we look into when Rosicrucian symbols and themes entered the Masonic system of degrees. Lastly, the chapter provides an examination of how the contemporary Rose Croix Degree of Freemasonry can be understood as a presentation of Rosicrucian psychospirituality.

ROSICRUCIAN HISTORY

THE MANIFESTOS

In the 17th century's second decade, a small, anonymously authored document made a noteworthy splash in the intellectual waters of Europe. It was entitled *The Fama Fraternitatis of the Meritorious Order of the Rosy Cross, Addressed to the Learned in General, and the Governors of Europe*. It is commonly referred to as the *Fama Fratenitatis*, or simply the *Fama*.[14] While versions of the *Fama* had apparently already been privately circulating for a few years, its first official publication was in 1614 in Germany. In 1615 it was followed by the *Confessio Fraternitatis*, also anonymously authored. The *Chemical Wedding of Christian Rosenkreuz* then appeared in 1616, which the German theologian and utopian Johann Valentin Andreae later admitted to writing. Andreae was a member of the Tubingen Circle, a group of Christian esotericists that Christopher McIntosh has argued collectively drafted the *Fama, Confessio*, and *Chemical Wedding*.[15] Together, these three documents are regarded as the introduction of Rosicrucianism to the world and are commonly referred to as the "Rosicrucian manifestos."

As we strive to make good use of these texts, it is helpful to know that they are part of larger literary, philosophical, and cultural movements. In general, they can be connected with Renaissance humanism urging a revitalization and synthesis of ancient wisdom in the Christian world. On the other hand, they also bear similarities with pre- and early Enlightenment calls for trusting the senses and reason in the study of Nature. There is also strong resonance with fictional and speculative explorations of Christian utopianism. Keeping these intersections in mind helps us better understand the context in which the author or

---

14. *Fama Fraternitatis* translates as "Fame of the Brotherhood."
15. Christopher McIntosh, *The Rosicrucians: The History, Mythology, and Rituals of an Esoteric Order*, first paperback edition (York Beach: Weiser, 1998), 19-30.

authors of the manifestos were envisioning change for a better world. There has indeed been progress in ways they hoped, but religion and politics have also changed in ways they could not foresee, and not always for the better.

Every aspiring Rosicrucian should be intimately familiar with the manifestos, but it is important to keep in mind that they were written within a specific culture and era, and that they were also meant to be inspirational. Their core desires for personal transformation and so-cial reform remain timelessly relevant and have been adapted by every generation since their appearance. It is therefore our task to hear and understand their spirit and its relevance for our lives today. In fact, the spirit of the Rosicrucian movement encourages us to use our God-given gifts of reason, intuition, and creativity rather than take these documents as crystallized doctrines demanding literalism and unthink-ing conformity. It is up to each of us to study, interpret, and develop them in ways fitting our own lives as individuals and in community with others.

THE FAMA FRATERNITATIS

The *Fama* tells the story of a brilliant young monk, C.R.C., who traveled to learn the greatest wisdom of the world, including time in Jerusalem, Arabia, Egypt, Fez, and Spain.[16] Among his studies were mathematics, medicine, magia, and Cabala. C.R.C. eventually re-turned to Germany, and in his desire to aid the reformation of the world, he built a temple and established the Orden des Rosenkreuzes (Order of the Rose Cross), a small, pious Christian brotherhood in which members were educated in the secret curriculum he had devel-oped, and in which they also produced works of their own.

After some time, the brothers resolved to travel apart from each other, taking their knowledge to be examined in secret by the most

---

16. In the *Fama*, he is actually first introduced as Father C.R., and then later in the document as C.R.C.. It is only in the *Chemical Wedding of Christian Rosenkreuz* that a name fitting the initials is provided.

learned, and to continue gathering the world's knowledge, reporting it back to each other. Before departing, they bound themselves to six agreements:

1. None of them should practice any other profession than to cure the sick, and that gratis.

2. None should feel constrained on account of the Brotherhood to wear a particular garb but should wear the attire of the country.

3. Every brother should appear on day C. at the House of the Holy Spirit or state the cause of his absence.

4. Every brother should look for a worthy person who might succeed him.

5. The word C.R. would be their seal, password, and sign.

6. The Brotherhood should remain undisclosed for one hundred years.[17]

According to the *Fama*, the Fraternity served its aims through a number of generations, and during that time the location of C.R.C.'s tomb was forgotten. Then, through a strange set of circumstances, a brother discovered the entrance to the tomb along with C.R.C.'s prediction that it would remain hidden for 120 years. He reported it to his brethren and, entering it together, they found a highly symbolic, fascinating, and seemingly miraculous structure, designed not only to contain C.R.C.'s physical remains, but also to preserve the corpus of his knowledge, including books, scientific instruments, and other artifacts.

The rest of the *Fama* offers further explanation of the Order's studies, ideals, and goals. It confesses Jesus Christ, reveres the Holy Bible, and pledges faithfulness to Christianity. After lauding the

---

17. *Rosicrucian Trilogy: Modern Translations of the Three Founding Documents*, trans. Joscelyn Godwin, Christopher McIntosh, and Donate Pahnke McIntosh (Newburyport: Weiser, 2016), 22.

alchemist physician Theophrastus Bombastus von Hohenheim (a.k.a. Paracelsus), it then decries those alchemists seeking to make actual gold, claiming that "true philosophers" have many better things to do.[18] Plato, Aristotle, Pythagoras, Enoch, Abraham, Moses, and Solomon are praised. Prophetic knowledge is claimed of unspecified changes that were expected to soon occur in Europe's politics.[19] The brothers declare their intention to provide secret help to the coming changes.

The document closes by inviting the learned to reach out to the Order. Those who bear sincere affection for it are promised benefits for all aspects of their well-being. Those who are motivated by greed are warned that they will come to "the greatest and deepest ruin."[20] It ends with a statement that "our building, even if a hundred thousand people had seen it from close to, shall forever remain untouched, unde-stroyed, unseen, and completely hidden from the godless world. *Under the shadow of Thy wings, Jehova.*"[21]

The Confessio Fraternitatis

Published the year after the *Fama*, the *Confessio Fratenitatis* pro-vides 37 statements about the Order's purposes and intentions. Rather than summarize the entire document, we here review three intersecting themes it expands upon from the *Fama*.

The first of those themes is fervent piety combined with a coura-geous and innovative attitude about how to be Christian. A significant amount of the *Confessio* asserts the Fraternity's Christian fidelity, while also claiming a better vision and expression of the faith than is often found in the world. They repeatedly uphold the Holy Bible as the most

---

18. *Rosicrucian Trilogy*, 31.
19. That prophetic view is clearly related to Martin Luther's views on the Four Monarchies, an eschatological perspective of history based on the Book of Daniel's apocalyptic vision. The author of this book does not hold to that view. To learn more about it, see Winfried Vogel, "The Eschatological Theology of Martin Luther, Part II: Luther's Exposition on Daniel and Revelation," Digital Commons @ Andrews Univer-sity, *https://digitalcommons.andrews.edu/cgi/viewcontent.cgi?article=1809&context=auss*.
20. *Rosicrucian Trilogy*, 32.
21. *Rosicrucian Trilogy*, 32.

valuable of guides and encourage their readers to make honest use of it, a radical stance for the times. Connected with this theme is the brothers' belief that Europe was on the cusp of a significant transition. They regard it as evidenced by an outpouring of new scientific knowledge and philosophical insight, as well as much fraud and charlatanism, and also by the emergence of new religious and political reforms. They have seen astrological omens, and they speak of the coming changes in ways that suggest various apocalyptic Biblical prophecies. It is their firm conviction that Heaven has ordained the passing of one era and the dawn of another during their own time.

On the topic of new knowledge, the *Confessio* affirms that even if all the world's books and writings were lost, truth and light could again be brought to the world with what C.R.C. discovered through his meditations. This theme includes the Fraternity's sense of duty to generously spread that knowledge, coupled with a responsibility to protect it from those who are unprepared to receive it, or are lazy, insincere, arrogant, driven by mercenary desires, or unvirtuous in other ways. At the same time, the brothers are aware of how often something of great value can be hidden in plain sight; "the Book of Nature is opened wide before the eyes of all, though few can read or understand it."[22] In fact, their closing comment confesses that nobody can know the Brotherhood or enjoy their benefits unless God wills it.

Finally, there are recurring statements on the theme of welcoming the sincere and virtuous into the Order of the Rose Cross, whomever they may be. There are also hints that becoming one of them is not actually a matter of joining an organization, but instead is about being a particular type of person. There is no comment clearer about the qualifications for the Order than this statement.

---

22. *Rosicrucian Trilogy*, 47.

Anyone who discerns those great letters that God has inscribed on the world-machine and renewed through all the vicissitudes of empires, and who can understand, read, and inform himself from them, is already one of us, though he may be unaware as yet.[23]

THE CHEMICAL WEDDING OF CHRISTIAN ROSENKREUZ

Of the three Rosicrucian manifestos, the *Chemical Wedding* is the least manifesto-like. Published two years after the *Fama*, it is an allegorical tale of C.R.C. as an elderly hermit, recounting his seven-day adventure in accepting an invitation to the wedding of a king and queen.[24] The story involves a constant use of esoteric symbolism from alchemy, astrology, and mythology. For that reason, it is the easiest to do injustice with a summary. Everyone sincerely interested in Rosicrucianism should ponder each of the manifestos for themselves, but this is most true of the *Chemical Wedding*. Studying the commentaries of others can also be helpful, and none can be more highly recommended than those by Jack Courtis and Adam McLean.[25]

The *Chemical Wedding* differs from the other two manifestos not only in style but also in message. It has thematic parallels with the *Fama's* story of C.R.C.'s early travels but goes into much greater depth and detail by metaphorically describing the process of self-transformation leading to the *conunctio* of psychospiritual alchemy.[26] Thus,

23. *Rosicrucian Trilogy*, 46.
24. It is noteworthy that Johann Valentin Andreae's family crest bears a red saltire cross and four red roses, both of which are prominent parts of C.R.C.'s attire in this tale. Also note that while C.R.C. of the *Chemical Wedding* is commonly regarded as the same character as in the *Fama*, some scholars regard them as different personages.
25. Jack Courtis, "Commentaries on the Chymical Wedding of C.R.C.," *Rosicrucian Library, Confraternity of the Rose+Cross*, Stepney Nominees Pty. Ltd., Trustee for Courtis No.4 Trust, 1998, *https://www.crcsite.org/rosicrucian-library/chymical-wedding-guide1*. Joscelyn Godwin and Adam McLean, *The Chemical Wedding of Christian Rosenkreutz*, Magnum Opus Hermetic Sourceworks Series: No. 18, (Grand Rapids: Phanes Press, 1991).
26. *Conunctio* is the integration and harmonization of the elements of our being. In alchemical literature it is often represented by the marriage and intercourse of a king, typically red, and a queen, typically white.

C.R.C. is not merely revered as an exceptional forebearer of mythic status, but instead becomes a relatable exemplar who successfully faces allegorical trials of the Great Work.

In effect, this text further clarifies the image of a Rosicrucian sketched by the *Fama* and *Confessio*. The first two give much attention to the study of books and pursuit of the arts and sciences. While all three indicate the importance of virtue and learning through the immediate experiences of life itself, the *Chemical Wedding* stresses these two elements. As one who reads and writes, C.R.C. apparently has some educational background, but he leads a simple rustic life and is a devout man of prayer, deep meditation, and visions, who also consults his dreams and attends to portents in Nature. His virtue is demonstrated in numerous ways, including his humility, good judgment, compassion, and willingness to take the necessary risks of exploring the mysterious and forbidden.

C.R.C.'s characteristics are important because they underscore that Rosicrucianism is not reserved for those with significant worldly resources. At the time the manifestos were written, books and education were still mostly reserved for the wealthy, members of the aristocracy, and clerics. The C.R.C. presented in the *Chemical Wedding* does not appear to be any of those and has no honors to declare for himself other than being "a brother of the Red Rose Cross."[27] Even so, by the end of the story he has earned the recognition of being made a Knight of the Golden Stone. The boons of Rosicrucianism and the Great Work are shown to be within reach of everyone, based only on the merits of their hearts and minds rather than their purse or social rank.

Perhaps most importantly, the *Chemical Wedding* clarifies the most essential element in accomplishing the Great Work. On the fifth morning of C.R.C.'s adventure, after a ritualized beheading of the royals on the previous night, he is secretly shown the sepulcher and beautiful, naked body of the Lady Venus. He also has a significant encounter

---

27. *Rosicrucian Trilogy*, 79.

with a cupid. Then, in preparation for restoring the royals to life so the marriage can be completed, a circle of nymphs sings this song:

I
Naught better is on earth
Than lovely noble love
Whereby we be as God
And no one vexeth his neighbour.
So let unto the king be sung
That all the sea shall sound.
We ask, and answer ye.

II
What hath to us life brought?
'Tis Love
Who hath brought grace again?
'Tis Love
Whence are we born?
Of Love
How were we all forlorn?
Without Love

III
Who hath us then begotten?
'Twas Love
Wherefore were we suckled?
For Love
What owe we to our elders?
'Tis Love
And why are they so patient?
From Love

IV
What doth all things o'ercome?
'Tis Love
Can we find Love as well?
Through Love
Where letteth a man good work appear?
In Love
Who can unite a twain?
'Tis Love

V
So let us all sing
That it resound
To honour Love
Which will increase
With our lord king and queen,
Their bodies are here, their souls are fled.

VI
And as we live
So shall God give
Where love and grace
Did sunder them
That we with flame of Love
May haply join them up again.

VII
So shall this song
In greatest joy

Though thousand generations come
Return into eternity.[28]

Love is thus praised as the philosophical fire that foments all the most important things in life. This poem reaches its crescendo in highlighting the necessity of love in our own psychospiritual transformation, figuratively illustrated by the resurrection and conunctio of the king and queen. This is a crucial lesson in the Great Work, and echoes St. Paul the Apostle's teaching on the centrality of love:

> *I may speak in different languages of people or even angels. But if I do not have love, I am only a noisy bell or a crashing cymbal. I may have the gift of prophecy. I may understand all the secret things of God and have all knowledge, and I may have faith so great I can move mountains. But even with all these things, if I do not have love, then I am nothing. I may give away everything I have, and I may even give my body as an offering to be burned. But I gain nothing if I do not have love.[29]*

Finally, C.R.C. and other wedding attendees successfully restore the king and queen with an alchemical operation. To honor their service, each is made a Knight of the Golden Stone and sworn to hold to these articles:

1. You Lord Knights shall swear to ascribe your Order not to any devil or spirit, but only to God your Creator, and to nature, his handmaiden.

---

28. "Chymical Wedding – Fifth Day," *Rosicrucian texts, Alchemy Web Site,* from the Foxcroft English edition of 1690, ed. McLean, Adam, and Green, Deirdre, for the Magnum Opus Edition, 1984, *https://www.alchemywebsite.com/chymwed5.html.* This poem bears more than a passing similarity to a poem written by Raymond Lully in the 13th century.
29. 1 Corinthians 12:1-3 NCV.

2. You shall abominate all whoredom, incontinence, and uncleanness, and not defile your Order with such vices.

3. Through your gifts you shall willingly come to the aid of all who are deserving and in need.

4. You shall not desire this honor to use for worldly show or high esteem.

5. You shall not wish to live longer than God wills.

In signing his name, C.R.C. selected for himself the enigmatic motto, *Summa scientia nihil scire*, meaning "the highest knowledge is to know nothing." Perhaps in this he is simply paraphrasing and subscribing to the *Socratic paradox*, "I neither know nor think that I know," which Socrates asserted was his only claim to wisdom. On the other hand, C.R.C. may be making an apophatic theological statement akin to the Via Negativa. In any case, this motto and the pretended incomplete ending of the story leave the reader with a lingering sense of mystery, and mysteries beg to be investigated.

THE ROSICRUCIAN FUROR AND THE MASONIC REVIVAL OF THE ROSE+CROSS

In *The Rosicrucian Enlightenment*, Frances Yates coined the term *Rosicrucian Furor* to describe the flurry of interest immediately generated by the manifestos.[30] Within a decade, hundreds of letters of application to the Fraternity of the Rose Cross were published, and praises, attacks, and defenses continued for decades more. The manifestos were referenced by others in their own writings on matters of alchemy, medicine, religion, and politics. Of course, there were hucksters using the whole scene as an opportunity to swindle the gullible, and in doing so, stained the name of Rosicrucianism for many others.

---

30. Frances A. Yates, *The Rosicrucian Enlightenment*, 1972, (New York: Barnes & Noble, 1996), 91-102.

Accepted and speculative Freemasonry has long been suspected of having Rosicrucian roots. As the operative lodges began accepting non-masons as members, and the philosophical and ritualistic elements of the Craft were more fully developed, some of the key figures were interested in Rosicrucianism or were alleged Rosicrucians, such as Elias Ashmole, Robert Moray, and David Ramsay. In fact, in 1638, a poem by the Scottish poet Henry Adamson, the *Muses Thernodie*, was published with these lines:

> *For what we do presage is not in grosse*
> *For we be brethren of the Rosie Crosse;*
> *We have the Mason word, and second sight,*
> *Things for to come we can foretell aright.*[31]

Those words became public in the midst of the Rosicrucian Furor, yet throughout the Furor, the Order of the Rose Cross appeared to remain silent and totally hidden, with no verifiable claims of anyone being admitted or stepping forward as an authenticated representative. Even Johann Valentin Andreae cast a pallor of doubt on the Rosicrucian movement. He died in 1654, and in his later years, he admitted to having written the *Chemical Wedding*, thus positioning himself as a member of the original Order if there ever was one. However, in that admission he labeled the *Chemical Wedding* as a *ludibrium*, meaning a "plaything." This confession, while not actually decrying the Rosicrucian movement, was nonetheless enough for many people to conclude that it was not worth taking seriously.

Although the Rosicrucian Furor had faded by the end of the 17th century, the manifestos and derivative works continued to attract

---

31. Henry Adamson, "Muses Thernodie – The Third Muse," *All Poetry*, *https://allpoetry.com/The-Muses-Thernodie:-Third-Muse*. For an excellent historical examination of the poem, see Ed Johnson, "The Muses Thernodie in Context," in *Heredom*, Vol. 27, ed. S. Brent Morris (DC: Scottish Rite Research Society, 2020), 63-102.

persons sincerely interested in the more recondite aspects of science and spirituality. In the middle of the 18th century, many of those people were Freemasons who felt moved to work Rosicrucian themes into their degree systems.[32] So it is that McIntosh refers to this period as beginning the "Masonic phase" of Rosicrucian history.[33] With regard to the creation of actual organizations, this renewal of Rosicrucian symbolism was highly active and produced long-lasting effects.

There had been rumors of Rosicrucian organizations existing ever since the *Fama*. Yet, during a 1761 anti-Masonic purge in Prague, a document of rituals and statutes emerged as the first solid evidence of a functional Rosicrucian society, Zur schwarzen Rose (The Black Rose).[34] Christopher McIntosh calculated that the order would have been in existence as early as 1757.[35] The order's rituals and teachings were significantly alchemical in nature and apparently reflected the work of Hermann Fictuld (c. 1700 – c. 1777), who was influential on a later order that was also concerned with psychospiritual alchemy, the Gold– und Rosenkreuzer (Golden and Rosy Cross), which was operational by 1777.[36] The legacy of the Gold– und Rosenkreuzer would later prove to be influential on the Masonic Societas Rosicruciana in Anglia, founded in 1865, and the non-Masonic Hermetic Order of the Golden Dawn, begun in 1887, with its inner order of the Rosae Rubeae et

---

32. As early as 1741, the term *Rosy Cross* had appeared in reference to a degree now included in the Royal Order of Scotland. See R. Stephen Doan, "Knight Rose Croix and Its inner Order," *The Plumbline: The Quarterly Bulletin of the Scottish Rite Research Society*, 28, no. 1 (2021): 3.

33. Christopher McIntosh, *The Rose Cross and the Age of Reason: Eighteenth-Century Rosicrucianism in Central Europe and its Relationship to the Enlightenment*, 1992, (Albany: SUNY, 2011), 39-58.

34. Tobias Churton, *The Invisible History of the Rosicrucians*, (Rochester: Inner Traditions, 2009), 396. McIntosh, *The Rose Cross and the Age of Reason*, 50.

35. 1757 is also the year in which a Brother Targe received a Masonic diploma in France showing him as a *Chevalier de l'Orient et Rose Croix*. See R. Stephen Doan, "Knight Rose Croix and Its inner Order," *The Plumbline: The Quarterly Bulletin of the Scottish Rite Research Society*, 28, no. 1 (2021): 3.

36. Tobias Churton, *The Invisible History of the Rosicrucians*, (Rochester: Inner Traditions, 2009), 396-397.

Aureae Crucis (Red Rose and Golden Cross). The main point here is that the mid-to-late 1700s produced a number of Masonic degrees or orders making use of the Rose+Cross symbol in an esoteric Christian initiatic rite. As another noteworthy example, in 1763 the Christian esotericist Jean-Baptiste Willermoz founded the Chevaliers del'Aigle Noir et Rose-Croix (Knights of the Black Eagle and Rose-Cross).[37]

If the manifestos and their early defenders were the foundation of the Rosicrucian historical edifice, then this era of Masonic revival was certainly when its numerous walls, floors, and rooms were constructed. Many have since crumbled and fallen, while others have been perpetuated into the present day. In any case, within Freemasonry the symbol of the Rose+Cross found a lasting home and continuing generations willing to draw inspiration from it.

THE ROSICRUCIANISM OF THE ROSE CROIX DEGREE

In this crucial period of the mid-1700s, Estienne (Stephen) Morin created the Order of the Royal Secret (1761), in which the 18th Degree was listed as "Knights of the White Eagle or Pelican, known by the name of perfect Mason, or knight of the Rose Cross."[38] In 1801, the degrees of Morin's order were included in a new system of 33 degrees that are still practiced under the banner of the Ancient and Accepted Scottish Rite. Today, the 18th Degree is most commonly known simply as "Knight Rose Croix," although it carries other titles connecting it with earlier versions, such as "Sovereign Prince Rose Croix of Heredom," "Perfect Prince de H-R-D-M," "Knight of the White Eagle or Pelican," and "Knight of the Eagle and Pelican."[39] In the following paragraphs, we consider how the degree's symbolism

---

37. McIntosh, *Rose Cross and the Age of Reason*, 41.
38. Arturo De Hoyos, *The Scottish Rite Ritual Monitor and Guide*, 3rd Ed. Rev. & *Enlarged*, (DC: The Supreme Council, 2010), 102-103.
39. De Hoyos, *Scottish Rite Ritual*, 439.

and teachings have evolved to more fully intertwine with common elements of Rosicrucianism.

Early versions of the 18th Degree *overtly* offer little more than a review of common Christian teachings on theology, damnation versus salvation, and the life, messages, and spiritual role of Jesus Christ. These points are embellished with the symbolism of temple destruction and rebuilding that is central to Scottish Rite Freemasonry, with special emphasis on the three Theological Virtues of faith, hope, and love/charity that are initially taught in many versions of the first degree, Entered Apprentice. There is nothing in the first versions of the Knight Rose Croix Degree that explicitly references the kinds of things found in esoteric Christianity, such as Neoplatonism, Hermeticism, Cabala, Gnosticism, or alchemy. More than one Masonic scholar has therefore concluded that there was never anything genuinely Rosicrucian about the Rose Croix Degree, including the encyclopedist Albert Mackey.

> *It is true, that about the middle of the eighteenth century, a period fertile in the invention of advanced Degrees, a Masonic Rite was established which assumed the name of Rose Croix Freemasonry, and adopted the symbol of the Rose and Cross. But this was a coincidence, and not a consequence. There was nothing in common between them and the Rosicrucians, except the name, the symbol, and the Christian character. Doubtless the symbol was suggested to the Masonic Order from the use of it by the philosophic sect; but the Freemasons modified the interpretation, and the symbol, of course, gave rise to the name. But here the connection ends. A Rose Croix Freemason and a Rosicrucian are two entirely different persons.*[40]

Other scholars, including McIntosh and Churton, have reasoned that there are indeed significant commonalities, and enough to regard the degree as a recognizable expression of the Rosicrucian spirit.[41]

---

40. Albert G. Mackey, *Encyclopedia of Freemasonry, Rev. & Enlarged by Robert I. Clegg, Vol. 2* (Chicago: Masonic History Company, 1946), 878.
41. McIntosh, *The Rosicrucians*, 137. Churton, *Invisible History*, 401-403.

However, seeing the commonalities requires interpretations of the degree's symbolism that are not offered by the degree itself, and such interpretation is the right of every Freemason, even a duty. To that end, you are encouraged to consult published versions of the early rituals as you consider the following points.[42]

1. The Rose+Cross: The authors of those early rituals were well aware of the background of this image and must have known it would be regarded as at least a symbolic connection with the movement started by the *Fama*. Perhaps more telling than the lack of any admission to an intentional connection through this symbol is the lack of any disclaimer. Had they not wanted the connection to be made, they could have said so, but they did not. At the very least, regarding the Rose Croix Degree as Rosicrucian is left an option.

2. The prominence of the colors black, white, and red: These colors are also central to alchemy, where they actually name the three most universally referenced phases of the Great Work – *nigredo*, *albedo*, and *rubedo* – the blackening, the whitening, and the reddening. Gold also fits into this sequence, since it is typically connected and sometimes even equated with red. One could further argue that the sequence of events of the degree ritual parallels these phases.

3. The cubic stone sweating blood and water: This is a combination of widely known Christian imagery based on Biblical references to Jesus as the chief cornerstone of the Church, his perspiring blood in the Garden of Gethsemane, and the water that gushed from the spear wound in his side as he hung on the cross. This imagery also

42. See *Masonic Rituals and Formulas Transcribed by Albert Pike in 1854 and 1855*, ed. Arturo de Hoyos, (DC: Scottish Rite Research Society, 2010), and Arturo de Hoyos, *Freemasonry's Royal Secret: The Jamaican "Franken Manuscript" of the High Degrees*, (DC: Scottish Rite Research Society, 2014).

speaks directly to alchemists, where the cubic stone signifies the primal material with which one works, as well as the work's goal, the Philosopher's Stone. The blood and water can likewise be regarded as representations of the fundamental solar and lunar elements within the stone, elements that many alchemical texts say must be properly extracted and reintegrated to accomplish the Great Work.[43]

4. The eagle: The eagle has two traditional meanings in ordinary Christianity that have further depths among esoteric Christians.

    a. Because the eagle is a sharp-eyed bird that freely soars closer to the heavens, it represents Christians who can "see the Light," have been baptized and born again, freed from the weight of their sins, and are thus closer to Heaven. The eagle has a somewhat resonant meaning in alchemy, where it represents essences that have been evaporated or sublimed from a substance, and it is thus generally symbolic of the spirit that animates matter. It is therefore also sometimes connected with the phoenix, which rises reborn from its flaming death.

    b. Second, the eagle is commonly associated with St. John the Evangelist and his gospel. Of the four canonical gospels, John's is the one that most addresses the heavenly or divine aspects of Jesus Christ. This common exoteric association with the Gospel of John is also meaningful among esoteric Christians. The first chapter addresses the divinity of Jesus as the *Logos*, a term that was very familiar to Greek philosophers. Among other meanings, it was the rational, animating aspect of the Divine,

43. A similar observation of this symbolism is found in Leon Zeldis, "An Esoteric View of the Rose Croix Degree," *Pietre-Stones Review of Freemasonry, https://www. freemasons-freemasonry.com/zeldis11.html.*

upon which each thing in creation is dependent for its existence. This understanding of Logos fits well with that of the Gospel of John, as does Philo of Alexandria's (c. 20 AD – c. 50 AD) concept of the Logos as being the first-born of God. The Gospel of John also speaks most clearly of Jesus' intention that his followers know the same unity with God that he knows, an idea that seems hidden in plain sight to many mainstream Christians.[44] Esoteric Christians commonly regard these statements as a mandate for seeking mystical realization or gnosis, a kind of liberation from illusion that is aptly represented by the high-flying eagle or reborn phoenix.

5. The pelican feeding its chicks with blood from its own breast: This is an ancient portrayal of salvation and spiritual nourishment provided to the faithful through Jesus' self-sacrifice. But alchemists also recognize it as depicting a kind of distillation vessel called a *retort*. In the Great Work, it facilitates the refinement, condensing, and

multiplication of the Philosopher's Stone so that it can then be used in the transformation of other things. Psychospiritually speaking, it signifies the stage of development in which one is preparing to apply their spiritual essence for the benefit of others, which nicely parallels the standard religious symbolism of the pelican feeding its young.

44. John 17:11, 21-24.

6. <u>The required meeting on Maundy Thursday</u>: Maundy Thursday is the day in the liturgical calendar on which Christians venerate the Last Supper, when Jesus taught his disciples the sacrament with bread and wine to remember the sacrifice of his body and blood. The word *maundy* literally means "mandatory," relating to Jesus's "new commandment" to love as he loved.[45] On the Rosicrucian side, Maundy Thursday is one candidate for the mysterious "day C" mentioned in the *Fama*, on which all Rosicrucian initiates are expected to spiritually commune in the House of the Holy Spirit, or report the reason for their absence.[46] According to an old statute for Masons of the Rose Croix Degree, if one is alone on this day, then it is imperative to meet "other Knights in the spirit."[47]

7. <u>Themes of personal transformation and social reformation</u>: The presence of these themes in Rosicrucianism has already been established. Furthermore, their presence throughout Freemasonry is beyond dispute. This degree presents those themes in its allegorical journey from darkness to light, along the way encouraging members to contemplate the disposition of their souls, to practice the virtues of faith, hope, and charity, and to emulate Jesus Christ in loving others.

Examination of these seven elements makes it hard to accept Mackey's assertions that Rosicrucianism and the 18th Degree have nothing in harmony but the Rose+Cross symbol and a Christian character, and that a Rose Croix Freemason and a follower of Rosicrucianism must therefore be fundamentally different persons. To the contrary, it shows that there are significant symbolic intersections and that

---

45. John 13:34-35.
46. C.R. Dunning, Jr., "The Mysterious Day C of the Rosicrucians," *Manifestos, Rosicrucian Tradition: Traditional Teachings of the Invisible Order*, 2020, *https://pansophers.com/day-c-of-the-rosicrucians*.
47. *Masonic Rituals and Formulas Transcribed by Albert Pike in 1854 and 1855*, ed. Arturo de Hoyos, (DC: Scottish Rite Research Society, 2010), 415.

a Knight Rose Croix and an aspiring Rosicrucian could easily be one and the same. From the first appearance of this degree, the congruence would have been apparent to anyone well versed with Rosicrucianism and alchemical or esoteric Christian interpretations of the degree's symbolism. This perspective is further punctuated by the possibility that the degree was first written by Jean-Baptiste Willermoz (1730-1824), a known esotericist and student of the theurgist Martinez de Pasqually.[48]

All seven elements are still integral to more recent versions of the degree. However, beginning with revisions made in 1861, more commonalities with Rosicrucianism were included. The current ritual of the Ancient and Accepted Scottish Rite Southern Jurisdiction was put in use within the first decade of the 21st century. Although the ritual still does not directly address Rosicrucianism, it and its official supporting literature reveal even more aspects connecting it with the movement. We now examine some of the content that has been made available to the public. The follow paragraphs reference the official guidebook for the degrees of the Scottish Rite Southern Jurisdiction, which is *The Scottish Rite Ritual Monitor and Guide*.[49]

The contemporary version of the 18th Degree is laced with alchemical references. Within the first paragraph of its synopsis is the declaration, "This Degree both reveals and conceals one of the great secrets of Alchemy…."[50] This is followed by an explanation of the difference between "Practical Alchemy" and "Spiritual Alchemy." It is then asserted that the latter type is initiatic and that its practitioners have sought to transform themselves, which is clarified as the work of

---

48. Churton, *Invisible History*, 402. Pasqually was the founder and head of the Elu Cohen (1754-1774), a Christian theurgic system of degrees in which members learned and practiced invocation and evocation of spiritual beings for the betterment of humanity and all of creation.

49. Arturo De Hoyos, *The Scottish Rite Ritual Monitor and Guide, 3rd Ed. Rev. & Enlarged*, (DC: The Supreme Council, 2010).

50. De Hoyos, *Scottish Rite Ritual*, 247.

this degree. Thus, this textbook explanation of the Rose Croix Degree firmly connects it with psychospiritual alchemy and thereby echoes the *Fama*.

Intertwining with the alchemical language are references to Nature that mirror those found in the Rosicrucian manifestos. For example, the Rose Croix lecture explains one esoteric meaning of the acronym INRI as *Igne Natura Renovatur Integra*, "All of Nature is Renovated by Fire." Further consideration of INRI includes this statement:

> *We apply reason to the Book of Nature and find a great truth written in the letters of light: there is a living God. The great law that governs the universe is harmony; the will of the Almighty God, always acting as the expression of His infinite love. Arriving at this result by applying reason to the decipherment on the great pages of the Book of Nature, we read the sacred initials thus....*[51]

For comparison, in the *Confessio* we find, "the Book of Nature is opened wide before the eyes of all, though few can either read or understand it."[52] Also, consider the *Fama* speaking of the importance of probing "all faculties, sciences, and arts, and all of Nature in order to determine certain infallible axioms...."[53]

The lecture additionally contains references to some of the same philosophers and sages lauded by the *Fama*, including an extensive examination of the Tetractys of the Greek philosopher Pythagoras.[54] That examination makes a connection with Cabala, which is also mentioned in the *Fama*. Furthermore, the Hermetic Axiom, *as above so below, as below so above*, is dramatically highlighted in the ritual in a way that must remain privy to those who have received the initiation.

51. De Hoyos, *Scottish Rite Ritual*, 459.
52. *Rosicrucian Trilogy*, 47
53. *Rosicrucian Trilogy*, 19.
54. De Hoyos, *Scottish Rite Ritual*, 462-465.

CONCLUSION

Rosicrucianism is rooted in the three manifestos of the 17th century. In the 18th century, the movement extended a branch into Freemasonry through a number of different rites and degrees that incorporated Rosicrucian symbolism, themes, and values. One of those degrees, Knight Rose Croix, has continued to evolve so that today it even more obviously reveals its resonance with Rosicrucianism. Becoming a Rosicrucian may not simply be a matter of joining an organization or passing through an initiation ritual, but doing those things can surely be instrumental. It is therefore perfectly reasonable to conclude that anyone who receives the 18th Degree, deeply contemplates its ritual, symbols, and teachings, and actively applies the light gained therefrom, may rightly be regarded as walking a genuine Rosicrucian path.

CHAPTER 3:
ON THE MASONIC ETHOS
THE LOVE OF VIRTUE AND THE VIRTUE OF LOVE

The Rosicrucian manifestos clearly assert the importance of virtue and love, and Freemasonry also has much to say about them.[55] This chapter is intended to more fully reveal the Masonic ethos that informs the Rose Croix Degree, and thus provide a clearer context and a firmer foundation for a Rosicrucian path stemming from that degree.[56]

55. Blue Lodge references are from the Preston/Webb family of rituals, and Scottish Rite references are from the Pike family of rituals in the Ancient and Accepted Scottish Rite, Southern Jurisdiction.
56. This chapter is adapted from C.R. Dunning, Jr., "On the Masonic Ethos: A Meditation on the Love of Virtue and the Virtue of Love," *The Plumbline: The Quarterly Journal of the Scottish Rite Research Society 27, no. 4* (2021): 1-7.

Every Masonic degree describes specific virtues that its initiates are admonished to practice, and many of them also extoll the benefits of love in some form. Even so, while there are many things implied about the relationship between love and virtue, that relationship is never thoroughly examined in the performance of Masonic rituals. Primarily in terms of Platonic and Aristotelian thought, this chapter conducts such an examination to arrive at a more complete understanding of Freemasonry's ethical ideals. Beginning with the development of working definitions for love and virtue, we proceed to consider how they are related, how Freemasonry urges initiates to more fully embrace them, and then finally we ponder their most profound possibility.

LOVE

The English word, *love*, as both a verb and noun, refers to a range of meanings that are separately named in other languages. In ancient Greek, the words *eros, philia*, and *agape* are among several terms used to distinguish one form of love from another.[57] In *Morals & Dogma*, the insights of the great Greek philosopher Plato and his teacher, Socrates, are repeatedly referenced with regard to love. This fact is not surprising, given that Plato's *Phaedrus* and *Symposium* (385-370 BCE) are generally regarded as two of the ancient world's most insightful dialogues on the nature of love.

These dialogues focus on eros as the most fundamental form of love. In fact, over three centuries prior to them, Hesiod claimed Eros to be the fourth of all the gods to appear.[58] In the generation just before

57. An excellent Masonic examination of the different Greek words for love can be found here: John S. Nagy, *Building Cement: Uncommonly Concrete Masonic Education, Vol. 7*. (Lutz, FL: Promethean Genesis Publishing, 2013).
58. Hesiod, *Theogony*, in Hugh G. Evelyn-White, *The Homeric Hymns and Homerica with an English Translation*. (Cambridge, MA: Harvard University Press; London, William Heinemann Ltd. 1914), line 120. *https://data.perseus.org/citations/urn:cts:greekLit:tlg0020.tlg001.perseus-eng1:104-138.*

Socrates, Parmenides even positioned Eros as the first of the gods.[59] These observations are significant because in *Phaedrus*, when Socrates reveals his own views on love, he starts by praising it as the god Eros, whom he refers to as the son of Aphrodite, the goddess of love.[60]

Love's divine status is important because, as Socrates states, "For if love be, as he surely is, a divinity, he cannot be evil."[61] His definition first and foremost establishes love as essentially and truly good in a way that cannot be undone by human beings. A similar view would be asserted hundreds of years later by the earliest Christians: "God is love, and those who abide in love abide in God, and God abides in them."[62]

Following Socrates' lead, the definition of love for this chapter begins with its divinity. Whether regarded as a deity itself or an attribute of a single all-encompassing Deity, love is here considered so fundamentally real and essentially good that it is ultimately beyond human corruption. As with all things divine, it must also remain somewhat mysterious, having dimensions transcending the limits of our senses, comprehension, and control.

Nonetheless, for humans to have a useful definition of love, we must further qualify how it can be known and expressed by us. On this point, it is again noteworthy that Plato's dialogues focus on eros as the fundamental form of love. In its most rudimentary sense, eros is simply our attraction to and desire for beauty. The basic truth of the relationship between eros and beauty is literally expressed in English by referring to beautiful things as "lovely." A range for this relationship

59. Parmenides, "On Nature," trans. John Burnet (1892), stanza 13. *https://philoctetes. free.fr/parmenidesunicode.htm.*

60. Plato, *Phaedrus*, in *Plato in Twelve Volumes*, Vol. 9, trans. Harold N. Fowler. (Cambridge, MA, Harvard University Press; London, William Heinemann Ltd. 1925), line 242d. *https://data.perseus.org/citations/urn:cts:greekLit:tlg0059.tlg012. perseus-eng1:242d.* Note that the Roman names of Eros and Aphrodite are "Cupid" and "Venus," characters with important roles in the *Chemical Wedding*.

61. Plato, Phaedrus, line 242e. *https://data.perseus.org/citations/urn:cts:greekLit:tlg0059. tlg012.perseus-eng1:242e.*

62. 1 John 4:16 NRSV.

is illustrated in *Symposium* when Socrates recounts how Diotima of Mantinea explained love to him as an ascent, which later scholars have treated as a metaphorical ladder:[63]

- The first and lowest rung is the love that is the attraction and desire to more fully experience the physical beauty we perceive in a particular thing or person. This view of love is the basis of how people most commonly understand eros today.

- The second rung is love as an appreciation for the physical beauty found in many things and uniquely expressed through the differences of each.

- A love for minds is the third rung, which is valuing an inner beauty not dependent upon external appearances.

- The fourth rung is love for laws and institutions, which characterize beautiful societies.

- A love for the sciences and participating in the beauty of knowledge is the fifth rung of eros.

- Finally, the sixth rung brings one to the love of beauty itself, in its divine state, which is revealed in Diotima's description:

  > *When a man has been thus far tutored in the lore of love, passing from view to view of beautiful things, in the right and regular ascent, suddenly he will have revealed to him, as he draws to the close of his dealings in love, a wondrous vision, beautiful in its nature; and this, Socrates, is the final object of all those previous toils. First of all, it is*

63. Emrys Westacott, "Discover What Plato Means About the Ladder of Love in His 'Symposium'." Thoughtco. 2020. *https://www.thoughtco.com/platos-ladder-of-love-2670661.*

*ever-existent and neither comes to be nor
perishes, neither waxes nor wanes; next, it is
not beautiful in part and in part ugly, [...]
but existing ever in singularity of form independent by itself, while all the multitude
of beautiful things partake of it in such wise
that, though all of them are coming to be and
perishing, it grows neither greater nor less, and
is affected by nothing. [...] so that in the end
he comes to know the very essence of beauty.*[64]

Before concluding this definition, two additional observations
are made. First, this analogy shows that love is not merely a passive attraction and desire to experience beauty. As effort is necessary to ascend
a ladder, so love also includes the active drive to pursue and express
these qualities in our lives. Loving the physical bodies of other people and things moves us to connect with and care for them. In loving
other minds, we naturally enter further into emotional, intellectual,
and spiritual communion with them. The love of laws and institutions
urges our participation in and service to them. The love of knowledge
drives the pursuit of truth and science, experimenting and exercising
the powers of observation, critical thinking, and precise communication. Second, the ascent of Diotima's ladder reveals not only an upward
movement toward the spiritual ideal of beauty, but also an expansive
movement that increasingly opens to a broader range of experiencing
and expressing beauty.[65] These active and expansive qualities of love
are highlighted in *Morals & Dogma* when it says of Plato's philosophy:

*With him, the inspiration of Love first kindled the light of arts
and imparted them to mankind; and not only the arts of mere*

64. Plato, *Symposium*, in *Plato in Twelve Volumes, Vol. 9*, trans. Harold N. Fowler.
(Cambridge, MA, Harvard University Press; London, William Heinemann Ltd.
1925), line 210e. *https://data.perseus.org/citations/urn:cts:greekLit:tlg0059.tlg011.
perseus-eng1:210e.*
65. A more fitting analogy for developing love could be moving outward from the
point at the center of a circle, rather than than ascending a ladder.

existence, but the heavenly art of wisdom, which supports the Universe. It inspires high and generous deeds and noble self-devotion.[66]

In summation, love is here defined as a divine attribute which humans experience and express as a relationship of active and expansive attraction, desire, pursuit, care for and participation in beauty.

VIRTUE

While Freemasonry is constantly speaking of specific virtues, the general meaning of *virtue* deserves closer scrutiny. The etymology of the term leads back to its first known use in Middle English in the 13th century to signify conformity to a standard of rightness. The word is derived from the Latin root *vir*, for "man," and thence *virtus*, meaning "manly" or "strong."[67] Thus, *virtue* suggests the admirable qualities expected of mature men or, more inclusively, mature adults. Even so, this word may be somewhat misleading in that it has been used in translation of the Greek *arete*, which simply means "excellence."[68] With regard to virtue, *arete* specifically refers to excellence in moral thought and behavior, which at present we seek to define more comprehensively.

Before advancing further in that task, it is necessary to acknowledge the divine basis for the various ways we recognize moral excellence, as was done in defining love. "In man they are virtues; in God, His attributes."[69] As before, this recognition helps us be mindful that virtue is a way in which we may align or connect with Deity, and also reminds us that it will always retain a degree of mystery.

66. Albert Pike, *Albert Pike's Morals and Dogma of the Ancient & Accepted Scottish Rite of Freemasonry, An Annotated Edition,* ed. Arturo DeHoyos (DC: Supreme Council, 33rd Degree, S.J., U.S.A. 2011), 802.

67. "Definition of Virtue," in Merriam-Webster Dictionary. 2019. *https://www.merriam-webster.com/dictionary/virtue.*

68. Henry George Liddell and Robert Scott, "Arete," *Greek-English Lexicon.* (Oxford. Clarendon Press. 1940). *https://www.perseus.tufts.edu/hopper/text?doc=LSJ%20a)reth/&lang=original.*

69. Pike, *Albert Pike's Morals and Dogma,* 816.

Once again it is worthwhile to return to Plato, because he has strongly influenced Freemasonry's view of moral excellence. Plato's works are where the Four Cardinal Virtues – prudence, temperance, fortitude, and justice – were first written about as an integrated set. In *Republic*, Socrates declares, "virtue is a kind of health and beauty and good condition of the soul," and "beautiful and honorable pursuits tend to the winning of virtue."[70] Therefore, the excellences we recognize as specific virtues are those "beautiful and honorable pursuits" that benefit the soul, each in some particular way.

It is significant that Socrates specifically references benefit to the soul. The Greek term for this good is *eudaimonia*, which is often simply translated as "happiness" or "wellbeing."[71] More literally, the word combines *eu*, meaning "good" or "well," with *daimon*, meaning "spirit." Thus, eudaimonia alludes to an inner goodness or wellbeing. While philosophers frequently connect eudaimonia with the physical and social pleasantries of life, it should also be acknowledged that sometimes the good of the soul demands physical and even emotional suffering. *Morals & Dogma* emphatically makes this point:

> *Suffering is the discipline of virtue; of that which is infinitely better than happiness, and yet embraces in itself all essential happiness. It nourishes, invigorates, and perfects it. Virtue is the prize of the severely-contested race and hard-fought battle; and it is worth all the fatigue and wounds of the conflict.*[72]

The most common example of this discipline of moral excellence is suffering in the present with the understanding or hope that it eventually contributes to a worthwhile benefit for oneself or others, which

70. Plato, *Republic*, in *Plato in Twelve Volumes, Vols. 5 & 6*, trans. Paul Shorey. (Cambridge, MA, Harvard University Press; London, William Heinemann Ltd. 1969), line 444d-e. *https://data.perseus.org/citations/urn:cts:greekLit:tlg0059.tlg030. perseus-eng1:4.444d.*
71. "Eudaimonia," in Philosophy Terms. *https://www.philosophyterms.com/eudaimonia/.*
72. Pike, *Albert Pike's Morals and Dogma*, 249.

is what often makes hard work virtuous. Another example is suffering (and perhaps even dying) in service to something judged a greater good, even without hope of any extrinsic benefit. This example is about doing good simply because it is good, such as unyielding commitment to a noble principle like truth, liberty, justice, or love itself; such a commitment is often considered the epitome of virtue. Before leaving this point, it is reiterated that suffering is sometimes required by virtue, but not always; suffering is neither a virtue nor necessarily leads to virtue.

To further clarify the nature of moral excellence, we now turn to Plato's student, Aristotle. His *Nicomachean Ethics* (350 BCE) remains a core text in academic studies of virtue. Within it, he elucidates additional aspects of virtue that distinguish it from other things: "Virtue, then, is a state of character concerned with choice, lying in a mean, i.e., the mean relative to us, this being determined by reason by which the man of practical wisdom would determine it."[73]

Choice is central to virtue. Aristotle claims virtue is a choice to act based on a deliberate desire for the good.[74] Such a desire is called "deliberate" because it arises with deliberation, making judgments about what actions are (and are not) good. This understanding does not reduce moral excellence to a list of rules and regulations specifying the right and wrong things for every possible situation, as if such a list were even possible. Another import to this aspect of virtue is that it necessarily values a person's motives or intentions. On one hand, a person may choose to act with entirely good motives and intending nothing but good effects, but there may nonetheless be bad outcomes. On the other hand, a person may choose to act in such a way that has good results despite bad motives and intentions. The first case remains an example of virtue, but the second does not. Thus, due to the necessity of making judgements, and to the relevance of motives and intentions,

---

73. Aristotle, *The Nicomachean Ethics*, trans. William David Ross, ed. Lesley Brown. (Oxford: Oxford University Press, Cop. 2009), 30-31.
74. Aristotle, *Nicomachean Ethics*, 44-45.

a proper concept of virtue includes recognizing individuals as moral agents with liberty to choose based upon deliberate desires.

Aristotle applies a *doctrine of the mean* to virtuous choice, arguing that all moral excellences are not fixed conditions, but are instead found along a continuum between two opposing extremes, which are the vices of excess and deficiency.[75] This aspect of moral excellence is classically illustrated with the virtue of fortitude, or courage, holding the middle ground between rashness, the vice of excess, and cowardice, the vice of deficiency.[76] The doctrine of the mean is helpful, in part, because it indicates a range of thinking and behavior by which one may be more (or less) virtuous, rather than removing moral excellence to a rarely attainable ideal of precision. It also provides a guide for exercising the "practical wisdom" of deliberation, which is to perceive the opposing extremes and choose a way of thought and action between them.

"Neither by nature, then, nor contrary to nature do the virtues arise in us; rather we are adapted by nature to receive them, and are made perfect by habit."[77] Aristotle thus addresses the necessity of habituation for instilling moral excellence as a matter of character. Repeatedly exercising deliberation and choosing to apply the doctrine of the mean results in consequences of pleasure and pain that refine one's ability to think and behave virtuously. Over time, one develops a more stable disposition to choose the good for its own sake, and to do so with less need for considering options. This observation reveals that, although the capacities necessary for virtue are innate, instruction and training help individuals learn to consistently apply those capacities toward moral excellence and thereby acquire virtue as a character trait.

True virtue aims not only at serving the benefit of one's own soul, but also the souls of others. It is plainly logical that to be

75. Aristotle, 24-25.
76. Aristotle, 50-51.
77. Aristotle, 3.

genuinely committed to the good for the sake of the good itself effectively requires the good to be served on behalf of everyone, everywhere, at all times. To desire and act for the good of all is thus the essence of justice. "Justice in this sense, then, is not part of virtue but the whole of virtue…."[78] The logic of this part of moral excellence is also innately driven, "since man is a political creature and one whose nature is to live with others."[79] Such an understanding of humanity is reflected in the Master Mason's beehive lecture:

> *It might have pleased the great Creator of heaven and earth to have made man independent of all other beings; but as dependence is one of the strongest bonds of society, mankind were made dependent on each other for protection and security, as they thereby enjoy better opportunities of fulfilling the duties of reciprocal love and friendship. Thus was man formed for social and active life—the noblest part of the work of God….* [80]

In consideration of Plato's and Aristotle's thoughts on virtue, the following definition is offered: Virtue, or moral excellence, is a character trait in which one has become habituated to choose actions, in the mean between excess and deficiency, for the wellbeing of the soul in oneself and others, even if it requires suffering. Specific virtues, such as temperance, are therefore more categorical ways of thinking and acting that serve moral excellence.

LOVE & VIRTUE RELATED

Up to this point, love has been addressed in terms of a relationship with beauty, and virtue as a relationship with goodness. However, Plato's philosophy strongly suggests a unity among beauty, goodness, and truth as interconnected divine attributes or transcendental

78. Aristotle, *Nicomachean Ethics*, 82-83.
79. Aristotle, 176-177.
80. Daniel Sickels, *General Ahiman Rezon and Freemason's Guide, Freemasonry, Internet Sacred Texts Archive* (New York: Masonic Publishing and Manufacturing Co. 1868), 211. *https://www.sacred-texts.com/mas/gar/gar56.htm.*

qualities of Being itself. Aristotle makes this unity more explicit, and it is later fully asserted among Neoplatonists such as Plotinus and Christian theologians like Dionysius the Areopagite and Thomas Aquinas.[81]

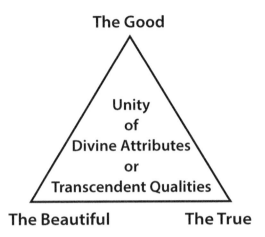

The Good

**Unity
of
Divine Attributes
or
Transcendent Qualities**

The Beautiful   **The True**

Morals & Dogma summarizes this view when it says, "The True, the Beautiful, and the Good are not three distinct essences: but they are one and the same essence, considered in its fundamental attributes...."[82] In other words, they are only named differently because each represents a different category for how humans experience and conceptualize the single divine essence manifesting in the people and things of this world. The good is therefore beautiful and true, the beautiful is good and true, and the true is beautiful and good. It follows that love is not only oriented toward beauty, but also truth and goodness. Likewise, virtue not only works for the good, but also the beautiful and the true.

Having established that love and virtue are both centered on the same divine essence of truth, beauty, and goodness, we now consider the similarities and differences in how they relate to that essence. To that end, each concept is examined by the other's definition.

81. Wouter Goris, and Jan Aertsen, "Medieval Theories of Transcendentals," in *The Stanford Encyclopedia of Philosophy*, ed. Edward N. Zalta. 2019. *https://plato.stanford.edu/entries/transcendentals-medieval/*.
82. Pike, *Albert Pike's Morals & Dogma*, 815.

To what degree does virtue fit the definition of love? Is it active and expansive in its attraction to, desire for, pursuit of, care for, and participation in beauty?

- Active and expansive: Virtue recognizes no limit or boundaries other than to avoid doing that which is not good. It does not regard the good, or therefore the beautiful, as something to know and do only under certain circumstances. It always seeks to serve and empower goodness and beauty for oneself and others.

- Attraction: Virtue includes an attraction to the good, and so also the beautiful. We must recognize and attend to goodness and beauty in order to understand and act with moral excellence.

- Desire: The definition of virtue specifies a deliberate desire for the good, and so it must also desire beauty. Desire for the beauty of goodness and the goodness of beauty motivates us to choose morally excellent thoughts and action.

- Pursuit: Virtue moves toward the ideal of the good in both thought and action, and in that way, it does indeed pursue beauty, both intellectually and materially. Furthermore, virtue not only does so for oneself, but for others.

- Care: Virtue strives to maintain and protect the good, and therefore also does so for beauty.

- Participation: Virtue works toward the good of its own development and refinement in oneself and within society, and thereby actively participates in beauty.

Virtue clearly meets all the criteria for loving thought and action, and so it may be rightly said that moral excellence is inherently loving.

Each specific virtue is therefore a more particular way of exercising loving thought or action. However, it is also apparent that virtue depends upon love. One does not seek to know and align with truth and goodness, nor does one care about moral excellence, without first loving truth and goodness.

To what degree does love fit the definition of virtue? Does it include serving the wellbeing of the soul for self and others, choice based on deliberate desire, residing in the mean, habituation, and the willingness to suffer?

- <u>Wellbeing of the soul for self and others:</u> Love is recognized as divine, which means it is inherently good for one and all. Socrates points out that even when the "divine madness" of love drives people out of their senses, it is nonetheless a gift that attracts the human soul to desire eternal beauty and truth and thus be drawn to the love of wisdom.[83] We experience and express such goodness both privately and socially, for our own benefit and that of others.

- <u>Choices based on deliberate desires:</u> Sometimes we instinctively appreciate and desire the beauty of people or things, so in that regard there is no choice. But love can also arise as a result of intentionally acting upon a deliberate desire to discover the previously unrecognized beauty and goodness in someone or something. In either case, we can and do deliberate and make choices about the time, energy, and means by which we attend to, strive toward, and join with the beauty and goodness we find.

- <u>Residing in the mean:</u> As previously noted, the most basic experience of love is simply our natural attraction to beauty, and thus goodness. It is our response

---

83. Sarah Patterson-White, "Love and Madness Theme Analysis," *LitCharts LLC.* 2019. *https://www.litcharts.com/lit/phaedrus/themes/love-and-madness.*

to such attraction, our expression of love, that either is or is not chosen within the mean between excess and deficiency. For example, Aristotle claims *philia*, brotherly love or friendship, "is a virtue or implies a virtue," which we can therefore conceptualize as residing in the mean between extremes like disinterest and codependency.[84]

- **Habituation:** Not all attraction and desire for beauty involves deliberation and choice, and so habituation cannot be part of every experience of love. Nonetheless, we can and do develop abiding appreciation for and even commitment to the beauty and goodness in things and people despite our first reactions to them as being totally unattractive or even off-putting. Diotima's ladder illustrates how we can develop a stable inclination to recognize, desire, pursue, care for, and participate in increasingly elevated kinds of beauty and goodness.

- **Willingness to suffer:** As with virtue, love includes the willingness to suffer, but not necessarily suffering itself. It is universally observed that the stronger the love, the more willing one is to endure hardship and pain in order to pursue, care for, or participate in that which is loved. Even in the most basic form of eros, our willingness to experience or express the beauty and goodness of something or someone can be such a strong emotional reaction that we call it "passion," the original meaning of which is endurance and suffering.[85] People also freely choose the difficulties of all sorts of committed loving relationships, and knowingly take on the hardships of philanthropy (literally "loving humanity") in serving the great causes of liberty, equality, and justice.[86]

---

84. Aristotle, *Nicomachean Ethics*, 142.
85. "Passion," Online Etymology Dictionary, *https://www.etymonline.com/search?q=passion*.
86. "Philanthropy," Online Etymology Dictionary, *https://www.etymonline.com/search?q=philanthropy*.

While our initial attractions and desires for beauty are good, these are often simply instinctive reactions, may not involve any deliberation or choice, are not necessarily the result of habituation, are not always restricted to a mean between excesses, but do include a willingness to suffer. Virtue is only a latent potential at this small point of love's nascence in human experience, but it is not love's nature to remain limited to this point. Love's attraction to and desire for beauty draws it to actively expand beyond its most basic manifestations, and therefore into more demanding and rewarding ways of knowing and doing the good, the beautiful, and the true. Thus, love has within it an inherent drive, or natural inclination, to increasingly develop itself with moral excellence. Consciously recognizing and choosing to engage that drive is the actualization of the virtue of love.

LOVE & VIRTUE IN THE MASONIC ETHOS

An ethos is the distinguishing moral character of a person, group, or institution.[87] Perhaps the most well-known way Freemasonry traditionally addresses its ethos is this: "A peculiar system of morality, veiled in allegory and illustrated by symbols." In other words, Freemasonry defines itself as a distinctively structured approach to goodness in human relationships, and thus also to their truth and beauty. A major "peculiarity" of that approach is the use of analogies with operative masonry and architecture in temple building, a body of lore well-suited to metaphorically emphasizing the active and expansive qualities of love and virtue. These allegories and symbols are partly necessary because goodness, truth, and beauty are essentially divine, and therefore ultimately beyond the power of human language to fully capture. All attempts at revealing the infinite reaches of these transcendent qualities cannot avoid also concealing them in finite words and images.

---

87. "Definition of Ethos," Merriam-Webster Dictionary. 2019. *https://www.merriam-webster.com/dictionary/ethos.*

Thus, rather than merely provide limited answers to the great questions and challenges of moral excellence, Freemasonry ritually employs symbolism and allegory coupled with inspiring rhetoric to stir our appreciation, desire, and pursuit of virtue. Consider the initial words of a common opening charge: "The ways of virtue are beautiful. Knowledge is attained by degrees. Wisdom dwells with contemplation; there we must seek her."[88] And reflect on these statements from a popular charge given at the closing of a lodge:

> *You are now to quit this sacred retreat of friendship and virtue, to mix again with the world. Amidst its concerns and employments, forget not the duties you have heard so frequently inculcated and forcibly recommended in this Lodge. Be diligent, prudent, temperate, discreet. [...] Let the world observe how Masons love one another.*

> *These generous principles are to extend further. Every human being has a claim upon your kind offices. Do good unto all.*[89]

In passages such as these, the Craft speaks to the interconnectedness of love and virtue, and continually encourages its members to further investigate, test, and improve their moral understandings in direct application throughout their lives. Freemasonry thereby displays all the qualities in the present definition of love, illustrating the *love of virtue* as key to the Masonic ethos.

In addition to the love of virtue, the Masonic ethos strongly encourages recognizing and acting upon the *virtue of love*, and especially in terms of charity. This Theological Virtue stems from 1 Corinthians 13, where the Apostle Paul describes all knowledge, talents, and works as lacking any virtue without love.[90] He says that after all such things have passed, only faith, hope, and charity remain, and charity

---

88. Sickels, *General Ahiman Rezon*, 23. *https://www.sacred-texts.com/mas/gar/gar11.htm.*
89. Sickels, 26, 27.
90. 1 Corinthians 13:1-3 NIV.

is the greatest.[91] That ranking of charity is illustrated in Freemasonry's allegorical depictions of Jacob's Ladder, where charity is placed at the top with faith at the bottom and hope in the middle. Its significance is punctuated with this statement:

> *Charity is the chief of every social virtue, and the distinguishing characteristic of Masons. This virtue includes a supreme degree of love to the great Creator and Governor of the Universe, and an unlimited affection to the beings of his creation, of all characters, and of every denomination. This last duty is forcibly inculcated by the example of the Deity himself, who liberally dispenses his beneficence to unnumbered worlds.*[92]

The divine nature of charity is also acknowledged when the ritual says it "extends beyond the grave, through the bound-less realms of eternity."[93] In fact, Freemasonry's use of the word *charity* derives from it being an English translation of Paul's Greek word, *agape*, for unconditional and universal love. Therefore, when Freemasonry speaks of charity as the most important virtue, it urges recognizing that there is nothing more virtuous than loving in a way that reflects Divine Love itself.

This lesson is provided in many degrees, certainly including those of the Scottish Rite. One of the most noteworthy examples is the degree of Knight Rose Croix, where the Theological Virtues are revisited before teaching candidates to follow the New Law of Love, which "is recognized as the simple but sublime expression of the divine nature."[94] In reference to the 26th Degree, it is said, "The true Prince of Mercy obeys the New Law of Love taught in the 18th Degree. He imitates the mercy, goodness, and beneficence of God the Father in heaven."[95]

---

91. 1 Corinthians 13:8-13 NIV.
92. Sickels, *General Ahiman Rezon*, 67-68. *https://www.sacred-texts.com/mas/gar/gar19.htm*.
93. Sickels, 77. *https://www.sacred-texts.com/mas/gar/gar26.htm*.
94. Hutchens, Rex Richard, *A Bridge to Light*. (D.C.: Supreme Council, 1995), 139.
95. Hutchens, *Bridge to Light*, 223.

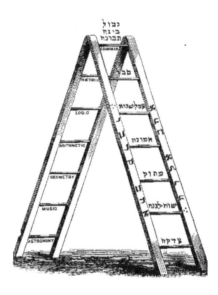

The 30th Degree likewise addresses the supremacy of love with the Mystic Ladder of the Knight Kadosh, which is two-sided, each side supporting the other.[96] One side is denominated "Love of God" and the other side is labeled "Love of Neighbor," with the rungs composed of various virtues and the Seven Liberal Arts and Sciences. The Mystic Ladder thus illustrates the role of the virtues as parts of love, as well as the interconnectedness between love of Deity and love of humanity. Furthermore, it reveals that the principles we usually call virtues are not our only tools of love. All the symbols, allegories, and charges of Freemasonry can be understood as means of magnifying one's ability to love. For example, in striking resonance with Diotima's speech in *Symposium*, the Mystic Ladder specifically presents the arts and sciences as vital to attaining the greatest heights of love. This fact also aligns with the Craft Lodge teaching that "Truth is a divine attribute, and the foundation of every virtue," for the arts and sciences are means by which we learn and communicate more truth, and thus more beauty and goodness. What we learn through the love of truth in turn

96. Hutchens, *Bridge to Light*, 280.

empowers us to be more loving and morally excellent with our fellow human beings.

Applying the word *mystic* to the Knight Kadosh's Ladder may be more than a simple reference to its place in this mysterious rite. In parallel with Diotima's affirmation that the ascent of love can arrive in knowing divine beauty itself, *mystic* also speaks to the potential for a direct encounter with truth, beauty, and goodness in their divine unity.[97] In fact, the saying *Ne Plus Ultra,* literally meaning "no more beyond," is traditionally associated with the Mystic Ladder, indicating it is either the degree's highest teaching or leads to the highest of heights, or both.[98] Here we recall the previous statement proclaiming charity as a "supreme degree" of love for Deity and "unlimited affection" for all creatures and, with it, the further declaration that "Charity is the brightest gem that can adorn our Masonic profession. [...] Charity is the Keystone to our mystic fabric."[99] Indeed, approximately 450 years prior to the formation of the United Grand Lodge of England, the very influential theologian Thomas Aquinas argued that Charity/Love is at once a proper name for Deity, the most excellent virtue, the cause and the end of all other virtues, and the means by which we most immediately realize union with Deity.[100] All our considerations in this chapter are consistent with his view, and we can therefore regard the Mystic Ladder as revealing that Freemasonry's ethos is not only a reverent guide to good human relationships, but also a mystical discipline. It is an active and expansive praxis of love and moral excellence capable of contributing to the fullest possible communion with Deity. This

---

97. "Definition of Mystical." *Merriam-Webster Dictionary,* 2019. *https://www. merriam-webster.com/dictionary/mystical.*

98. Pike, Albert, *The Magnum Opus, or, Great Work: Pike's First Version of the Esoteric Work and Lectures of the Scottish Rite Rituals.* (Kila, Mont.: Kessinger. 1992), XXX.7.

99. Sickels, *General Ahiman Rezon,* 79. *https://www.sacred-texts.com/mas/gar/gar26.htm.*

100. Thomas Aquinas, "The name of the Holy Ghost-Love (Prima Pars, Q. 37)," and "Charity, considered in itself (Secunda Secundae Partis, Q. 23)," *Summa Theologiae, New Advent. https://www.newadvent.org/summa/1037.htm#article1,* and *https://www. newadvent.org/summa/3023.htm.*

praxis may be summarized with words attributed to one of Masonry's traditional patrons, Saint John the Evangelist:

> *Dear friends, let us love one another, for love comes from God. Everyone who loves has been born of God and knows God. [...] No one has ever seen God; but if we love one another, God lives in us and his love is made complete in us.*[101]

CONCLUSION

Far from being a mere code of right behavior or list of dos and don'ts, the Masonic ethos nurtures the love of virtue and teaches the virtue of love. It employs a ritualistic, symbolic, and allegorical revelation of profound ways of contemplation and action that arise from our natural attraction to the divine light of goodness, truth, and beauty. More importantly, it includes the freely chosen obligation to actively pursue those ways in the loving, mutual support of kindred spirits and to extend them to all others. This ethos is therefore offered as a guide to individually and collectively reflect, participate in, and commune with Masonry's and Rosicrucianism's shared aspiration of making real "that spiritual temple – that house not made with hands – eternal in the heavens."[102]

---

101. 1 John 4: 7-12 NIV.
102. Sickels, *General Ahiman Rezon*, 70. *https://www.sacred-texts.com/mas/gar/gar21.htm.*

Part Two:
Reflections

Introduction

Each of the following chapters began as a meditation on something relevant to the Rose Croix Degree and Rosicrucianism. There has been some attempt to go back and make appropriate citations, but I freely admit that I have not referenced other sources as often as in previous chapters. That is because much of the content is built upon or includes ideas that have become integral to my own conceptualization of things. Nevertheless, I have tried to provide citations where I think they are most due.

The overall thrust of part two is to provide a richer landscape in which to consider the possibilities of engaging the Great Work. Picking up on the ethical themes of the previous chapter, Chapter 4 deals with the chivalrous aspect of the Rose Croix Degree and its relevance to Rosicrucianism. The images of knighthood in popular culture are often skewed by historical ignorance and juvenile notions about masculinity. Therefore, I believe it is very much worthwhile to consider what a Rosicrucian chivalry might actually look like, taking Masonic chivalry as our guide. The next two chapters complement each other in addressing key symbolic elements of the degree from the perspective of psycho-spiritual alchemy. They more fully address the processes and potential outcomes of personal reformation and why the work is important. For these reasons, they can be very useful to anyone proceeding to do the actual work laid out in the third part of this book.

On the topic of Rosicrucian chivalry, I wrote the following poem many years ago when I was fascinated with the Knights Templar and how they might have been related to some of the esoteric movements in the Christian world. I had been meditating on this matter in various ways when it came to me to use active imagination, putting myself in the place of a Templar knight in the Crusades. In a flash, I received all the imagery and insight of this poem. I trust you will appreciate how it weaves together both personal and social transformation as inseparable aspects of the Great Work, and both internal and external labors of the heart and mind.

THE SWORD AND TROWEL

I

Due to an oath of service
It has come that I must stand
Within this foreign country
On this strange enchanted land,
To raise the ancient Temple
So long lost beneath the sand
Of time and Man's corruption,
And thus must I have at hand
Both sword and mason's trowel,
So to serve the Lord's command.

II

Princes, kings, and potentates
Sent us all across the shore

To cut down the infidels
In a bloody holy war.
They promised righteous glory,
Even life forevermore,
And so we've battled inward
Boldly taking on the chore,
Serving up our enemy
To the mercy of our Lord.

III
But in a lonely vigil
On a cold and eerie night,
Blew a moaning mournful wind
That filled my heart with fright.
I, glimpsing an invader,
Thrust my sword with all my might
Into an airy phantom,
My own shadow by moonlight,
And thus my eyes were opened
And my soul was given sight.

IV
Within that silent moment
I was graced with Light shot through,
And for what seemed an hour,
Yet within a breath or two,
I was freed from all my sin
And stood with the Christ anew
As he vanquished my true foe,
Not pagan, Muslim, or Jew,

But the hubris, hate, and greed
Sitting on my heart's back pew.

V
And now I know my duties
Are most truly to protect
The Cross from all dishonor
And the Temple to erect.
Not with metal sword or tool,
But by love must I perfect
The site of Christ's next coming
Where His Light shall intersect
The heart of a true brother
Though he's of another sect.

VI
So, I take the sword and trowel
As the tools that I must test,
Not upon a foreign land
But within this human breast,
To conquer evil forces
And intolerance arrest,
Building a fraternity
That will serve the noble quest
To spread illumination
And True Glory manifest.

Chapter 4:
Psychospiritual Chivalry

The title of this chapter highlights a theme of immense importance to Knights Rose Croix, a theme of wisdom, strength, and beauty that is sorely needed in present times.[103] Many Masonic degrees confer the title of *Knight* on their initiates and teach impressive lessons on the noble virtues Masonic knights should embody and the principles they should serve. We shall examine what the Scottish Rite

---

103. This chapter is adapted from C.R. Dunning, Jr., "Spiritual Knighthood for the Common Good," in *The Oklahoma Scottish Rite Mason*, September (2020): 6.

teaches about those virtues and principles, and how we can employ those lessons for the benefit of all.

Just as Craft Masonry makes speculative use of the language and imagery of operative stonemasonry and architecture, so does the Scottish Rite symbolically employ stories and scenes of knighthood as allegories for making ourselves better human beings. Properly understood, the path of Masonic and Rosicrucian chivalry does not lead us to become literal warriors ready to do violence against other people. Instead, we honor and seek to emulate the knightly virtues of discipline, devotion, courage, and perseverance in service to our highest ideals. In fact, to be whole and healthy human beings working well together in good social relationships, we need the assertive passion of the knight dedicated to worthy service. Well integrated knightly energy empowers us individually and collectively to ask and hear the hard questions, to speak uncomfortable truths, and to challenge ourselves and others to accomplish worthy but difficult goals.

Every good knight of old served a cause, creed, or tenets valued as more important than one's own life. Such a reference point provided inspiration to begin great quests and campaigns, direction when the path seemed unclear or confusing, and motivation during bleak times of frustration and despair. Masonic knights remember that their Principal Tenets are Truth, Relief, and Brotherly Love, and not only to be shared with each other, but with everyone. As a traditional closing charge for the Craft Lodge puts it, "all persons have a claim upon your kind offices." This ethos is expanded upon by the Scottish Rite's official creed:

> *Human progress is our cause,*
> *liberty of thought our supreme wish,*
> *freedom of conscience our mission,*
> *and the guarantee of equal rights*
> *to all people everywhere our ultimate goal.*

What does it mean to be a psychospiritual warrior with such a lofty creed? To be a warrior presumes some enemy, but who or what are our true enemies? In the 30th Degree, Knight Kadosh, initiates learn that the enemies are always *ignorance, fanaticism,* and *tyranny*. They are taught that they should not only fight against these enemies, but that they also have a duty to protect, defend, and liberate those who are oppressed by these destructive forces. The degree further teaches that if one is to be a speculative knight rather than an operative combatant, one must understand that our battles are not waged by taking up arms to shed blood. Our campaigns are of the heart and mind, first and foremost within ourselves, and then in the way we conduct ourselves with others.

Just as an actual knight was prepared to leave behind his home and family and shed his own blood, so may we also be called to make great sacrifices for our ideals. Wielding the sword of truth and justice within ourselves, we must be willing to confront, acknowledge, and battle with our own ignorance, prejudice, intolerance, cruelty, and arrogance. We find these inner "enemies" lurking within the shadows of our own souls, such as in our wish to appear more knowledgeable or certain than we actually are, in the temptation to feel proud and self-righteous in comparison to others, or in the desire to win an argument rather than have mutually beneficial dialogue. We also find these ruffians in our unquestioning submission to our religious and political communities, or siding with them to the point of ignoring their own shortcomings and failings while exaggerating those of other communities.

Behind all these conflicts, we find very ordinary human fears and the understandable instinct to protect ourselves and loved ones from the threats we perceive (and easily imagine) in this complicated world. Fear is always behind the armor of our defensiveness, yet the more we try to shield ourselves behind the appearance of toughness and fearlessness, the more fragile and defensive we become. These conditions produce even more conflict within oneself and with others, which leads to further pain and fear. Therefore, a psychospiritual knight's first duty is to face one's own fears with genuine courage, not in the misguided attempt to destroy them, but to accept and understand them, and find constructive, healthy, life-affirming ways to manage them. The extent to which we have come to reasonable terms with our own fears determines the extent to which we are able to authentically respond with the "kind offices" of Truth, Relief, and Brotherly Love to the fears of others, even to their fears of us and our communities.

While our first duty is vigilance within ourselves, the greatest tests and trials of our chivalry often arise in our dealings with others, whether in our immediate circles, through social media, or in the political friction between groups with different perspectives and beliefs. Differences between individuals and groups are simply natural, and that diversity facilitates the development of much wisdom, strength, and beauty in the world that would otherwise not exist. Yet, differences can also be uncomfortable, challenging, and even seem dangerous, especially when we do not truly understand them. These natural complications are further amplified by the common effort to polarize all our differences into irreconcilable opposites of right and wrong, good and evil, true and false. It can be easy to start thinking about everything of importance in terms of combat, an all-consuming war in which every individual and every group is either an ally or an enemy, and where even our comrades must continually be tested to prove their loyalty lest they become traitors in our midst.

There are terrible costs to habitually thinking and acting in terms of binary oppositions or conflicts of only two sides with irreconcilable differences. In this framework, we too easily ignore the subtleties, nuances, and complexities that allow for many more perspectives, positions, and possibilities, and too easily forget the essential unity of all humanity. In effect, we leap into combat where it does not need to happen, ignoring and even destroying the middle ground and surrounding territories of thought and behavior. We lay waste to psychological, social, and political space where it would otherwise be possible to find and value our commonalities with other people, and to discover and enjoy the richness of our differences. The late Dr. Jim Tresner, 33° G.C.,[104] has spoken about this destruction as "losing our center."[105]

In this context, the center is not a position of avoidant neutrality, a naïve or rigid defense of the status quo, or an expectation that every ideal must be completely and permanently sacrificed to compromise. It is instead the tireless, courageous, and sometimes heroic effort to establish, maintain, and develop the commonalities in which as many as possible can, in Masonic language, "best work and best agree." That kind of work requires all the prudence, temperance, fortitude, and justice a person or a group can muster. These virtues enable us, individually and collectively, to demonstrate the patience, tact, diplomacy, empathy, and compassion demanded for achieving mutual understandings and acting for the greatest mutual benefit.

For a moment, let us return again to the internal campaign of a psychospiritual knight. One of the greatest obstacles to being victorious in that campaign is pride. Spiritual pride is what we feel when we regard our own efforts toward enlightenment and harmony as so superior to others that we no longer question or adjust ourselves, let alone extend our hands with faith, hope, grace, and humility. In spiritual pride, our focus increasingly becomes how others need to admit and atone for their faults, how others need to realize and remedy their ignorance, or how others need to be willing to compromise, collaborate, and make peace. What is actually happening in such moments of arrogance is often more about moral and spiritual laziness, and behind that is the fear of humbling ourselves and continuing to address our own ignorance and temptations to fanaticism and tyranny.

---

104. The Thirty-Third Degree is the highest of Scottish Rite Freemsonry, and the initials G.C. represent "Grand Cross," the highest honor that can be bestowed upon a Thirty-Third Degree Mason.

105. Jim Tresner "Strengthening the Center," *The Scottish Rite Journal, Vol CXXV, No. 2, https://scottishrite.org/blog/journals/march-april-2017/.*

In reflecting on the existence of evil and its opposition to the good, the 18th Degree reminds its participants of an alchemical operation known as the *resolution of contraries*. That operation involves taking what seem to be two opposite, even antagonistic, elements and bringing them into harmony with each other. This work is necessary in order to transform the crude metals of the soul into the philosophical gold of an enlightened being, which in turn enables one to shine that golden light out to the world. But the operation requires a fluxing agent, a third element to integrate the others. A Knight Rose Croix learns that this agent is love and is given the New Law of Love as the banner one must always faithfully follow and valiantly serve. The Knight Rose Croix is also reminded of the wise teacher from Nazareth, who charged his followers to love even their enemies, reminding us of the Divine Love that embraces and dwells within all. This charge transcends political ideologies, sectarian alignments, and all other popular divisions of humanity. If we accept this charge, then we can perform the greatest resolution of contraries possible in this world we inhabit together, and thus move things ever closer toward the ideal of peace and harmony "on earth as it is in heaven."

CHAPTER 5:

FROM THE CUBIC STONE TO THE MYSTIC ROSE

A JOURNEY OF TRANSFORMATION

The Great Work is, before all things, the creation of man by himself, that is to say, the full and entire conquest of his faculties and his future; it is especially the perfect emancipation of his will....[106]

Like the Builder's Art of Freemasonry, the Great Work of psychospiritual alchemy and Rosicrucianism is a journey of transformation. But what do we mean by transformation? The earliest known use of

106. Eliphas Levi, *Transcendental Magic*, trans. A.E. Waite, Rider Pocket Edition (London: Rider, 1984), 113.

the word *transform* dates back to the 14th century, where it was a verb specifically referring to a change of composition or structure. That sense of the word *transformation* is apparent when we think about the symbolism of a stone somehow becoming a rose. If you were to examine a stone with all your senses, it probably would not naturally occur to you that it could become a rose. Likewise, if you were to carefully examine a rose, you probably would not surmise that it could have once been a stone. Nonetheless, that very transformation is dramatically portrayed in many versions of the Knight Rose Croix degree, and its relevance to both Freemasonry and Rosicrucianism makes it a touchstone for contemplation.

Even in a perfectly natural, less allegorical, sense, if we did not know what a seed was, how would we ever suspect that a hard, dry, dull-colored little kernel could ever transform into a magnificent bush of fragrant, flowering, colorful, silky beauty? What a journey of transformation has the essence of life in that seed undertaken! The Great Work urges us to engage in a similar act of transformation, just as Masonry urges its members to build their moral edifices, but transformation is not something most people want, even most Masons and Rosicrucian students. Instead, we want minor changes, like simply taking off some of our rough edges, polishing ourselves a bit, making ourselves a little more refined in some ways. We shy away from transformation because if we allow ourselves to truly transform, to actually change in composition or structure, then our old selves must die to make way for a new being that we cannot entirely foresee.

What would happen if some of your beliefs and attitudes became significantly different, like those about religion, politics, or what to do with your time, energy, and money? How might such changes affect your most important relationships? What would people think of you if you became a genuinely different person?

Most of us have learned to become more or less comfortable with who we are, probably liking many things about ourselves. Even if we are not entirely pleased with who and what we are, it is at least familiar to us, and we have learned how to get by with our particular set of strengths, weaknesses, vices, and virtues. If it ever does occur to us that transformation is possible in our lives, feeling comfort with what we know, fear of disturbing our social relationships, and fear of the unknown, most people simply avoid it.

Yet, here we are, drawn to the traditions of Rosicrucianism and Freemasonry, with all their imagery, language, and ritual focused on transformation. Is our interest in these traditions simply due to some meaningless set of circumstances? Is it simple curiosity? An ego trip? Or is it because there is a truly inspiring light within them?

Somehow our souls have been drawn to one or both of these traditions like moths to a flame, and most of us flutter around and around that flame, instinctively attracted to it but also understandably avoiding direct contact with it. Even so, flying into the flame of transformation is exactly what these traditions urge us to do. INRI – *Igne Natura Renovatur Integra!* All Nature is renewed by fire! Renewal, rebirth, resurrection, rejuvenation, reintegration -- all of these words induce an inspiring sense of faith and hope about what awaits us if we will take up this journey into the unknown.

In the journey of Freemasonry, right off the bat, initiates learn that the apprentice's primary work is to strive to perfect the ashlar, which represents the personal self. The perfecting of the stone is done through removing vices and superfluities and developing the several virtues introduced in that degree. They are also told that the Entered Apprentice represents the cornerstone of the lodge, bringing new life and new possibilities to the social and spiritual edifice of our Fraternity. But then, somewhat strangely, the symbolism of the stone does not get the same kind of overt and literal attention in the Fellow Craft (2nd) and Master Mason (3rd) degrees, although everything within them is still directly relevant to it.

The theme of a special stone reappears in the higher degrees beyond the Craft Lodge, but then as something mysteriously discovered in the course of one's labors. In the 13th Degree of the Scottish Rite, this discovery happens in a process of descent into the depths of a vault in the earth. What is found must be brought back up and identified by those who know or can decipher its meaning. Keep that movement in mind – descent and ascent – because we will come across it again. This context of *discovering* the special stone rather than *producing* it is highly significant. It suggests that while the moral and social ideal represented by the perfect ashlar, keystone, or cornerstone is something we should work toward, the special stone also alludes to something already existing, seed-like, deep within us, that needs to be uncovered, nurtured, and freed.

That Masonic ritual also suggests we benefit from the assistance of others helping us get down in there to find that treasure, and to then bring it up and out into the light of day. This is an important thing to remember, because so much of the language of transformation emphasizes its private personal dimension, but such work involves risks. We simply need the support of trusted companions to help us navigate those risks.

What was lost has been found, raised up out of obscurity, but what is the significance of this perplexing discovery? Again, tradition tells us that we need the help of others to make sense of it. We should seek the counsel of wise elders, who then assist us in understanding the profound significance of this magnificent discovery. In the 14th Degree, it is put in its proper place, a place of reverence, respect, and protection. There is a great lesson here, for such a treasure is not something to be paraded around in foolish pride.

According to the symbolism of the Scottish Rite, the answer to our question about its meaning is found by deciphering the image on a special stone one has discovered in the previously mentioned descent. That image is the Hebrew letter *Yud* within a triangle, which is also the emblem on the ring worn by Masons of 14th Degree. The motto inscribed inside that ring is *Virtus Junxit Mors Non Separabit*. The simplest or most direct translation of the motto is "Virtue unites, death does not separate," or "'What virtue has joined, death shall not separate."

This motto naturally raises a question: What does virtue join that death cannot separate? Some Masonic writers have suggested the answer is that the practice of virtue creates an eternal bond of love between the hearts of Masons, and between the generations of Masons through history. That view is understandable in part because some versions of the 14th Degree ritual state that the ring represents not only devotion to virtue, but also commitment to others who share that devotion. The motto has sometimes even been translated as "*Whom* virtue unites, death shall not separate." However, this is a more interpretive than literal translation.

In any case, the ring itself simply presents the emblem found on the cubic stone, which is explained as portraying the Divine dwelling within us. By tradition, the ring may place that emblem of the Divine around the same finger on which a wedding ring is worn, and thus It assumes the same meaning as the union of the triangular plate with the cubic stone, the union of the Divine with the human. In summary, the Mason who wears this ring is theoretically one who, through contemplating and practicing virtue, has discovered, or is at least committed to discovering, something perfect, beautiful, and eternal hidden within oneself, something that reveals one's intimate connection with the Divine, the very essence of one's own being.

That is indeed a journey of transformation, but there is much more to know about how that transformation happens. Furthermore, it is important to realize that the journey is not finished. The revelation of the significance of the stone and the emblems on it is not a stopping place, but a place for a new beginning, for intentionally taking further steps.

One thing we have learned through this symbolism is that the processes of joining, uniting, and harmonizing things are vital to this work. In fact, Masonry is constantly reminding its members of this truth in one way or another. For example, the opening of a Masonic lodge is symbolically represented by joining the square and compass. The square is associated with the material world because right angles are crucial to the strong stable construction of buildings, and the compass is associated with the spiritual because it is used in working out the movements of heavenly bodies. Thus, the act of bringing them together at the opening of the lodge illustrates that the lodge should be regarded as a place where heaven and earth, the Divine and the human, intersect in harmony. It marks the lodge as a sacred space for the purpose of members helping each other make the internal descent and ascent to realize that same harmony with the Divine within their own souls.

In our effort to better understand these processes of transformation, it is helpful to reflect for a moment on the antiquity and universality of this symbolic use of the square and compass. The phrase *kuci chü* is used in modern Chinese to signify "the way things should be, the moral standard," but it literally means the compass and the square. This terminology traces back 5000 years in the legend of Fuxi and Nuwa, the spiritual beings who are the father and mother of creation. Here you see them intertwined, with Fuxi holding a square to which is also attached a plumb bob, and Nuwa holding a compass. Above them is the sun, below them is the moon, and around them are constellations of stars.

The Chinese philosopher, Mencius, who lived between 372 and 289 BCE built upon that symbolism when he wrote:

> *A Master Mason, in teaching apprentices, makes use of the compasses and the square. We who are engaged in the pursuit of Wisdom must also make use of the compass and the square.*

The square and compass are also incorporated into this famous *Rebis* image, which was first presented in the work *Azoth of the Philosophers* by Basil Valentine in 1613.

Note that this speculative allegorical use of the square and compass was 21 years before the first recorded instance of non-operative members being accepted into Scottish Craft lodges, and 33 years before Elias Ashmole's initiation into Accepted Freemasonry. Interestingly, 1613 is also just one year prior to the publication of the *Fama Fraternitatis*, soon followed by the *Confessio Fraternitatis* and the *Chemical Wedding of Christian Rosenkreuz*. These documents clearly express an interest in alchemy, and one of the wonderful things about this image is that it makes a direct connection between the symbolism of the square and compass and that of psychospiritual alchemy, and thus it offers more depth and detail about the Masonic journey of transformation.

Rebis (from the Latin *res bina*, meaning dual or double matter) is a result of the Great Work in alchemy. It represents the various qualities of the human soul, once opposing and at odds with each other, now integrated into a functional whole. They include the sun and moon; Mars and Venus; and Saturn and Jupiter; the rational, solar masculine, and the intuitive, lunar feminine. Valentine's emblem shows that they have all been united by the harmonizing effects of Mercury at the top center. This integration puts the raw instinctive energy of life, represented by the dragon, under the creative command of the illuminated philosopher instead of being ruled by it through uncircumscribed passions and desires.

In 1782, at the tail end of an era in which the so-called high grades of Masonry had been rapidly appearing all over Europe, and overtly incorporating Rosicrucian and alchemical themes, Adam Friedrich Böhme published a document with the long and intriguing title, *Hermes Trismegistus, Old and True Natural Path OR: The Secret of How To Prepare The Great Universal Tincture Without Glassware, For Humans And Metals, by a True Freemason.*

In that text we find this illustration where the themes of union and harmony are represented in a manner very similar to the previous Rebis image. It includes the sun, moon, planets, the dragon, and the

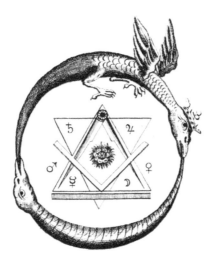

earthly square and heavenly compass. He has even included the gauge or rule just beneath the square and compass. Böhme also attached Latin comments to offer more direction, which you see here translated into English:

> *Hermes*
> *He rises from earth to heaven, and from there back down*
> *to earth, and he receives the power of all the higher and lower things.*
> *It combines the red Sun and the white Moon,*
> *a path and a skillful arrangement.*

The top portion are lines from a famous alchemical document, the *Emerald Tablet of Hermes*, communicating a message of vertical movement that parallels the descent and ascent of the Masonic process we previously reviewed. The words immediately following that passage in the *Emerald Tablet*, which Böhme did not include, are "By this means you shall have the glory of the whole world and thereby all obscurity shall fly from you." Instead, he has written about combining the red sun and white moon to emphasize that the work of integrating opposites, particularly the solar masculine and lunar feminine, is central to the process of transformation. Böhme has clearly made his own connection between the Builder's Art of Masonry and the Great Work of psychospiritual alchemy, and through this document publicly suggested that they are one and the same.

Also note that the Universal Tincture mentioned in Böhme's title is called "Azoth" by many alchemists, and Azoth is the keyword in the title of Basil Valentine's work from which we have the previous image of Rebis. Azoth represents that perfected substance that holds the powers of all the other elements in equilibrium, and it is also often referred to as the alchemical element mercury, and *Hermes* is the Greek name for the god Mercury.

This image is also entitled *Azoth*. It was published by Stolzius von Stolzemburg in his *Theatrum Chymicum* in 1614, the same year as the publication of the first Rosicrucian manifesto. As with the other images, we have the sun and moon, heaven and earth, the planets, and the fiery solar king and watery lunar queen. We also have land and sea, smaller emblems of seven alchemical phases between the rays of the planets, and a cube identified as *corpus*, meaning the body, the raw matter of our material existence, in a triangular arrangement with *anima*, meaning soul, and *spiritus*, the spirit. Between the rays in the rim of the circle are seven Latin words. Furthermore, the rays are numbered, proceeding clockwise from Saturn at the bottom. Moving in that order, the Latin words form the saying, *Visita Interiora Terrae Rectificando Invenies Occultum Lapidum*, which means "visit the interior of the earth and by rectification find the hidden stone." These words make an even stronger connection between the Great Work of Rosicrucian alchemy and the Masonic descent to find a special stone.

Among the most interesting things about this diagram is the pair of human legs extending down from the emblem, and human hands held out from its sides. Just as with the Masonic gavel and ashlar, this emblem suggests that the work happens within us, that we are the earth of which the interior must be visited and in which the operations of rectification, or putting things in right order, are to be done.

We have repeatedly seen certain ways that Freemasonry, alchemy, and Rosicrucianism urge us to take this journey of transformation, and we have been given numerous hints about what that journey of inner work includes. The details of this image make the particulars of one way of doing that work even more apparent, and at last we begin to consider them more fully.

The seven rays represent seven fundamental energies of creation that are not only external to us but also present within our own being. Those energies are primarily represented by Saturn, Jupiter, Mars, the Sun, Venus, Mercury, and the Moon, each of which can be associated with particular virtues, personality traits, states of consciousness, spiritual beings such as the gods and goddesses of the Roman pantheon (for which the planets are named), but also the archangels of Western monotheism, and even the divine attributes of God. Each ray likewise has corresponding vices and superfluities to overcome, and passions and desires to manage. The numbering of the rays indicates an order to be followed in studying, invoking, contemplating, and rectifying their respective associations. The seven alchemical emblems between the rays represent challenges and changes experienced as one advances in the work.

For example, the first ray is that of Saturn, the god of death, the Grim Reaper. In meditating upon this ever-present element of Nature, we recognize that nothing in the material world is permanent, and so reflect upon our own mortality, as represented by the raven sitting upon the skull. We may also take this as an allusion not only to physical death, but to ego death, which is necessary for psychospiritual transformation. That is hardly all there is to fully working with Saturn's associations, but it should give you a better sense of what it means to begin intentionally engaging a comprehensive process of true transformation from the inside out.

While again noting the order of the planets, sun and moon, let us recall that one of the most common descriptions of Rosicrucianism is a combination of *magia, chymia,* and *Cabala.*

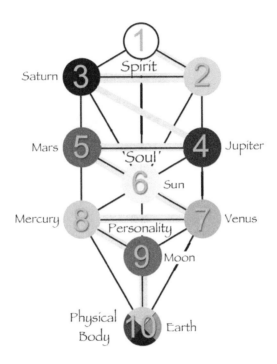

And here we find the very same order of planets within the Lightning Flash of Creation, shown in light gray, manifesting in the Cabalistic Tree of Life with its ten sefirot, or spheres of emanated light. It strikes down from Keter, the first sphere, through the second, Hockmah, neither of which have planetary associations because the planets beyond Saturn were not known in the ancient world. Then it moves into the third sphere, Binah, associated with Saturn, then to the fourth, Hesed, associated with Jupiter, and so on, in the exact sequence of the previous Azoth image.

In the tradition of Cabala, whether the Jewish forms or the Hermetic and Christian forms, each sefira on the Tree of Life is understood to have a set of associations like those mentioned with the rays in the Azoth image. Furthermore, each sphere of emanated light corresponds with a particular location relevant to the human body, as shown here.

One significance of these associations is that it helps make the process of the Great Work even more relevant to our personal being.

In every culture there are esoteric traditions and systems of working with the vital energies of the body, mind, and soul. Perhaps the most well-known of those systems is that of the seven chakras found in the various schools of yoga, and the chakras also have their correlations with planets, virtues, vices, and so on. The image on the next page shows an alignment of glowing disks arranged vertically like the chakras of yoga, with the symbols of the planets, sun and moon, in the same order from top to bottom that we saw in both the Azoth image and the Lightning Flash on the Tree of Life. It also shows several associated vices that must be overcome in the process of spiritual

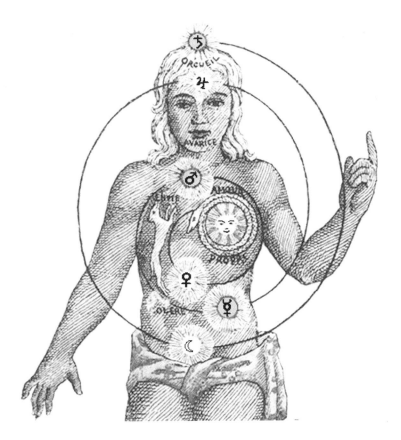

illumination. Interestingly, what you are seeing is not from a school of yoga, but rather from a text by the Christian theosopher Johann Georg Gichtel, *Theosophia Practica* (1696).[107]

Gichtel makes it very clear that the work of rectification is not just about following a list of dos and don'ts with external behaviors, but is also, and more importantly, an internal process like that we have been considering. Gichtel says:

> *If we want to contemplate and observe man in his deep inner generation, with our soul we need to leave the elemental life and the earthly astral and turn to the Divine inner life of Jesus Christ; We must appeal to the grace of this dear doctor, that He*

107. For a good English translation, see Johann Gichtel, "Theosophia Practica," trans. Ramon Light, in *Rosicrucian Tradition* (2018), *http://pansophers.com/theosophia-practica-gitchel/*.

*may deign to open our eyes, closed until then by the devil from Paradise, so that we may recover our **eye of light** to recognize and contemplate God in us.*

[...]

When the reader, friend of Wisdom, seeks God in his miracles and wants to contemplate in himself the occult Ternary, he must first of all return to himself and learn to know himself to the bottom in its genesis and its triple life, for it is in itself the eternal image of God according to the worlds of darkness and light.[108]

Gichtel adds:

the benevolent reader must meditate by himself until he has attained intelligence, and, as he might desire, to recognize himself and to contemplate himself in the light of Divine wisdom, that he is interiorized with ardent application, in the most profound center of his soul

In short, Gichtel is declaring that genuine transformation requires us to stop occupying our energies, our attention, care, and concern, only with what is going on in the world around us and our thoughts and feelings about it. We need to dive deep within ourselves to reconnect with our Divine essence, just as Freemasonry, alchemy, Cabala, and Rosicrucianism have been telling us, each in their own ways.

So, let us say we have done that. We have descended into the depths of our souls, have discovered the perfect cubic stone bearing the Divine spark of God, brought it up into our ordinary conscious awareness, and begun the work of rectifying and harmoniously reintegrating the elements of our being. Now we may come to know without doubt that we are always and everywhere in communion with the Creator. Is that the completion of the Great Work? Are there further steps?

---

108. The *occult Ternary* is literally the "hidden Trinity" within us. Also notice the language of descent paralleling that of various Masonic rituals.

According to the allegory with which we started, this process of transformation requires that the cubic stone itself must change.

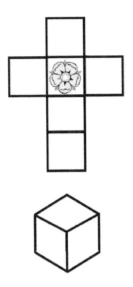

The six square surfaces of the cube unfold to form the six sections of the Christian cross, which represents the gift of the Light and Living Word of God offered as a sacrifice to the entire world. As the first chapter of the Gospel of John tells us, it is the Light with which everything was made, including each of us. Thus, the next step in this view of the Great Work is to open ourselves, freely sharing our Divine essence and radiating all those rectified qualities for the benefit of others. It is the most truly charitable expression of love for all God's children and creation.

That may sound wonderful and inspiring, but, as with the entire process of transformation leading up to this point, it can be very challenging, hard work. Here we recall the words of Jesus in Luke 9:23-24 ESV:

> *If anyone would come after me, let him deny himself and take up his cross daily and follow me. For whoever would save his life will lose it, but whoever loses his life for my sake will save it.*

In this context, these words describe the cross taken up by one who is sacrificing the old self in the process of transformation, and they provide the caveat that embracing and sharing the Divine Light we find within us can sometimes also be a burdensome act of sacrifice in itself. Nonetheless, it is the most beautiful, liberating, and joyful thing any of us can do with our lives, and so the blossoming of that beauty out of our core is represented by the delicate red rose of passion and sacrifice. Fittingly, Böhme also placed a rose at the center of his Masonic emblem of the Great Work.

Despite being distracted from it by our own ignorance, fears, vices, and superfluities, deep within us is a longing to manifest this mystic rose in our lives. That is why many people are drawn to Freemasonry and Rosicrucianism like moths to a flame. Under the pseudonym "Fiona MacLeod," the poet William Sharp, a member of the Hermetic Order of the Golden Dawn, touchingly and inspiringly captured that longing in the poem, "The Rose of Flame."

Oh, fair immaculate rose of the world, rose of my dream, my Rose!
Beyond the ultimate gates of dream I have heard thy mystical call:
It is where the rainbow of hope suspends and the river of rapture flows—
And the cool sweet dews from the wells of peace for ever fall.

And all my heart is aflame because of the rapture and peace,
And I dream, in my waking dreams and deep in the dreams of sleep,
Till the high sweet wonderful call that shall be the call of release
Shall ring in my ears as I sink from gulf to gulf and from deep to deep—

Sink deep, sink deep beyond the ultimate dreams of all desire—
Beyond the uttermost limit of all that the craving spirit knows:
Then, then, oh then I shall be as the inner flame of thy fire,
O fair immaculate rose of the world, Rose of my dream, my Rose!

As illustrated by the Rose Cross Lamen of the Hermetic Order of the Golden Dawn, the outpouring of the Divine Light and Love through a transformed human being is a living expression of the very essence of all the vital powers and processes of creation. Such souls are crucial to sustaining the wellbeing and progress of humanity. Or, as this image states, "the rose gives the bees honey." This is taken from the

text, *Summum Bonum*, meaning the "highest good," published in 1629 by Robert Fludd under the name Joachim Frizius. Fludd wrote three works in defense of the Rosicrucians in 1616 and 1617.

This final development in the transformation of the cubic stone into the mystic rose upon the cross of light is itself never-ending. There is no point before death at which the soul who is becoming a living Rose+Cross can say, "It is finished." Indeed, even after death the work of such souls and the energies they have poured out continue to affect the world, and their wisdom, strength, and beauty may continue to live in the hearts and minds of others, even for generations to come.

CONCLUSION

Recall this chapter's opening quote from Eliphas Levi:

The Great Work is, before all things, the creation of man by himself, that is to say, the full and entire conquest of his faculties and his future; it is especially the perfect emancipation of his will.

What Levi suggests is that your true will, your deepest spiritual instinct and drive, is to transform, realize, and express yourself as a living Rose+Cross, and so become a blessing of Divine Love to the world around you. That is the Great Work, the Builder's Art, which both Masonry and Rosicrucianism are constantly prompting us to perform.

CHAPTER 6:
THE ALCHEMICAL MYSTERY OF THE ROSE CROIX

This chapter carefully examines a key symbol of the 18th Degree and, placing it in context with certain references from one of the Scottish Rite's textbooks, *Morals & Dogma*, and also drawing from other esoteric works, it provides an interpretation of the Rose+Cross as an alchemical emblem summarizing the Great Work.[109] Finally, it

---

109. This chapter is adapted from Charles R. Dunning, Jr, "The Alchemical Mystery of the Rose Croix," in *Ad Lucem XII*, Masonic Societas Rosicruciana in Civitatibus Foederatis (2005), 13.

provides reflections on the nature of that work and crucial considerations in its pursuit.

DISSOLVING AND DISTILLING THE SYMBOLISM

In the ritual of the Rose Croix, initiates find the letters *I-N-R-I* prominently displayed. While the secret work of that degree supplies Masons with a special meaning to this acronym, in *Morals & Dogma* and other sources we learn that it has many interpretations. Among all Christians, INRI is regarded as a reminder of the spiritual authority of Jesus the Nazarene, yet there are esoteric and mystical meanings that are not so widely known.

Among Rosicrucian students, the acronym provides further clues to the performance of the Great Work. The following two are of utmost importance: *Iebeshah, Nour, Ruach, Iam* and *Igne Nitrum Roris Invenitur*. Although not an exact translation, Rosicrucian students interpret the first as Hebrew words representing the four elements of classical philosophy – respectively Earth, Fire, Air, and Water. This interpretation is of general importance to Cabalistic symbolism, which is at the heart of the Rosicrucian movement. We shall see that it unlocks the Rose+Cross as a symbolic framework or context for the performance of the Great Work. The second is interpreted as Latin for "by fire the niter of dew is extracted." This statement receives special attention because of its overtly alchemical language, and because *Morals & Dogma* refers to it as an aphorism framed by "Alchemical or Hermetic Masons." Using these two interpretations as a key, we can use the acronym INRI to unlock the symbolism of the Rose+Cross and reveal a formula for personal transformation.[110]

---

110. Albert Pike, *Albert Pike's Morals and Dogma if the Ancient & Accepted Scottish Rite of Freemasonry, An Annotated Edition*, ed. Arturo de Hoyos (DC: Supreme Council, 2011), 363.

THE CROSS OF THE FOUR ELEMENTS

In the previously noted quote from *Morals & Dogma*, attention is drawn to INRI, and thus the Rose Cross, as a symbol having special meanings to Alchemical or Hermetic Masons. It is interesting to note that the cross and the four elements are brought together in the second of the only two places where *Morals & Dogma* refers to "Hermetic Masons." Here is the statement and illustration:

The four Elements, the four symbolic animals, and the re-du-plicated Principles correspond with each other, and are thus arranged by the Hermetic Masons:[111]

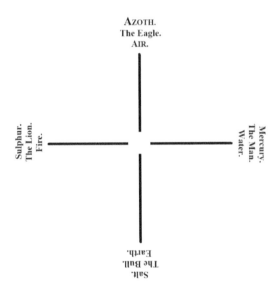

While this diagram provides some intriguing associations with the zodiac through the four archetypal creatures, that is not our present concern.[112] Rather than aligning the elements with the constellations

111. Pike, *Morals & Dogma, Annotated*, 894.
112. Pike adapted this image and much of his chapter on the Knight of the Sun from *Dogme et rituel de la haute magie*, by Elphas Levi (1861). The most intriguing aspect of this diagram is that it provides unusual associations between the four archetypal creatures and the four elements. The eagle, or the constellation Aquila, near Scorpio, is typically associated with water. The man, or the constellation Aquarius, is typically associated with air. The attributions of Azoth and Mercury could also be questioned.

and the points of the compass, we are placing this arrangement onto the vertical and horizontal axes of a cross. It is worth noting that these oppositions of the elements are present on the Cabalistic Tree of Life. The following diagram is thus constructed using the image of a Rose Cross, the Hebrew words corresponding to INRI, and the alchemical signs for the elements.

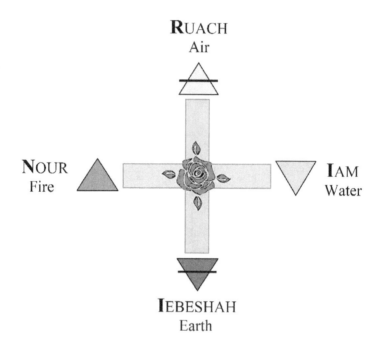

RUACH
Air

NOUR   **I**AM
Fire   Water

IEBESHAH
Earth

Morals & Dogma goes on to say:

> *As all the great Mysteries of God and the Universe are thus hidden in the Ternary, it everywhere appears in Masonry and in the Hermetic Philosophy under its mask of Alchemy. It even appears where Masons do not suspect it; to teach the doctrine of the equilibrium of Contraries, and the resultant Harmony.[113]*

Taking this passage as a guide, we can consider the rose upon the cross of the elements as itself somehow representative of that doctrine and the harmony it begets. What has yet to be addressed is

113. Pike, *Morals & Dogma, Annotated,* 895.

exactly how this symbolism can help us proceed with the Great Work of transformation.

THE FOUR ELEMENTS OF THE SOUL

Among Rosicrucians, and in other esoteric traditions, the four elements are often employed in an allegorical system of classification for different faculties and functions of the soul. While the specific attributions can vary, these are not uncommon:

- Air represents the impersonal higher intellect, including abstraction, analysis, and contemplative insight.

- Fire associates with one's will and desires, how they manifest in one's conscious sense of self in the world, and thus the personality.

- Water corresponds with the emotions and the unconscious and their effects upon the conscious self, which are partly reflected in dreams and visions.

- Earth refers to the physical body and its basic functions and needs.

That the various influences from these elements of the soul are often "contrary" to one another needs no explanation; we all know it from personal and sometimes painful experience. In this context, the Rose+Cross illustrates polarities that warrant closer examination. It also suggests that the blossoming of a very special and beautiful harmony occurs as the result of equilibrium among the elements.

First, we note that Fire and Water are placed opposite of one another on the horizontal axis of the cross. It could be reasonably

NOUR
Fire

IAM
Water

argued that the discipline of psychology, at least in the therapeutic field, is based on establishing a healthy working relationship between the personality and the unconscious. In fact, approaches such as Jung's Analytic Psychology and Assagioli's Psychosynthesis specifically point to such psychological integration as their purpose. Their methods and aims are based upon the observation that the health, maturity, and progress of a human psyche depend upon the degree to which its various parts work together in harmony. Special emphasis is placed on using the higher intellect to identify and resolve conflicts and oppositions between the personality and the unconscious. Techniques like active imagination and dreamwork draw out unconscious content, and these combined with analyses of conscious desires, fantasies, and intentions help the individual attain a more holistic understanding of self. Such an understanding supports more informed decisions, healthier behaviors, and fewer self-defeating patterns of thought and action.

Next, the vertical axis presents a polarity of Air and Earth, of the higher intellect and the physical body. Plato regarded the higher

RUACH
Air

IEBESHAH
Earth

intellect as the means by which humanity perceives the divine realm of ideal or perfect forms, the metaphysical archetypes of everything in existence. It is also noteworthy that the word *ruach* not only refers to the air of the atmosphere but is also a word for spirit. In Genesis, the spirit of life was *breathed* into humanity by God. This reference draws our attention to the role of Earth in this polarity, for it tells us that the body of Adam was formed from the dust of the earth and brought to life by the breath of God. Thus, the physical body is a vessel or vehicle for the spirit that animates it.

Just as psychotherapy addresses itself primarily to the dynamics of the horizontal axis, the dynamics of the vertical axis are the special interest of spirituality and religion. Religion concerns itself with the proper relationships among creatures in this world and their Divine Creator, and it serves those ends by providing guidelines for a healthy lifestyle, ritual observances and moral codes for the physical domain, and metaphysical doctrines and disciplines of meditation and prayer to nurture the higher intellect.

It is no surprise that the vertical line of spirituality intersects the horizontal of psychology. We have already seen how the higher intellect is called upon to facilitate the integration and harmonization of the psyche, and anyone who has aspired to fulfill the ideals of any religion can attest to the psychological challenges it can present. How fitting it is that among the central aims of religion is an intimate awareness of the spirit, the very breath of life from God, realized by the human psyche while in a physical body. This is the psychospiritual crux of the alchemical cross, and here we find the image of a rose.

The Alchemical Rose

At the meeting place of the four elements – at the intersection of heaven and earth within the human psyche – we find the rose, universally regarded as a symbol of beauty and love. However, to Rosicrucian aspirants, the rose can have other and more esoteric meanings. In pondering the meaning of the rose, we return to the second interpretation of INRI: *Igne Nitrum Roris Invenitor*, or "by fire the niter of dew is extracted." In the context of the four elements, this formula introduces both niter and dew as new symbols relevant to the Rose Cross and worthy of special attention.

Since it is from the dew that the niter is to be extracted, we begin by noting that Godfrey Higgins and A.E. Waite both held that the name *Rosicrucian* was not merely derived from *Rose Cross*, but that it is also a play on the Latin *ros*.[114] This word means dew, and dew is a common and important element of alchemical literature and imagery. Consider these excerpts from Rosicrucian and alchemical texts:

> *I am the moisture which preserves everything in nature and makes it live, I pass from the upper to the lower planes; I am the heavenly dew and the fat of the land; I am the fiery water and the watery fire; nothing may live without me in time; I am close to all things yea; in and through all things, nevertheless unknown.*[115]

> *...fire, water, air, earth be proceed from the first Chaotic Waters..., they produce the Universal Sperm [...] they continually regenerate the Chaotic waters for generation, preservation and Regeneration of all Things. This Universal Sperm is generated by condensation and evaporation of Vapours, which are circulated in the great Alembic of the Air, until they are sufficiently impregnated or animated by fire, when they are again condensed and resolved into water. This Chaotic Waters are commonly called Dew....*[116]

114. The origin of *ros* being equated with dew has been variously attributed to Eusèbe Renaudot (1646-1720) and Johann Lorenz von Mosheim (1693-1755).
115. "Secret Symbols of the Rosicrucians," trans. Unknown, *The Alchemy Website*, *https://www.alchemywebsite.com/secret_s.html*.
116. Anton Josef Kirchweger, "The Golden Chain of Homer," trans. Sigismund Bacstrom, *The Alchemy Website*, *http://www.levity.com/alchemy/catena1.html*.

Thus, the alchemical rose is dew, and dew is literally the moisture that has evaporated from the earth into the air to condense once more upon the earth when the proper balance of heat and humidity occurs. Dew is thus a most fitting analogy for the quintessence of being, the prime metaphysical emanation from which all forms of life and states of consciousness are generated. The power of this dew is spoken of in both scripture and esoteric literature.

> *Your dead shall live, their corpses shall rise. O dwellers in the dust, awake and sing for joy! For your dew is a radiant dew, and the earth will give birth to those long dead. (Isaiah 14:9)*

> *From the Skull of the Ancient Being wells forth Dew, and this Dew will wake up the dead to a new life. (The Zohar, "Idra Rabba.")*

THE NITER OF DEW

Niter is literally a chemical often used as a fluxing material in the refinement of metals. Niter thus serves two purposes: (a) to help metal liquefy more easily, and (b) to aid in removing impurities. In Anton Josef Kirchweger's *Golden Chain of Homer*, we discover more of the meaning of niter in psychospiritual terms. This alchemical text suggests that the alchemical dew has within it two basic potentials that work together to give rise to all things. The following list shows some of their associations:

Niter	Salt
Acid	Alkaline
Spirit	Body
Father	Mother
Universal Agent	Universal Patient
Hammer	Anvil

Where salt accounts for the *receptive* and *preservative* qualities in dew, we can see that niter represents the *active* and *transformative* potentials in dew. Continuing the analogy with a chemical fluxing material, when used with skill and knowledge, this psychospiritual niter has a dynamic and forceful role in refining the various elements of the soul, softening those that have become hardened and removing the impurities that are our vices and superfluities. The hammer and anvil associations should grab the attention of even the newest Entered Apprentice!

Mark Stavish has also explored this meaning for niter. He writes:

> *The energies of Niter are also referred to as the force of Kundalini, or spiritual forces. In alchemy, this is the Secret Fire. To the Salt, belongs the force of Prana, or Vital Energy.*
>
> *The function of the Vital energy is to maintain physical life forms and existence. It is completely instinctual and unconscious and is heavily influenced by cosmic cycles, astrological pulses, and other natural phenomena. The function of the Secret Fire is to increase in humanity, the only place where it is present, its sense of self, or "I". At the lowest level or functioning, this is the ego, at its highest, it is Divinity incarnate, as both are two sides of the same coin. One is 'self' in relation to the physical world and others; the other is 'self' in relationship to all of Creation and as a co-creator.*[117]

This statement leads us directly back to INRI and the four elements of the soul, where Fire is said to represent the conscious sense of self in this world, including one's more or less unique will and desires. We see here that the Secret Fire of alchemy, the niter of dew, is the essence of the allegorical fire that each of us experiences as "me." Recall also the Latin formula of INRI, which is now understood to say that this Secret Fire is extracted from alchemical dew by our self-awareness.

117. Mark Stavish, "Secret Fire: The Relationship Between Kundalini, Kabbalah, and Alchemy" *The Alchemy Website, http://www.levity.com/alchemy/secret-fire.html.*

How does the lesser Fire of the conscious self extract the greater Fire that is the transformative force within the quintessence? Heat is the quality most naturally associated with actual fire. To "put the heat on" something is a metaphor that speaks of an unrelenting intensity of attention, passion, and desire focused on that one thing.

Having dissolved so much of the symbolism of the Rose+Cross and INRI, we now distill from it this partial solution to the mysteries of the Rose Croix: When one has achieved the psychospiritual integration and harmony necessary to reveal the quintessence of one's being, then a continued fervency of attention to the work may in time enable a more refined use of the transformative force of creation and regeneration.

Performing the Great Work

Solved mysteries almost always lead to further questions, and there is still much about the Great Work that we have not examined. Exactly how does one achieve such a state of psychospiritual equilibrium? Once that is accomplished, what specifically must be done to extract the power of transformation? Once that power has been extracted, what is one to do with it?

Equilibrium

To some extent, the process of achieving psychospiritual equilibrium has already been addressed in this chapter. Recall that in examining the polarities and dynamics of the two axes on the psychospiritual cross, we discussed various practices of psychotherapy as well as guidelines and information provided by religion. Because the Great Work concerns itself with harmonizing both the psychological and the spiritual dimensions of consciousness, it follows that we need to apply heat in both dimensions.

Modern society offers many options for people drawn to psychospiritual evolution. Therapists, counselors, life coaches, support groups, and self-help books abound. Most of these resources offer some degree of valuable insight and assistance to people seeking psychological balance. On the spiritual side of things, the world's major religions continue to have a powerful presence, and in the more progressive nations there is an unprecedented opportunity for experimentation with different traditions. The New Age movement has also delivered a plethora of non-sectarian approaches to spiritual life and nurtured the development of new religions, many of which are attempts to revive traditions that were swept away by militant Christian evangelism.

Today's psychospiritual treasure chest may be overflowing, but there is nonetheless much dross to separate from the gold. The challenges facing the modern seeker certainly include making well-informed and wise decisions with regard to which psychological and spiritual sources will be tapped. The sheer number of options itself can lead many would-be illuminates to fall into the relatively unproductive pattern of hopping and skipping from one approach to another, sampling a little on the surface of each, but never really penetrating to the greater depths that any single system or tradition has to offer.

Should one make careful and definite choices, and assuming that the selected sources are legitimate, there are also common problems that arise from the psychological and spiritual realms being addressed separately. Psychology and religion have become so compartmentalized that the experts of each field can be defensive if not hostile with regard to the other. This situation makes it easy for people to assume that their psychological and spiritual quests must be pursued somewhat separately, and sometimes it seems that one path must be chosen over the other. But if the Great Work begins with equilibrium, then the labors of the two axes must be integrated. On a positive note, it is true that many clergy are now trained in counseling and increasing numbers of psychotherapists are becoming educated in religion and spirituality. Unfortunately, we do not easily find such helpers with extensive personal experience in the union and harmonization of both kinds of work, and even fewer still who are able to transcend the usual limitations that mainstream psychology and religion place on human consciousness.

To perform the Great Work, one must be willing to venture into the most mythical and magical realms of depth psychology and ascend to the most sublime heights of gnostic and mystical spirituality. Working within one of these two domains compliments the work of the other in both symbolism and philosophy. There are, therefore, advantages to pursuing them together in a coordinated manner. This is the calling of alchemical traditions and orders of initiation like those in the Rosicrucian movement and the Hermetic Masonry referenced in *Morals & Dogma*. We turn to it again for a clue as to how we might actually begin the Great Work.

> *He who desires to attain to the understanding of the Grand Word and the possession of the Great Secret, ought carefully to read the Hermetic philosophers, and he will undoubtedly attain initiation, as others have done; but he must take, for the key of their allegories, the single dogma of Hermes, contained in his Table of Emerald....*[118]

Following *Morals & Dogma's* lead and studying the Emerald Tablet, we find an alchemical description of a mysterious "one only thing" that, while never actually called dew, certainly fits the metaphor.

> *The father of that one only thing is the sun, its mother is the moon, the wind carries it in its belly; but its nurse is a spirituous earth. That one only thing is the father of all things in the Universe. Its power is perfect, after it has been united with a spirituous earth.*

The text continues with instruction on how to work with the dew.

> *Separate that spirituous earth from the dense or crude by means of a gentle heat, with much attention. In great measure*

---

118. Pike, *Morals & Dogma, Annotated*, 883.

it ascends from the earth up to heaven, and descends again, newborn, on the earth, and the superior and the inferior are increased in power.[119]

The wording here is strikingly similar to instructions for a meditative exercise sometimes called the *Fountain of Light*. In this exercise, the practitioner draws energy up through the body to the top of the head, where it then pours out like a fountain to rain down all around and through the body again. Many psychospiritual traditions, such as Yoga and Qi Gong, use some variation of this exercise. The energy being employed is visualized in the imagination as bright light and felt as a warm and tingling sensation in the body, which is likened to electricity or magnetism. This energy is often referred to as the *astral light*, which *Morals & Dogma* refers to as "the grand magical agent" and "Azoth, the universal magnetism of the Sages."[120] This statement in the Emerald Tablet may be taken as encouragement to practice such operations as beneficial to the Great Work.

Dew, the Universal Agent, or Azoth, is seen in the mind's eye as the Astral Light, but that is not all there is to it. With just a little reflection on the actual workings of the eyes and brain, we can also know that the Astral Light is the quintessence of *all* that is seen, and not only of what we imagine. Even a materialist, who believes we are nothing but atoms and molecules, knows that the brain does not actually reflect physical light in the phenomena of vision. In the materialistic explanation, photons strike the rods and cones of the retina, which in turn stimulate the optic nerve that carries a chemically encoded message to the visual centers of the brain for decoding. As far as that part of the brain is concerned, vision is vision, no matter if it is the result of the physical sense of sight or of fantasies, dreams, hallucinations or psychic visions. Basically, the same dynamics apply to all our other senses.

---

119. Manly P. Hall, *An Encyclopedic Outline of Masonic, Hermetic, Qabbalistic and Rosicrucian Symbolical Philosophy*, (Los Angeles: PRS, 1977) CLVIII.
120. Pike, *Morals & Dogma, Annotated*, 894.

Thus, everything we experience, remember, or imagine, all of known existence, is actually perceived in and by the energy of the mind. We can speculate, hypothesize, and experiment about external things that might stimulate this energy to move and take form, yet those operations are themselves processes and events moved and shaped by the internal processes of the mind.

> *"Know this," he said. "That which sees and hears within you is the Word of the Lord, and Nous [Mind] is God the Father. They are not separable from each other, for their union is life."*
>
> *"Thank you," I said.*
>
> *"But perceive the light and know it," said Poimandres.*[121]

While the Fountain of Light exercise closely parallels the description given in the Emerald Tablet, it would be an oversimplification to assume that this one exercise is all that the Tablet was meant to communicate or that it alone is sufficient for the Great Work. There are many ways that our alchemical dew can be heated to ascend and descend, and many ways to increase the power of the superior and the inferior, each with their own particular contributions to the Great Work. For instance, techniques offered later in this book involve a number of different energy circulations. With any system such as this, devoted and careful practice is intended to produce improved physical and psychological health, give rise to a more abiding sense of inner harmony, and aid the intellect in preparing for the most profound depths of spiritual contemplation – all the conditions of equilibrium alluded to by the Rose+Cross.

---

121. *The Way of Hermes: New Translation of The Corpus Hermeticum and The Definitions of Hermes Trismegistus to Asclepius*, trans. C. Salaman, D. Van Oyen, W. Wharton, and J. Mahe (Rochester, VT: Inner Traditions, 2000), 18.

EXTRACTION

In effect, if not in fact, our metaphorical dew, the energy of mind, is the divine quintessence of our being. To intellectually grasp this concept can be ground shaking, but it is nothing short of a spiritual revelation to actually experience and realize its truth. That blossoming of consciousness is the alchemical rose upon the cross of the soul. To genuinely achieve that insight is the beginning of the extraction of niter, drawing out the active and transformative power inherent in the essence of mind. In actual fact, we are always working directly with niter, for we could not think or do anything creative without it. Everything done to achieve greater equilibrium is accomplished only because niter is employed to that end. In conventional terms we would simply say that one's desire, attention, and intention are focused on greater equilibrium, and this heat drives the thoughts and behaviors that, in time, actually bring about the transformation.

To extract niter is not to bring forth some new power, but to actually recognize the transformative power for what it is, refine it, and be able to consciously use it more efficiently and effectively. Recall that niter is connected with kundalini, which many people automatically equate with sexual energy. It is true that kundalini is intimately involved in sex, which is obvious when we consider how much sexual behavior is a matter of desire and personal will, but this is only one of its manifestations. Many traditions refer to kundalini as the *serpent energy*, and it is known in Cabala by the name *Nehustan*, which was the brazen serpent on the staff of Moses. That serpent, like those on a caduceus, represents the subtle energies of life ascending and descending through the psychophysiological energy centers along the spinal cord. Each of these energy centers, when stimulated by Nehustan, or niter, generates its own class of drives, desires, thoughts, virtues, and vices. There is also a reciprocal dynamic, such that giving conscious attention to a certain class of desires and thoughts actually directs the transformative energy to the associated energy center. Tradition holds that the centers in the lower half of the body are concerned with survival, sex, and social status. So long as a person's consciousness remains primarily focused on those matters, there is relatively less stimulation of the centers from the heart upward. But when one begins to attend to the greater mysteries of life – such as the spiritual depths of beauty, justice, love, understanding, and wisdom – then the transformative energy is drawn up from its enmeshment in the lower centers to stimulate even further development and awakening in the higher. To knowingly and intentionally use the proper meditative techniques to pull the transformative energy up, direct it into specific operations, and then re-circulate it down, is what we mean by "the extraction of niter." It is much the same kind of work as practiced to achieve psychospiritual equilibrium, only now with greater understanding, awareness, and precision. In effect, the work of equilibrium never stops; it only becomes refined and applied in new ways.

The Emerald Tablet says the Great Work is accomplished "by means of a gentle heat, with much attention." The raw energy of transformation is like a wild beast that must be tamed, yet it is far safer and more rewarding to tame this beast with a mild hand and warm affection than with a whip and blistering domination. This point is important because one's equilibrium can be disturbed by too much fervency, yet a steady commitment and patient fortitude is indispensable. Focusing too fiercely on the stimulation of any one or few energy centers can result in the associated principles and dynamics being pushed to an extreme at the expense of others. That kind of *dis-ease* is readily apparent in people with obsessions related to the lower centers. Examples include cases where unrestrained sexual addictions or constant battling for social power have robbed people of the higher faculties of deep compassion or sound moral judgment. Similar dynamics can occur with the upper centers, and convenient illustrations are the spiritual escapist who has suppressed all concerns for worldly matters, or the aspiring psychic who has instead slipped into psychosis. To be sure, both the superior and inferior require gentle but constant attention. An ongoing refinement in the art and science of Rosicrucian alchemy is its own most crucial level of practice, for it provides the practitioner with the knowledge, skills, and power to accomplish other labors in the Great Work.

APPLICATION

Until now, we have spoken of the Great Work as the process of transformation within the practitioner, but these aims cannot be the sole end of one's labors. To truly realize the quintessence that informs one's personal being is to know spiritual unity with our fellow human beings as an actual fact. We are all children of the One God, and our souls all partake of the same dew and manna from Heaven. The illuminated alchemist loves neighbor as self, because both are known to be extractions of the same Divine Self. So it is that wherever the Rose+Cross has bloomed, one naturally feels obligated to help further the Great Work in the lives of others.

There are many different ways that niter can be employed on behalf of others. As stereotypical examples we might think of spiritual healing, or teaching and mentoring others in esoteric knowledge and practice. Both of those pursuits are legitimate and laudable undertakings, but not everyone is talented in these ways. Some people would be doing others and themselves a disservice by not pursuing different forms of service. For example, in addition to things that might seem more glamorous and magical, the Apostle Paul also lists *giving* and *administration* as spiritual gifts.[122] In any case, to be acquainted with and accepting of one's special talents and gifts and to employ them in the service of others are signs of an emerging adept.

In the scope of this chapter, we cannot do justice to considering all or even a few forms of service, but we can more closely examine one that should be dear to the hearts of many Rosicrucian students and to

122. Romans 12:6-8.

Alchemical and Hermetic Masons – the magic of ritual initiation. In recounting the rites of the ancient mystery religions that so inspired earlier generations of Masons, *Morals & Dogma* clarifies exactly why initiation has an important place within traditions of the Great Work:

> *Though Masonry is identical with the Ancient Mysteries, it is so in this qualified sense; that it presents but an imperfect image of their brilliancy....*[123]

> *The object of the ancient initiations being to ameliorate mankind and to perfect the intellectual part of man, the nature of the human soul, its origin, its destination, its relations to the body and to universal nature, all formed part of the mystic science; and to them in part the lessons given to the Initiate were directed. For it was believed that initiation tended to his perfection, and to preventing the divine part within him, overloaded with matter gross and earthy, from being plunged into gloom, and impeded in its return to the Deity.*[124]

As *Morals & Dogma* has noted, Masonic initiations do not, at least typically, match the power of the ancient initiations. This failure is because ritual initiation, in order to attain its potentials, must offer the candidate more than an experience of hollow secrecy, rote performance of liturgy, obligatory presentation of unvalued symbols, spiritless recitation of standardized prayers, and farcical threats to enforce obligations to common moral codes and ethical values. To be optimally effective in aiding the psychospiritual transformation of an initiate, ritual and all its elements must come alive as inspired and intentional expressions of transformative power. As John Michael Greer writes:

> *An initiation is a formal process for bringing about specific long-term changes in human consciousness. [...] Magical*

123. Pike, *Morals & Dogma, Annotated*, 96.
124. Pike, *Morals & Dogma, Annotated*, 472.

initiation is to the new initiate what consecration is to a talisman: something inert and unformed receives energy, shape, direction.[125]

Many conditions should be in place for a truly magical initiation to occur. Most fundamentally, the initiators ought to have already proven themselves in the work of their own transformations. They should understand how to manipulate the Astral Light to establish an atmosphere fine-tuned to the purposes of the given initiation. The skill to access and harness the powers and principles they would seek to evoke within the new initiate is required, as is the ability to invoke the archetypal characters represented by the various roles of the drama. The candidate needs to be adequately prepared with instruction and other measures contributing to a receptive and fertile state of consciousness. To crown all of their work, the initiators revere it as a rite of sacred love and mystical reunion among spiritual kin, a holy sacrifice dedicated to the Glory of the One God.

What greater work can be performed in the service of another? To administer a magical rite of initiation as an act of the Great Work is a true blessing, not only to the initiate but also to the initiators. It is a psychospiritual healing as surely as any form of therapy, and a giving of most rare and precious gifts. When emerging from such an experience, the new initiate is certain that mysterious forces have been applied to inspire the soul, forces that urge movement toward transformations the initiate intuitively desires, yet only dimly foresees.

CONCLUSION

The quest of the Knight Rose Croix is identical to the aims of the Rosicrucian alchemist. We begin by seeking psychospiritual transformation. If by our fervency, skill, and divine grace we witness the

---

125. John Michael Greer "The Magical Lodge," *Hermetic Library, https://hermetic. com/caduceus/articles/lodge1.*

blossom of the alchemical rose upon the cross of our souls, it is only to realize our truest selves living within the hearts of our fellow human beings. It is then that we know our labors are never finished until the hope expressed in the Rose Croix Degree is fulfilled:

> *when the great plans of Infinite Eternal Wisdom shall be fully developed; and all God's creatures, seeing that all apparent evil and individual suffering and wrong were but the drops that went to swell the great river of infinite goodness, shall know that vast as is the power of Deity, His goodness and beneficence are infinite as His power.*[126]

---

126. Pike, *Morals & Dogma, Annotated*, 361.

PART THREE:
RESOURCES

INTRODUCTION

The following pages are no longer limited to providing history, theory, and inspirational visions of the Great Work, but also clearly describe engaging activities that can produce real results in the psychospiritual transformation discussed in previous chapters. The organization of this part reflects the idea that Rosicrucianism consists of three interwoven branches of work – Cabala, magia, and chymia – and it then addresses service. While these topics are hardly discrete from each other, there is a natural progression in the given sequence that supports a stable and consistent approach to the Great Work. The various exercises have been carefully integrated, and you are *strongly advised* to develop practical fluency with the content in one chapter before moving on to the next. Skipping elements will detract from the overall results and may also risk psychospiritual imbalance.

It should also be noted that although these chapters focus on individual practice, many things presented here can easily be adapted for group work.[127] Groups operating independently of another organization are limited only by their own resources and imaginations.

---

127. For more guidance on group work within a Masonic context, see my previous book, *The Contemplative Lodge: A Manual for Masons Doing Inner Work Together*, and also the online resources of the Masonic Legacy Society.

Others, such as Masonic Knights Rose Croix, wishing to incorporate this work into their chapter meetings or to form a working group with a Masonic or another organization's initiation as a prerequisite should first be thoroughly familiar with their governing bodies' regulations.

The introductory poem for this part presents three interconnected perspectives on a deep and essential question about a practical aspect of the Great Work.

CONSECRATION

A Voice

With senses keenly focused within and without,
Carefully chosen scents billowing in a cloud,
Precisely breathing and weaving the priestly spell
With the waving of hands and a ringing bell,
Amplifying all the most fitting emotions
While reciting the traditional devotions,
Concentrating in finely tuned intellection,
Chanting and entranced in rapt attention,
Intonations reverberating sacred names,
Internal vision traversing across the planes,
Charging every implement of the ritual
Through the astral, etheric, and material,
Drawing the holy circle with dedication,
We make things right though theurgic consecration.

A Second Voice

Sitting in silence with the One,
With senses and thoughts all undone,
Desires and passions pacified,
The soul and spirit opened wide,
With grace flowing out from the core,

Recalling the Presence once more,
Eyes open and welcome the light,
Knowing that everything in sight
Is ever filled with the Divine,
And so is every place a shrine.
Without an equivocation,
Nothing needs a consecration.

A THIRD VOICE

Is it a matter of convenience,
Or perhaps arrogance or ignorance,
That we view anything apart from God,
And are not forever over-awed
To wander around in pure ecstasy
Amid creation's hallowed legacy?
But still, regardless of the real reason,
The essence of all things is forgotten.
Thus, the sacerdotal arts have their place
In recollecting the Spirit's embrace –
Reminding ourselves through affirmation
Is the prime purpose of consecration;
All ceremony is part of the dance
Of Heaven and Earth's eternal romance.

CHAPTER 7:
CABALA

We begin by reviewing the traditional place of Cabala in Rosicrucianism with special attention given to the Tree of Life, the most widely used symbolic system of Cabala. That examination is followed by consideration of the tradition's contemplative methods and their applications on a Rosicrucian path. Before proceeding into these matters, we have a duty to acknowledge that many non-Jews have claimed Cabala with little or no homage given to the Jewish source tradition. Some have failed to recognize that there are very significant differences between the source tradition and non-Jewish appropriations and adaptations. Some Christian Cabalists have arrogantly assumed a superior understanding of Cabala simply because of being Christians, and others have even used it to try converting Jews to Christianity. Those of us on contemporary Rosicrucian paths should deeply contemplate our ethical responsibility for our inheritance and strive to not repeat the wrongs of our predecessors.

CABALA AND ROSICRUCIANISM

The *Fama* clearly references Cabala as one of C.R.C.'s major areas of study, using the term to denote a kind of esoteric theosophical teaching that appears in different forms depending on its religious context. The word *cabala* originated in Hebrew to signify a received tradition of wisdom in Judaism, one supposedly first revealed directly from God and then passed on through secret teachings from one generation to another. It also refers to the direct reception of mystical insight, or gnosis, imparted by the Divine to the minds of properly prepared devotees. Among the methods of the original Jewish tradition are profound contemplations on scripture, which yield layers of different meanings for the same reference, from the literal to the allegorical and moral, to comparisons with other references, and finally to the esoteric and mystical, which come through inspiration and cannot always be adequately expressed in words.

Cabala has its roots in much more ancient traditions, but publicly surfaced in the late 12th century with publication of the *Bahir*. That text referenced an earlier privately circulated work, *Sefer Yetzirah*, which appears to be much older. While Cabala began in Judaism, according to Gershom Scholem it "can be defined as the product of the interpenetration of Jewish Gnosticism and neoplatonism."[128]

---

128. Gershom Scholem, *Kabbalah* (New York: Dorset, 1987), 45.

Not long after the *Bahir* was published, the Cabala became known and studied by people of other faiths. The first Christian scholar to demonstrate significant familiarity with Cabala was Raymond Lully (c. 1225 - c. 1315). He made use of it in his own efforts to reform scientific investigation and to argue for the interconnectedness of Nature and God, objectives that were directly relevant to those of the *Fama* a few hundred years later. From Lully, throughout the Renaissance into the time of the Rosicrucian manifestos, Cabala significantly influenced many Christian scholars, theologians, reformers, and mystics, who adapted its theories and methods to their own faith and interests like alchemy and medicine. Following the lead of our Rosicrucian forebears, we can also make good use of certain concepts and contemplative methods found in Cabala.

THE TREE OF LIFE

Every theosophical system, because it is a system, has some sort of conceptual map used by practitioners as a guide for their work and for understanding the experiences that come from it. Cabala provides Rosicrucianism with the *Tree of Life*. The Tree of Life takes its name from the Tree of Life (*Etz Chaim* in Hebrew) in the Garden of Eden. The essential elements of the Tree of Life were first described in the *Sefer Yetzirah*, based upon the numbers one through ten and the twenty-two letters of the Hebrew alphabet. Each of the ten numbers was associated with one of the fundamental principles of creation, thus showing how existence progresses from the simple singularity of 1 to the complex diversity represented by 10. Correspondences were also made with things such as the zodiac, the directions of space, planets, four elements, and parts of the human body. These were eventually arranged into a diagram of ten sefirot with a number of interconnections, or paths, associated with the Hebrew letters. These paths illustrate important ways that the forces of creation interact with each other. The first known publication of that diagram appeared on the cover of *Portae Lucis* (1516), a Latin translation of Joseph ben Abraham Gikatilla's *Sha'are Orah* (*Gates of Light*). The artwork is attributed to the Catholic humanist, Johannn Reuchlin (1455-1522).

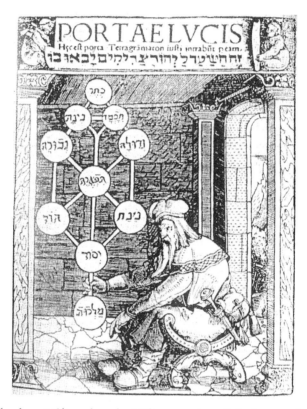

In the late 16th and early 17th centuries, Cabalistic scholars were experimenting with many different versions of the Tree, including multiple variations by the same author, and at the time of the Rosicrucian manifestos, despite widespread familiarity with the concept, there was no standardized arrangement. Then, in the early 1650s, Athanasius Kircher, a German Jesuit, published his version, which is relevant to Freemasonry because it shows parallels with the Tabernacle and the Temple of King Solomon.

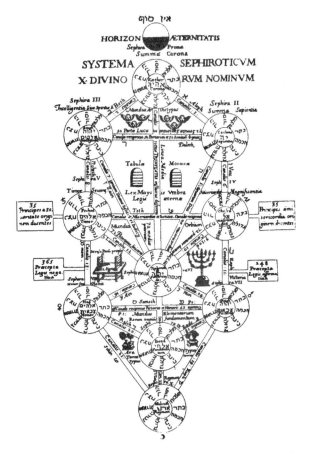

In the late 19th century, the Kircher diagram was adapted by the Hermetic Order of the Golden Dawn. It was central to their syncretic theurgical system involving esoteric Christian, Rosicrucian, Cabalistic, Hermetic, and Egyptian elements, among others. Their version of the Tree included extensive symbolic correlations for each sefira and path, including a precise set of colors for each. Since then, it has served as the most widely known diagram. There are still different schools of Cabala, including varying designs of the Tree, even within the Jewish tradition, but the Golden Dawn version is popular among persons involved with the Rosicrucian movement and is the basis of the Tree employed in the present text.

The designs on the Tree at once represent the inner workings of two categories of reality: (1) creation as an ongoing and orderly interaction of Divine powers emanating from the Godhead, or the design of the macrocosm, and (2) the psyche or soul as a more or less self-aware embodiment of those powers, or the microcosm. As proclaimed in *Genesis*, we are created in God's image, and so we might say the Tree is like a metaphysical x-ray of that image. The Tree's analogy of these two categories reveals a parallel between Cabala and the Hermetic axiom, *as above so below, as below so above*, positing that the macrocosm is reflected in the microcosm. One of the most important implications here is that the Tree is meant to help us work with the great mysteries of existence, both within us and beyond us.

THE STRUCTURE OF THE TREE OF LIFE

The Tree of Life is arranged in a manner intended to reveal many dynamics of creation, which is considered to be an ongoing process rather than something that occurred once, long ago. In the illustration on the following page, you see three concentric semi-circles above the Tree. They represent the Godhead in its highest transcendence of creation. They are collectively referred to as the *Veils of Negative Existence*, terminology that emphasizes their mysteriousness. We speak of the Divine Source with the greatest reverence when we do so by negation, saying what IT is *not*. IT is *not* a thing, hence *Ayn*, which means "nothingness." IT is *not* limited to space and time, thus IT is named *Ayn Sof*, where *sof* is translated as "limitless" or "boundless." And yet, we say IT is *like* light because IT emanates, and so we also call it *Ayn Sof Aur* the "Light of the Limitless No-Thing." It is important to understand that these negations deny neither that we are created in the image of God nor the axiom *as above, so below*. Rather, it is congruent with both in acknowledging that the mystery of God and the mystery of one's own being reflect each other.

The Tree of Life

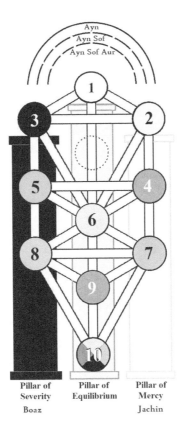

Pillar of Severity	Pillar of Equilibrium	Pillar of Mercy
Boaz		Jachin

Note that the ten sefirot align in three vertical columns, which are the Pillar of Equilibrium in the middle, the Pillar of Mercy on the right, and the Pillar of Severity on the left. The left and right pillars correspond to the pillars on the porch of King Solomon's Temple, which are *Boaz*, meaning "strength," and *Jachin*, meaning "establishment." One significance of the pillars is how they reference the relationship of force and form, or energy and structure, two inter-related principles that are present in everything. Every sefira naturally includes both force and form, but this arrangement reveals whether one principle is dominant, or if they are held in balance. Those on the white Pillar of Mercy are more oriented to force, those on the black

Pillar of Severity to form, and those on the Pillar of Equilibrium integrate force and form.

Among the dynamics illustrated by the Tree is the order in which the ten sefirot emerge. Likely reflecting a Pythagorean influence, the sefirot correspond to the first ten natural numbers, and some systems of Cabala represent their emergence as a series of concentric circles, with Keter ("crown") at the center and Malkut ("kingdom" or "dominion") at the outer ring. However, the Tree presents them as shown in the diagram below, as if a lightning flash reaching from the highest heaven down to earth. It begins with the sefira Keter and terminates in the sefira Malkut.

The Lightning Flash of Creation

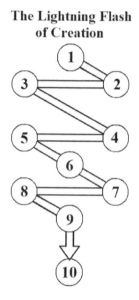

We are now ready to introduce each sefira, bearing in mind that many volumes have been written in their contemplation. Each therefore deserves further study and meditation, and opportunities for doing so are provided in later exercises. Please note that there are different pronunciations of the various names, and suggestions are provided in the glossary at the end of this book. Further associations are tabulated in the appendix. For now, the following information is provided for contemplation on each sefira:

1. Its name and a general description, including its location on the Tree of Life and relationships with other sefirot.

2. God Name: This name is a means of invoking, recognizing, and attuning with a particular divine attribute, and thereby coming to greater clarity about how the Divine begins emanating itself in different ways.

3. Archangel: A spiritual being further differentiated from the Godhead than the God Name, who serves as a kind of governor for those principles and dynamics associated with a particular sefira.

4. Celestial Object: The astrological correspondent of the sefira, including the relevant gods or goddesses from ancient pantheons.

5. Spiritual Experience: True knowledge and integration of a sefira's reality and meaning comes through experience, not just conceptualization. Such experiences manifest at many levels, including intuitively, emotionally, and physically, in spontaneous meditative visions, dreams, and moments of synchronicity in one's material and social life. They can sometimes be very powerful and dramatic, and other times quite subtle, each contributing to a never-ending depth of familiarity, understanding, and competence with the given sefira. There is never one experience that bestows all.

6. Illusion: On the one hand, the illusion of each sefira can be a misunderstanding of reality that prevents or distorts its spiritual experiences. On the other hand, it can also arise from spiritual experience that has not been well analyzed and integrated and therefore contributes to a mistaken perception of reality. Cognitive distortions and ego defense mechanisms are typically involved.

7. Virtue: This is the moral excellence traditionally considered most relevant to the divine attribute of the given sefira. It suggests the particular behavioral mean for deliberation and habituation that best serves the aspects of truth, beauty, and goodness corresponding to that divine attribute.

8. Vice: Each sefira other than Keter has a traditionally assigned vice, a behavioral excess or deficiency that is customarily considered an obstacle to or avoidance of the corresponding positive qualities of the sefira. Aristotle also explained that every virtue relates to two vices, one of excess and one of deficiency, and so two such vices for each sefira's virtue are also suggested.

THE SUPERNAL TRIAD

Together, the first three sefirot are referred to as the *Supernal Triad*. They represent an indivisible trinity in which one cannot be properly appreciated without reference to the other two. Everything else in the Tree can be thought of as different manifestations of their interacting fundamental principles. While they have correlates in the human soul, in themselves they are considered to be transcendent of individual consciousness.

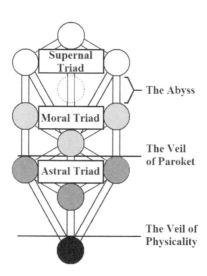

The first sefira is *Keter*, which means "crown," and thus represents the Divine Crown, or Divine Will, emanating as the pure force of all forces and form of all forms, the primal energy and inviolable law of creation. It contains within it all the potentials that unfold in the rest of the Tree. With regard to the elements, Keter is associated with Aether, which is the quintessence from which the classical elements – Air, Fire, Water, and Earth – are derived. It is associated with the crown of the human head, and in the human psyche it represents the fundamental drive to exist and all the archetypes that can be manifested in human life.

- God Name: *Eheyeh*, meaning "I am." It is sometimes written as the full answer to Moses' question to the burning bush about God's name, *Eheyeh Asher Eheyeh*, "I am that I am."

- Archangel: *Metatron*, the chief archangel about whom much has been written in esoteric literature. The exact meaning of the name is unclear, but Metatron is also called the Prince of Countenances, the Prince of the Presence, and the Lesser YHVH.

- Celestial Object: In the ancient system observed by this book, Keter correlates with the "First Swirlings" of the universe, which may be regarded as the beginning of the Big Bang. Keter is sometimes assigned Neptune in more recent versions of the Tree.

- Spiritual Experience: Union with God

- Illusion: False Attainment, delusions of completion, perfection, or final enlightenment

- Virtue: Attainment

- Vice: Not applicable, as attainment would be a state of perfection in and/or transcendence of all the virtues

Hockmah, the second sefira, means "wisdom," but the Hebrew roots also suggest "the potentiality of what is." It is the emerging essential force of all to be manifest in creation and is thus associated with the element of Fire. The transcendent wisdom of Hockmah is the wordless imageless awareness of and openness to the Divine Will of Keter, open not only for receiving that light but also transmitting it into Binah where it can begin gestating into form. In the human body, it is visualized at the left side of the head but corresponds best with the function of the right hemisphere of the brain.

- God Name: *YHVH*, which has no exact translation, but may be interpreted as "The Ever-Becoming." While this name has often been pronounced as "Jehova," or "Yaweh," the actual pronunciation has been lost. Out of respect for the significance of this name it is here pronounced by each of its Hebrew letters – Yud-Heh-Vav-Heh.

- Archangel: *Ratziel*, which means "Secret of God."

- Celestial Object: The Firmament of the Heavens, or the zodiac, is the ancient association we maintain, and Uranus is a modern option.

- Spiritual Experience: Vision of God, face to face

- Illusion: Separation, the misperception that we are disconnected from God and each other

- Virtue: Devotion

- Vice: The traditional vice is evil. The suggested vice of excess is ungroundedness, and the vice of deficiency is nihilism.

Binah means "understanding" or "intelligence." Here in the third sefira, the archetypal forms begin to coalesce into the transcendent ideas of creation. Associated with water, one title of Binah is the Great Sea, the primordial depths from which all life emerges. It is the womb that receives the seminal energy from Hockmah, and within which all structures of existence are ineffably "conceived" in accord with the Divine Will of Keter. It is visualized to the right of the head, while the functions of the left hemisphere of the brain best reflect it.

- God Name: *Elohim*, traditionally translated in the Bible simply as "God." The root *eloh* is feminine for "god," and the masculine *-im* suffix indicates the plural. In the *Book of Genesis*, it is Elohim that says, "let Us make man in Our image, … male and female He created them."[129] Some Christian theologians see an allusion to the Holy Trinity in this name.

- Archangel: *Tzafkiel*, "Contemplation of God"

- Celestial Object: Saturn

- Spiritual Experience: Vision of Sorrow

- Illusion: Death

- Virtue: Silence

- Vice: The traditional vice is avarice or greed. The suggested vice of excess is uncommunicativeness, and the vice of deficiency is indiscretion or logorrhea.

THE ABYSS AND DAAT

Between the Supernal Triad and the other sefirot is a region known as the *Abyss*. It has this title because there is no way to ascend through it and retain any sense of individuality. All notions of separateness, distinctness, and uniqueness are lost in mystical union. Thus, crossing the Abyss is not achievable through individual desire or effort, although both the approach and the response to it are necessarily individualized.

129. Genesis 1:26-27, NAS.

In the wake of such an event or state, as individuality is reborn and reforms or reconfigures, enlightened knowledge of the Supernal Triad may take shape in one's consciousness. Such knowledge is Cabalistically called *Daat*, which literally means "knowledge," and it is also appropriately referred to as *gnosis*. Daat is *not* a sefira in itself but is instead a reflection of mystical experience of the Supernal Triad projected onto the Abyss from an individualized consciousness of the lower sefirot. It is sometimes referred to as a "pseudo-sefira," and is assigned the God Name *YHVH Elohim*, combining those of Hockmah and Binah. Daat is often shown with a dashed circle in the midst of the Abyss, as in the preceding illustration, and is associated with the throat. There is much significance in this location's association with respiration, ingestion, and speech, and their allegorical relevance to Daat's role.

To reiterate, Daat, unlike a sefira, cannot be experienced; it *is* both an experience and the knowledge received through that experience. The gnosis of Daat may be qualified by integration of the three virtues of the Supernal Triad. In this mystical sense, the silence of Binah is known as abandonment of any form of language, feeling, or perception in simple awareness of the presence of the nascent duality of existence, which is only analogized with words such as "light and darkness" or "force and form." The devotion of Hockmah is known as the steadfast single pointedness of the emerging light of the Divine Self reflecting on Itself, like an "unspotted mirror" offering no substantive differentiation between the knower and the known. The attainment of Keter is the eternally self-attained unity that is unattainable except in IT simply being IT. Daat is the *knowing* of these truths; they are no longer merely elements of faith, doctrine, abstraction, or inference.

THE MORAL TRIAD

Just beneath the Abyss, the sefirot Hesed, Gevurah, and Tiferet constitute the *Moral Triad* on the Tree of Life. They are the fundamental Divine principles of creation functioning at a level that is perceptible at the highest reaches of individual consciousness, the intuitive and inspirational levels just above ordinary thinking in words and images. The term *moral* is applied to them not because they are the only sefirot with ethical significance, but because they guide our deepest convictions about, and most noble efforts toward, realizing goodness, justice, and beauty in all things.

The fourth sefira and first of the Moral Triad, *Hesed*, means "loving kindness." As a force sefira associated with Water, it is the incessant outpouring of Divine Grace, the eternal font of God's infinitely abundant love. In terms of the macrocosm, this can be witnessed in the sustained act of creation itself, the ongoing evolution of existence. Hesed is the torrent of reproduction in Nature, whether as the propagation of species or of stars and planets. In the human soul, it is our capacity for charity, compassion, mercy, forgiveness, and our drive to bring more life and bounty into the world. Hesed correlates with the left shoulder because the left side of the body is traditionally associated with our more creative potentials.

- God Name: *El*, simply translated as "God."

- Archangel: *Tzadkiel*, "Justice of God"

- Celestial Object: Jupiter

- Spiritual Experience: Vision of Love

- Illusion: Self-Righteousness

- Virtue: Obedience

- Vice: The traditional vice is bigotry, gluttony, hypocrisy, or tyranny. The suggested vice of excess is servility, obsequiousness, or tribalism, and the vice of deficiency is rebelliousness or faithlessness.

Gevurah means "severity," "strength," or "power." This fifth sefira's relationship with Hesed reflects that of Binah's with Hockmah.

Gevurah is a Fire sefira that takes Hesed's flood of creative waters and channels it into greater structure and order. In the macrocosm, this structure and order is perceived in the laws of consciousness and physics that in turn govern chemistry and biology, giving rise to the processes of Nature. The "severity" of these matters is encountered whenever we push too hard against those laws, thereby generating disturbing consequences that can be shockingly destructive. These macrocosmic operations of Gevurah are also present in the microcosm of our individual being as well as in our social coexistence. In the human soul, Gevurah gives rise to our passionate instinctive sense that there are proper, right, and just ways for things to be, and that such things warrant strict and assertive management. This sefira is associated with the right shoulder, on the side of the body traditionally connected with strength and labor.

- God Name: *Elohim Gibur*, "Powerful God" or "God of Power"

- Archangel: *Khamael*, "Seer of God"

- Celestial Object: Mars

- Spiritual Experience: Vision of Power

- Illusion: Invincibility

- Virtue: Courage

- Vice: The traditional vice is cruelty. The suggested vice of excess is rashness, and the vice of deficiency is cowardice.

The final sefira in the Moral Triad is *Tiferet*, meaning "beauty." Hesed and Gevurah represent a fundamental dichotomy in existence and a polarity experienced at every level of our being. In the absence of a harmonizing principle, they would be in constant violent conflict cycling back and forth in dominance over each other. In its excess,

Hesed would generate change so quickly and frequently that nothing could persist long enough to realize its greatest potentials, and the most basic energies could not sufficiently combine in order for the more complex forms of creation to emerge. By contrast, the domination of Gevurah would, on the one hand, strive to shut down all change in an effort to maintain the status quo. Yet, on the other hand, Gevurah's inherent perfectionism would also be constantly driven to utterly destroy the present circumstances because of their inadequacy – the finite and temporal can never fully capture the infinite and eternal.

The nature of the sixth sefira is to bring all oppositions into dynamic productive equilibrium. Tiferet is therefore the harmonizing principle that effectively integrates Hesed's unrelenting cascade with Gevurah's fiery harshness. An analogy in physics are the neutrons that facilitate arrangement of positively charged protons and negatively charged electrons into all the various elements beyond the most basic hydrogen isotope. Another analogy is the intelligence that brings together force and form to build a steam engine within which the potentials of fire and water are both harnessed for industrious purposes.

Tiferet, an Air sefira, is thus always acting as a mediating, moderating, integrating principle in the macrocosm, in our psyches, and in society. It is associated with the breast, and especially the heart. Physiologically speaking, the heart is the central pump that ensures the elements of life are equitably distributed to every cell, tissue, and organ. The metaphorical heart of the psyche is the meeting place and harmonizer of all our various functions – intuition, inspiration, thought, emotion, sensation, instinct, and behavior. Socially, the principle of Tiferet is epitomized by those great-hearted leaders and institutions that have effectively brought peace and harmony to otherwise clashing elements of humanity, healing old wounds, bridging divides, welcoming all to common ground, and exemplifying how to "best work and best agree" for the greater good.

- God Name: *YHVH Aloa Ve Daat*, which can be understood as "Ever Becoming God of Knowledge," is also regarded as expressing "God Manifest in the Mind." The name also suggests an important relationship between Tiferet and the pseudo-sefira Daat.

- Archangel: *Rafael*, "Healer of God"

- Celestial Object: Sun

- Spiritual Experience: Vision of Harmony, Vision of the Mysteries of Crucifixion

- Illusion: Personal Identification of the Self

- Virtue: Devotion to the Great Work

- Vice: The traditional vice is pride or arrogance. The suggested vice of excess is fanaticism, and the vice of deficiency is apathy.

THE VEIL OF PAROKET AND THE ASTRAL TRIAD

Immediately beneath Tiferet is a boundary known as the *Veil of Paroket*, which literally renders as "veil of the veil." The Hebrew *paroket* references the veil of the Tabernacle and later that of the Temple of Solomon, which concealed the most holy place where the priests of Israel communed with God. On the Tree of Life, it marks the line of transition between the higher transpersonal levels of the soul and the lower levels in which personality develops as an instrument for the soul's engagement with the world of social and physical reality.

Beneath the Veil of Paroket is the *Astral Triad* of Netzach, Hod, and Yesod. *Astral* literally refers to the stars, and to the ancients it was a name for the world just above the earthly world to which humanity seemed tethered. Over time, *astral* began to be used less literally, referring instead to a level of being and awareness just beyond the five senses and more directly accessible through the conscious mind and emotions. Thus, the Astral Triad is the level on the Tree directly corresponding to the psychological dimension of existence, and through which all the principles of the previous sefirot influence our personal perceptions, understandings, decisions, feelings, and actions.

As a whole, the Astral Triad may be best understood in human terms as the imagination in its broadest sense. We often speak of the imagination as merely that part of us which consciously daydreams, supposes, speculates, and envisions possibilities. A little deeper reflection reveals that the imagination is also engaged in all problem-solving activities and even in the formation of the words, numerals, and other symbols we internally see and hear during the course of ordinary thinking. In fact, it is within the imagination that everything we categorize as perceptions of the five senses are actually consciously experienced. An even more comprehensive view acknowledges that imagination is also the part of us in which our sleeping dreams occur, and within which our intuitions and creative impulses arise and take shape. The imagination is therefore not limited to the conscious mind; it also has myriad unconscious aspects and processes.[130]

Netzach, the first of the Astral Triad, is a Fire and force sefira, and its name means "victory." The force of this seventh sefira is that of instinct and emotion, from the most basic feelings in every creature's drive to survive and reproduce, to the most refined sentiments evoked by beautiful music. Netzach is also the creative urge, flame of inspiration, and the will to act felt by everyone at various times, but these are especially known by lovers, romantics, artists, prophets, and visionaries. The victory of this sefira is in its constant aspiration toward the greatest possible experience and expression of beauty in Nature at all her levels, about which the Platonic understanding of eros/love explored in Chapter 3 offers much insight. Netzach is visualized at the left hip.

---

130. For a more thorough consideration of imagination in metaphysics, see the works of Edward Douglas Fawcett, *The World as Imagination* (1916), and *Divine Imagining: An Essay on the First Principles of Philosophy* (1921).

- God Name: *YHVH Tzabaot*, meaning "YHVH of Hosts." "Hosts" actually refers to armies, which in this case are the many different metaphysical intelligences and forces operating just behind the scenes of the natural world to implement its manifestation.

- Archangel: *Haniel*, "Grace of God"

- Celestial Object: Venus

- Spiritual Experience: Vision of Beauty Triumphant

- Illusion: The Ego Defense of Projection

- Virtue: Unselfishness

- Vice: The traditional vice is wantonness or lust. The suggested vice of excess is self-abuse or self-neglect, and the vice of deficiency is selfishness.

Visualized at the right hip, the eighth sefira and second in the Astral Triad is *Hod*, which means "splendor." As a form and Water sefira, it provides fitting structures for the energies of Netzach, as faithfully as possible representing their intentions in patterns recognizable to conscious awareness, patterns that shine with the splendor of truth. In the macrocosm, Hod includes the laws of Nature and physics foreshadowed by the organizing principles of Gevurah. Within the microcosm, words, numbers, and other symbols are all products of Hod, as is their coherent assembly according to the boundaries of logic, syntax, semiosis, mathematics, and music. This sefira is the seat of the processes of abstraction, analysis, and association we use in conceptualizing our experiences and determining what we wish to do. Combining and coordinating all these activities is how Hod makes communication possible.

- God Name: *Elohim Tzabaot*, "God of Hosts." In Hod these hosts are the countless metaphysical forms and beings available for organizing the forces of Netzach

- Archangel: *Mikael*, "Likeness of God"

- Celestial Object: Mercury

- Spiritual Experience: Vision of Splendor

- Illusion: Perfect Order

- Virtue: Truthfulness

- Vice: The traditional vice is falsehood or dishonesty. The suggested vice of excess is imprudence, and the vice of deficiency is deceitfulness or willful ignorance.

Just as the polarity of Hesed and Gevurah needs the harmonizing principle of Tiferet, so do the fiery forces of Netzach and the watery forms of Hod require the integration of *Yesod*. It is an Air sefira serving an administrative function that brings these metaphysical forces and forms together, maximizing their potentials and moving them toward manifestation. In the natural world of our planet, air surrounds, interpenetrates, and moves both fire and water. Fire needs air in order to continue its existence and help it spread, and water needs air to make it more supportive of life. Thus, the name of this ninth sefira, meaning "foundation," befits its role in the macrocosm as the metaphysical matrix within which emerges the phenomena of the material world in conformity with the designs of Hod and the drives of Netzach. In the microcosm, Yesod corresponds to the incarnational portion of the soul, which, like the moon receiving and reflecting the light of the sun, predisposes the earthly personality to respond to its experiences and develop its unique identity in ways reflecting the intentions of the higher individuality.

- God Name: *Shaddai El Chai*. *Shaddai* means "almighty", and *chai* means "life," so the name is understood as "Almighty God of Life" or "Almighty Living God"

- Archangel: *Gabriel*, "Strength of God"

- Celestial Object: Moon

- Spiritual Experience: Vision of the Machinery of the Universe

- Illusion: Personal Security

- Virtue: Independence

- Vice: The traditional vice is idleness or sloth. The suggested vice of excess is aloofness or incompassion, and the vice of deficiency is dependence or conformity.

THE VEIL OF PHYSICALITY AND MALKUT

Between the ninth and tenth sefirot is the *Veil of Physicality*, a boundary analogous to the Veil of Paroket. In this case, the veil marks the transition in creation from metaphysical emanations to physical manifestations. This veil seems rigid and impenetrable for people who strongly adhere to a materialist view of existence. However, it is in actuality quite thin, and most people's attention frequently passes back and forth through this veil without even realizing it. Indeed, it could be argued that our attention is focused beneath the veil only when we are closely attuned to the perceptions immediately arising from the physical senses. This indicates that what we typically call "the mind" is not really located in the material world but observes and interacts with it through the mechanisms of the body. On the other hand, it also suggests that Malkut *is* within the greater reality of Mind, or the consciousness that spans all of creation, which is something we can easily fail to recognize while our attention shifts to and fro.

The last sefira, assigned to the element of Earth, is *Malkut*. In the macrocosm it represents the whole of the physical universe in all its resplendent diversity, and each of our material bodies in the microcosm. Its name means "kingdom" or "dominion," which immediately reveals that all of creation, all the way down into every earthly creature and the densest depths of crude matter, is divine, sacred territory. The material world is neither an accident, nor a mistake, nor a place of exile, but is an intended outcome of creation's continual emanation from God. It is the Garden of Eden, or at least it could be, if we would stop allowing ourselves to be misled by the illusion of separation and all the vices it begets.

Keter and Malkut may also be thought of as the two poles between which the currents of existence continually flow. Just as the Lightning Flash of Creation delivers the forces and forms of life down into their stabilization in Malkut, so does that sphere echo and reflect the results back up through the Tree. The Divine Will is always witnessing and responding to its own becoming.

Within personal experience, one way this dynamic of projection and reflection is engaged is in the Vision of the Holy Guardian Angel. The Holy Guardian Angel is conceptualized in various ways by different authorities. For some, it is a being with its own identity apart from the soul of the aspirant. For others, it is an aspect of the aspirant's own soul at a higher level of being. In any case, it is understood that the relationship between the aspirant and the Holy Guardian Angel provides instruction, protection, guidance, tests, and challenges to assist one toward fulfilling their potentials as a unique embodiment of the Divine in this world. It is a conduit by which part of the back-and-forth flow of communication occurs between Keter and Malkut within one's own life. Thus, the spiritual experience of Malkut delivers a clearer understanding of and attraction to one's distinguishing talents and callings. In the process, one may internally encounter the personified form of a spiritual being serving as a special mentor, protector, and inspirational exemplar of one's own psychospiritual potentials. Please note that this vision does not constitute the Knowledge and Conversation of the Holy Guardian Angel, which is a further development attributed to an unfolding of potentials in Tiferet.

- God Name: *Adonai ha Aretz*, literally "Lord of the Earth"

- Archangel: *Sandalfon*. This name has uncertain meaning, but may be interpreted as "Co-Brother" or simply "Brother" in reference to a special relationship with Metatron

- Celestial Object: Planet Earth

- Spiritual Experience: Vision of the Holy Guardian Angel

- Illusion: Materialism

- Virtue: Discernment

- Vice: The traditional vice is avarice or inertia. The suggested vice of excess is intolerance or prejudice, and the vice of deficiency is gullibility or inattentiveness.

THE FOUR WORLDS

Most theistic religions propose a series of planes of emanation between the Divine Source and material existence, with different categories of beings corresponding to each level. Among today's Christians, these matters are unfamiliar to most mainstream Protestants, although they are still recognized in Anglican, Episcopalian, and Methodist traditions. For Orthodox Christians and Roman Catholics, interacting with these spiritual beings and seeking their assistance has always been a part of religious practice for both laity and clergy.

In the Cabalistic approach, so far, we have been considering the emanation of creation as a sequential process down through the sefirot and levels of the Tree of Life. However, there is another model intersecting with the Tree of Life that often proves useful in conceptualizing finer details and dynamics of creation. That model is the *Four Worlds*, as follows:

1. Atzilut, the World of Emanation
2. Briah, the World of Creation
3. Yetzirah, the World of Formation
4. Assiah, the World of Action

Atzilut holds the Divine essence and potential for each sefira. The process of emanation begins to differentiate from immediate identification with the Divine in Briah. In that world, the various potentials within Atzliut become creative intentions that guide the immaterial forms taking shape in Yetzirah. These forms in Yetzirah steer and bind energy into its various manifestations as we perceive them in Assiah through the physical senses, including all the known forces and particles of physics.

As shown below, these worlds can be correlated with different levels on a single diagram of the Tree, but they can also be illustrated with a complete Tree in each world.

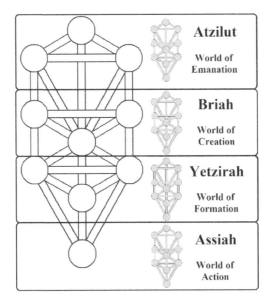

Another way to visualize the Four Worlds is as concentric rings within each sefira of a single Tree. This approach communicates the view that there is only one Keter, only one Hockmah, Binah, and so forth, but that all four levels of emanation are present within each sefira, or that each sefira is simultaneously present in all Four Worlds.

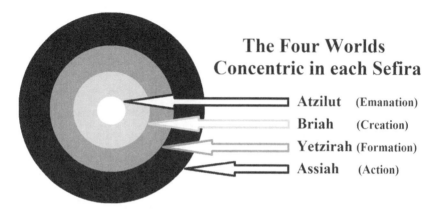

The Four Worlds Concentric in each Sefira

Atzilut (Emanation)
Briah (Creation)
Yetzirah (Formation)
Assiah (Action)

Every visualization of the Four Worlds has its strengths and shortcomings, each in its own way conveying useful implications about relationships between the different levels of emanation. What is most important is developing a practical familiarity with the levels and their relationships. For example, in the macrocosmic view, there are different categories of beings native to each world and relating to each other as follows:

1. In Atzilut, there are the energies and attributes of the Divine closest to the Godhead, which are expressed through the God Names of the sefirot.

2. In Briah, the archangel of each sefira provides governance over its functions in differentiating from the unity of Atzilut.

3. In Yetzirah, angels serve with greater specialization in moving those functions toward physical manifestation.

4. In Assiah, physical beings participate in the material processes of manifestation.

From a microcosmic view, the various aspects or functions of the soul also correspond to each of the Four Worlds, and so it is possible for us to interact with the beings and forces at each level. In Assiah, we interact through our physical bodies with its senses and behaviors, including speech, and here is where the virtue of each sefira becomes a complete reality. In Yetzirah, we engage through the mind with concepts, images, and emotions, and thus overcoming the illusion and perceiving the spiritual experience of each sefira are relevant to this world. In Briah, we work through psychospiritual faculties just beyond the ordinary range of human consciousness, tapping into intuitive and inspirational energies that give rise to thoughts and feelings but are not limited to them. Communing at the level of Atzilut is an even more mysterious matter, yet it is ever present in the most profound silence and stillness of our deepest depths.

Applying the model of the Four Worlds, we can work with the archangels through ritual and meditation as a means of fine tuning our consciousness and contemplative efforts. Knowing which archangel or archangels are most pertinent to those changes guides the rituals we perform in Assiah, and the mental and emotional forms we generate in Yetzirah, to express our intentions in Briah. If the creative intentions are properly focused and suitably resonant with the Divine Will and Laws of Nature, then they reflect back down in a cascade effect through Yetzirah and into Assiah, where they are more likely to produce the desired changes in our lives. These are, in fact, the mechanics of magia, which are further addressed in the next chapter.

It is important to proceed with an understanding that the Tree of Life and the Four Worlds are meant to be guides, tools with practical value, yet they also have limitations. As an analogy, consider that architects and engineers can diligently try to provide flawless blueprints for the construction of a building and take great pride in their meticulous labor. Nevertheless, corrections and adjustments are inevitably made onsite by the tradespersons who actually use those blueprints.

Likewise, it would be foolish to expect that we could either discover or devise a version of the Tree and Four Worlds that flawlessly represents things beyond our ability to fully cognize, let alone capture them in visual images. Thus, while the present forms are not perfect, many people have found them to be reliable trestleboards with designs more than adequate for the construction and refinement of their own spiritual temples. Cabala takes us further in that work with the practice of contemplation.

VARIETIES OF CONTEMPLATION

While the word *contemplation* sometimes has more specific meanings within different traditions, it is here used as an umbrella term to represent a broad range of intentional efforts to practice awareness of something. It therefore includes mindfulness, many different forms of meditation, imagery, breathwork, chanting, and prayer. In fact, ritual of the sort offered in many Rosicrucian and Masonic organizations is itself a contemplative practice. In the following paragraphs, we consider how an assortment of traditional Cabalistic contemplative methods can be adapted to our purposes.

According to *The Kabbalah Handbook*, there are five different forms of meditation:

- Inwardly-directed, unstructured – attending to something spontaneously happening within oneself, like thoughts, emotions, feelings, and physical processes

- Inwardly-directed, structured – sustained concentration upon a particular faculty, state, quality, or action

- Outwardly-directed, unstructured – spontaneously attending and reacting to, possibly participating in, something arising external to oneself

- Outwardly-directed, structured – intentional, planned concentration on and/or participation in something other than oneself

- Undirected – avoids perceptions of either internal or external phenomena to instead rest in stillness or emptiness[131]

In *Meditation and Kabbalah*, the scholar and physicist Rabbi Aryeh Kaplan asserted that the most common of these types are (1) the outwardly-directed, structured, (2) the inwardly-directed, unstructured, and (3) the undirected.[132]

The first of these three, the outwardly-directed, structured form, is exemplified by the use of a sound, word, or phrase that is chanted either aloud or silently for a given number of repetitions or over a specific period of time. Another example is gazing steadily at a particular image or a flame. Rituals, specific prayers, and meditations on particular scriptures, concepts, symbols, or virtues also fall into this category. Practices such as these tend to eliminate thoughts and feelings about anything else, freeing your mind from the distractions of its usual conditions and perhaps invoking deeper inspiration, intuition, or insight relevant to the focal point.

For inwardly directed unstructured meditation, there is a kind of prayer in which you spontaneously pour out your thoughts and feelings before God. This type of meditation can also be performed by simply observing the thoughts and feelings passing through your awareness. It is often described like sitting on the bank of a stream to watch it continually flow past. Its bubbles, swirls, and floating objects pass into and out of sight as the watcher sits still upon the bank. These methods increase familiarity with the dynamics of consciousness and develop greater self-awareness, self-honesty, and equanimity.

131. Gabriella Samuel, *The Kabbalah Handbook: A Concise Encyclopedia of Terms and Concepts in Jewish Mysticism* (New York: Jeremy P. Tarcher/Penguin, 2007), 208-209.
132. Aryeh Kaplan, *Meditation and Kabbalah*, First Paperback Edition (York Beach: Red Wheel/Wieser, 1985), 11-12.

Undirected meditation is somewhat harder to describe without saying that it is intentionally *not* doing any other forms of meditation or intentionally *not* attending to anything. While other forms of meditation can serve as pathways into an undirected state, it can also be entered more directly. Try to recall some moment in your life when you were instantly stunned into silent immobility by something of great beauty, awesome wonder, confusing absurdity, or incomprehensible horror. Or perhaps you know what it is like to experience fasting, sleep deprivation, or simply a prolonged repetitive experience, draining you of thoughts, emotions, and responsiveness. Consider moments when you might have been awakening from or falling into sleep, wordlessly knowing you were awake, yet unaware of any sensory perceptions and internally still and quiet. Such moments are analogous, if not proximate, to the emptiness of pure, undirected, undifferentiated consciousness. It is often only in their wake that we can find or make meaning of them, seeing how their vacuousness punctuated, perhaps even provided, the significance of what came before and after, while also parting the veil to an unfathomable and indescribable mystery beyond the circumstances and their meanings. That enigmatic state of unknowing points toward what Cabalists refer to as the *Ayn Sof*, the Limitless No-Thing, the Divine in its puzzling transcendence of both existence and non-existence.

These different forms of meditation take into account that we are multidimensional beings – physical, emotional, intellectual, and spiritual. Among the most common experiences of meditators are discovering how little awareness and control we often have over these dimensions. We notice how fixed some things seem to be that we know could be more flexible, and how volatile other things are that we know could be more stable. Yet, there is hope for reformation within our personal microcosms. Each of the different kinds of meditation can span all four dimensions, and each kind can intersect with or naturally lead into the others. Therefore, with time and the blessings of Deity, a committed, comprehensive approach to our practice can bring order to the chaos while also recognizing that chaos itself is an inherent element of the greater order of creation and Nature.

In speaking of these different dimensions, Kaplan references the Jewish philosopher Maimonides to discuss bringing them together in meditation as "the path of love."

> *...when a person deeply contemplates on God, thinking of His mighty deeds and wondrous creations, he becomes profoundly aware of His wisdom, and is brought to a passionate love for God. ... where the emotion is so intense that every thought is exclusively engaged with its object. ... This is considered to be one of the highest possible levels of enlightenment....*[133]

In these potentials for personal reformation and mystical love, we see the relevance of Cabalistic contemplative methods to Rosicrucianism. Ever since its inception, people within the Rosicrucian movement have understandably adapted and applied those methods, and especially the outwardly directed structured approach. They have done so in a variety of ways with different scriptures, concepts, and symbols as their focal points, while also retaining elements of the Jewish tradition, like the Tree of Life.

DEVELOPING THE SKILLS OF CONTEMPLATION

If you are a beginning meditator, the following instructions can provide you with a solid foundation for your current and future spiritual practices. If you are an experienced meditator, it is recommended that you enjoy this time of revisiting the basics, to which many traditions return as the very pinnacle of their methods. Beginning meditators are advised to build up to at least 15 minutes per session of basic meditation. Basic meditation can be practiced on its own or made the focus of your work after opening and before closing your oratory. It is not necessary to open your oratory to practice basic meditation, though you are encouraged to do so as often as possible.

133. Kaplan, *Meditation and Kabbalah*, 13-14.

To begin basic meditation, sit upright in a chair, or on the floor with crossed legs. If you sit on the floor, it can be helpful to use a cushion thick enough to keep your hips elevated slightly higher than your knees. Your spine should be held in a straight and comfortable position. Use some kind of back support if necessary. Avoid slouching or tipping your head too far forward, backward, or to one side. If you are sitting in a chair, it is ideal to sit with your hips a little higher than your knees and your shins perpendicular to the floor. Sitting on the front edge of the chair prevents uncomfortable pressure on the backs of the thighs. Rest your hands in your lap or on your legs. Either close your eyes or allow your eyelids to droop as you stare blankly.

Mentally scan your body from one end to the other, taking note of and releasing any tension you do not need to remain sitting in a healthy posture. If you wish, offer a short prayer asking for divine assistance. Then take a few deep, full breaths, paying careful attention to the air flowing in and out of your body. Be conscious of the entire airway and all the muscles in your chest and abdomen that are involved in breathing. Each time you exhale, allow your mind and body to sink into a deeper state of calm relaxation. After the deep breaths, simply allow your breathing to settle into a peaceful natural rhythm. Continue to attend to the breath. Thinking "in" as you inhale and "out" as you exhale can improve focus and eliminate distractions.

Allow your mind to become as still and quiet as possible. It is no longer necessary to focus on the breath as you become more aware of the stillness and quietness between and around your thoughts, feelings, and sensations. If you become distracted by anything, simply allow it to pass away as you return your focus back to stillness and quietness. If necessary, turning your attention again to the breath can help clear your mind.

When you feel the time for meditation is over, take a deep breath and fully open your eyes. It is a good idea to massage and stretch your muscles before and after standing. Sometimes people feel a little spacey coming out of meditation. To assist yourself in returning to a more ordinary state of consciousness, rub your face with your hands, clap sharply once or twice, rub or stomp your feet on the floor, or combine one or more of these actions.

Beginning meditators often express concern about distraction. Here are a few tips on managing it during meditation. First, understand that distraction is perfectly normal; even the most highly experienced meditators can be distracted from time to time. When this happens, it does not mean that you are failing at meditation. If you think of it as failure, then you may become upset, and this would only further distract you from the stillness and quietness. Second, when you reach the stage of attending to your breath's natural rhythm, mentally count the breath like so: "in one, out one, in two, out two…." Do this through ten complete breaths. If you lose count, then start over. Be patient with yourself and in time it will come easily. Once you have developed this level of concentration, it will be easier to focus on the stillness and quietness surrounding and between your thoughts, feelings, and sensations.

Meditation is best understood through experience rather than conceptualization, yet we must use concepts to communicate something about the experiences of meditation. For our purposes, it is enough to say that meditation is an intentional act of clearing, focusing, and applying consciousness. Meditation is thus an important addition to the typical ways of pursuing spirituality and philosophy. It automatically makes your work something much deeper than merely talking, reading, or writing. It can also open the heart and mind beyond the confines of your ego and its defenses, deceptions, and manipulations. When properly practiced, meditation reduces stress and promotes both physical and mental health; in fact, the word *meditate* comes from a Latin root that means "to remedy." Meditation brings clarity and discipline to the imagination. It opens the mind to deeper levels of insight, intuition, and inspiration. It engenders greater levels of self-honesty and is an exercise in integrity that naturally assists you in manifesting the truth of this ancient aphorism – "As one thinks, so one becomes." Thus, the practice of meditation forms a bridge from speculative philosophy to operative wisdom.

Three areas are especially recommended for your consideration during your continuing practice of meditation – silence, contemplative reading, and contemplative reflection on your dreams.

SILENCE

In the Pythagorean School at Crotona, it was mandatory for initiates of the first degree to practice silence. Among its many benefits, practicing silence helps us realize how much uncontrolled noise is in the mind, and how much of the time we are just chattering away to ourselves without any real purpose. This is only the first discovery that can come from the practice of silence. Another realization is that within you is an "observer" and a "chatterer," the latter of which is sometimes referred to as the "monkey mind." Thus, there is part of you within the mind that is chattering and another part hearing that chatter. Evidence of this fact arises from the observation that the chatter does not necessarily stop simply because the observer wants it to stop.

Interestingly, the observer can choose different positions or attitudes with regard to the chatter. One attitude is complete surrender, in which case the distinction between the observer and the chatterer is all but lost. Many of us spend far too much time in this state. This frame of mind leaves us easily distracted, unfocused, irrational, and insensitive. It prevents us from accurately perceiving the world around us as well as ourselves. As we begin to become aware of these dynamics, it can be a substantial challenge just to catch ourselves when we have slipped into this state.

A more developed position is that of detached observation, in which the observer patiently attends to all the chatter without any attempt to interrupt or change the flow in any way. This position offers a heightened state of self-awareness in which you have the opportunity to explore the way that particular part of your mind typically works. You can observe the patterns of thinking and feeling that influence your behaviors. Without this awareness, we move through life like an automaton, simply obeying our programming. But the more you practice detached observation, the more you become empowered to overcome such an unconscious and robotic way of life.

Another attitude is one of almost complete detachment, in which it seems that the observer actually "tunes out" or ignores the chatterer. It might seem as though the chatterer itself is actually settling down and pouring out less and less inner noise. This state is not unlike what happens when you become focused on an important activity and no longer hear the background noise surrounding you. A similar process occurs when you begin falling asleep. Conscious awareness gradually withdraws from your senses and finally from your emotions and thoughts. Assuming this attitude, you can come to the same state of quiet, open mind, yet not fall asleep, because your mind maintains both attention and intention. Your attention is focused upon the silence and stillness itself, and your intention is to keep turning the attention in that direction.

In this state of detachment or stilling of the chatterer, the observer can experience gaps between the words and images streaming through the mind. The observer may then realize that all of this mental activity is happening within and arising from silence. Yet in that silence, there is still a *presence*. If there is nothing to observe, then that presence must be more than just an observer. When one realizes that one's being cannot be reduced to either the chatterer or the observer, both the observer and the chatterer are recognized as parts, aspects, or functions of something even more fundamental. In this state, where both the chatterer and the observer seem to vanish, what remains? Only the silence, that mysterious "place" in which all your thoughts and perceptions live and move and have their being. You are that Divine Silence, and that

Divine Silence is you. In communing with the Divine in this way, in this loving of God, your silent meditation becomes the *Prayer of Silence* in the highest meaning of the word *prayer*.

What else can we say of that silence? It is mysterious. It is indescribable except through the use of negative terms. It is not a thing, not a thought, without any observable qualities, and yet everything that you can know arises within it, including what you usually think of as yourself. When you realize the state of quiet, open mind, it has a purifying and healing effect on your consciousness. This state can pave the way for reflection on any matter of concern you might have, aiding you to perceive and understand it more clearly. From this position, what comes to your awareness out of the silence is often more significant, meaningful, and insightful (perhaps even revelatory) than what you would derive through conventional ways of thinking. Such a spontaneous emergence can be an *intuition* in the best sense of the word, which means direct or immediate insight that is not dependent on ordinary thought processes. Pythagoras advised his students to converse with the gods, and, given his respect for silence, perhaps this sort of meditative prayer is what he had in mind.

CONTEMPLATIVE READING AND REFLECTION

Many of us are quite good at devouring books, and some of us could be accused of being literary gluttons, but are we always getting the most that we can from our reading? In the Great Work, we want our reading to be more than mere entertainment or the superficial gathering of information. Spiritual and philosophical literature require deep reflection and critical consideration if they are to be as meaningful and useful as possible. You are therefore advised to practice a contemplative approach to your readings.

As an analogy for contemplative reading, consider the practice of walking meditation. The goal is not merely to get from point A to point B, but to fully experience the walk itself. Similarly, with contemplative reading (or mindful reading), you simply slow down and take the time to consider individual words or phrases much more carefully, to visualize the imagery more clearly, and to better attend to your feelings about what you are reading. In effect, you make reading a more holistic experience, rather than a merely intellectual exercise.

You should also practice contemplative reflection by setting aside a couple of days per week to meditate upon one short passage or excerpt from something you are reading. As you read, highlight or make a note of those sentences or phrases that most grab your attention. You might find some of them to be particularly enigmatic, or perhaps they touch you in some way. Then, before you begin meditation, quickly memorize just one short excerpt to make it a point of contemplation after sitting with a quiet, open mind for a few minutes. Allow the excerpt to float at the center of your attention for 15 to 30 minutes and discover what new insights, associations, and questions arise. You might receive some insight that is directly related to your personal life or relationships, or it may be more philosophical and abstract. Whatever happens is fine, even if it seems like you got nothing new at a conscious level. You should know that contemplative reflection helps to implant the reading in the unconscious mind where it can continue to connect with other information and experiences.

It is also very helpful to make notes about any new insights, associations, and questions immediately after the meditation. As with our dreams, it can be easy to forget the experiences of meditation. Making notes helps to anchor these experiences in your conscious mind, and putting insights on paper or on screen is one of the ways you can begin to manifest the inner light to the outer world.

CONTEMPLATIVE REFLECTION ON DREAMS

Contemplative reflection on your dreams is also a useful practice, because it is a powerful method for deepening self-awareness. It is not presently necessary to examine the many theories about the process of dreaming. For our purposes, it is sufficient to know that people on Rosicrucian paths have found it worthwhile to pay attention to their dreams. In contemplating the nature of dreams, more than one sage has found that existence itself may be likened to the dream of the Creator. Dreaming has been the subject of extensive research and application in the field of psychotherapy. Dream analysis has been used to help countless people achieve greater levels of self-awareness, health, and happiness. Clearly, ancient seers and modern psychotherapists agree on the potential value of dreams.

It is best to begin making notes about your dreams. It is not necessary to keep a daily log, but you are advised to record dream imagery that has been especially vivid or intriguing to you. Then, on occasion, you may use your meditation time to reflect on the dream, just as you would in contemplative reflection on your readings. Allow yourself to swim through your memory of the dream for 15 to 30 minutes and discover what new insights, associations and questions arise. You might receive some insight that is directly related to your personal life or relationships. It might speak about your own psychological dynamics, or it may be more philosophical and abstract. With dreams, it is not unusual for there to be many layers of parallel and intersecting interpretations. It is not nearly as important to come up with a single best answer as it is to explore the possibilities, though sometimes a particular interpretation will seem to hold more significance than others. Remember to make notes about your interpretations and questions immediately after the meditation.

Keep in mind that the purpose of this work is to increase self-awareness by bringing conscious attention to the imagery produced by the unconscious. In effect, you are working at increasing the clarity and depth of communication between these two realms of who and what you are. With time, this communication will flow with greater ease, and the significance of your dreams may become more immediately apparent.

INITIAL ROSICRUCIAN CONTEMPLATIONS

If you have been practicing with the methods and skills previously described, then it is time to begin actually applying them for a deeper dive into the spirit of the Rosicrucian movement. The following sections focus on images and concepts from the manifestos and from the Rose Croix Degree of Freemasonry. The importance of performing these contemplations cannot be overstated, especially for those who feel drawn to connect with Rosicrucianism or proceed into the work of the next two chapters. It is also strongly recommended that you consider possible connections between these items and what you are learning about Cabala. These focal points are provided without interpretation, because the effort of deriving your own interpretations is vital not only to forming and illuminating your rapport with Rosicrucianism but actually facilitating the greater awareness, actualization, and integration of your own psychospiritual faculties. Such work takes priority over learning the interpretations of others, although reading and dialogue with other sincere contemplatives is also of great value and should be included for each item.

We begin with symbolic images because there are many centuries of traditional practice as well as modern research showing their value to learning. It is no wonder that the psychospiritual quest of Freemasonry is traditionally called a search for light, the energy that makes things visible. Most people find it easier to recall pictures than words, and that phenomenon has its own scientific name, which is the *Picture Superiority Effect*. Another advantage to images is that even relatively simple ones can convey nuances and possibilities of meaning that would require volumes of written words. Pictures therefore allow more opportunities for interpretation and the development of multiple and layered meanings. Furthermore, images more readily connect with both conscious and unconscious parts of the soul where words and numbers have less utility and significance. For example, consider how dreams are dominated by visual imagery as opposed to other kinds of content.

In light of these observations, it is advised that some of your meditations on a picture should be spent gazing steadily at it, memorizing its details to accurately reproduce it within your imagination, thereby allowing it to sink deeply into your psyche. In this approach, avoid analyzing or interpreting it at a conscious level, and instead rest assured that it is being processed by other aspects of your being. This procedure can be facilitated by choosing a short word or phrase for repetition, thereby occupying the chatterer while attention is mainly given to the image itself. For example, mentally say "rose cross" as you look at a picture of one. This practice is especially recommended when first beginning to work with an image. Followed by other forms of meditation and study, it can yield noteworthy results, some of which may not be as immediately apparent as those from the other forms of contemplation, but instead slowly emerge like sprouts from deeply planted seeds.

EARLY ROSE+CROSS IMAGES

Of all images, none is more important to Rosicrucianism than that referenced by the movement's very name. Even so, the manifestos never actually describe the Rose+Cross, and so there have been countless versions. Yet, there are a few options from the time of the manifestos and Rosicrucian Furor that deserve careful attention. Finding larger color versions online is highly recommended. Use them as you wish, but each is worthy of at least one week of focused contemplation, both within and without ritual.

The Luther Seal or Luther Rose (1530)

Black cross, red heart, white rose, sky blue field, gold rim

Shield from the Andreae Coat of Arms

The roses and saltire cross are red.

In *The Chemical Wedding of Christian Rosenkreuz*, there are

parallels with C.R.C.'s attire.

From the frontispiece of Speculum Sophicum Rhodostauroticum (1618)

The earliest known image conjoining a cross with roses in Rosicrucian literature.

This text is sometimes referred to as the "Fourth Manifesto."

Dat Rosa Mel Apibus (1629)

"The Rose Gives the Bees Honey," from Robert Fludd's *Summum Bonum*

Monas Hieroglyphica

While not a Rose+Cross per se, it is the only cross symbol actually illustrated within the original texts of the three Rosicrucian manifestos. That uniqueness likely serves to highlight its significance. Found in *The Chemical Wedding* (1616), this symbol had appeared in John Dee's book, *Monas Hieroglyphica* (1564), which offered it as unifier of Cabala, alchemy, and astrology, and as a magical key to investigating and manipulating reality and reforming the world.

Finally, with regard to early Rosicrucian images, there are a number of things described in visual terms that serve as focal points for Rosicrucian meditation. These include many things from the tomb of C.R.C., the entirety of which is central to the Golden Dawn's initiation into the Rosae Rubeae et Aureae Crucis. The forms of the constellations mentioned in the *Confessio* are another example, as are numerous particulars within the *Chemical Wedding*.

EARLY ROSICRUCIAN CONCEPTS

Fortunately, the manifestos, and especially the *Fama* and *Chemical Wedding*, draw our attention to certain ideas by laying them out in lists or encapsulating them in mottos or inscriptions.[134] This is not to say that only these concepts should be attended to, or even that they are necessarily the most important. Instead, we take some of them as starting places for our esoteric efforts to become more familiar with the spirit of Rosicrucianism. As with images, it is most important to begin by allowing the memorized words to sink deeply into the soul with mental repetition in silence. After a number of such sessions, focus on developing your own initial understandings beyond the literal, seeking insight about their esoteric implications. Persons with Christian backgrounds will find some of the words familiar and loaded with preconceptions, such as the name *Jesus*. Such persons are encouraged to take that sense of familiarity as a cue to not settle for their old understandings, but to open themselves to new possibilities. In any case, after having sought your own insight, you are better prepared for later work in this book and to pursue further reading and conversation with others.

---

134. All following references are from Godwin, et al., *Rosicrucian Trilogy*.

FROM THE FAMA FRATERNITATIS

Each of the five agreements among the Brothers of the Rose Cross deserves to be a single focal point of its own.

1. None of them should practice any other profession than to cure the sick, and that gratis.

2. None should feel constrained on account of the Brotherhood to wear a particular garb, but should wear the attire of the country.

3. Every brother should appear on day C. at the House of the Holy Spirit or state the cause of his absence.

4. Every brother should look for a worthy person who might succeed him.

5. The word C.R. would be their seal, password, and sign.

6. The Brotherhood should remain undisclosed for one hundred years.

After completing contemplation of the agreements, take up these mottos.[135]

- Hoc universi compendium unius mihi sepulcrum feci

- Jesus mihi omnia

- Nequaquam Vacuum

- Legis Iugum

- Libertas Evangelii

- Dei Gloria Intacta

- Granum pectori Jesu insitum

- Ex Deo nascimur, in Jesu morimur, per Spiritum Sanctum reviviscimus

- Sub umbra alarum tuarum Jehova

---

135. These and other mottos are translated in the glossary.

From the Chemical Wedding of Christian Rosenkreuz

This text also has many inscriptions and mottos to be examined, but there is one inscription at a fountain about which the narrator, C.R.C. himself, says "I will give here for anyone to meditate on:"

HERMES PRINCEPS.
POST TOT ILLATA
GENERI HUMANO DAMNA,
DEI CONSILIO:
ARTISQUE ADMINICULO,
MEDECINA SALUBRIS FACTUS
HEIC FLUO.
Bibet ex me qui potest: lavet, qi vut :
Turbet qui audit:
BIBITE FRATRES ET VIVITE.

(Prince Hermes. After so many injuries done to the human race, by God's counsel, and the aid of art, here I flow, made a healing medicine. Drink from me who can; wash who wishes; stir who dares; drink, brethren, and live.)

Here is a selection of mottos for your continuing contemplations:

- Ars Naturae Ministra

- Temporis Natura Filia

- Summa scientia nihil scire

Finally, there are the five articles for Knights of the Golden Stone:

1. You, Lord Knights, shall swear to ascribe your Order not to any devil or spirit, but only to God your Creator, and to Nature, his handmaiden.

2. You shall abominate all whoredom, incontinence, and uncleanness, and not defile your Order with such vices.

3. Through your gifts you shall willingly come to the aid of all who are deserving and in need.

4. You shall not desire this honor to use it for worldly show or high esteem.

5. You shall not wish to live longer than God wills.

ELEMENTS OF THE ROSE CROIX DEGREE

The contemporary 18th Degree of the Scottish Rite is a gold mine of meditative focal points. In addition to all the dialogue, action, scenery, and furnishings of the degree, there are the traditional jewels, aprons, and tracing boards. Like all Masonic degrees, every bit of it is meant for contemplation, yet this degree has the special merit of communicating many things about both Rosicrucianism and Freemasonry.

ROSE CROIX IMAGES

Only a few of the available images have been chosen for introduction to the symbolism of this degree. Their complexity combines several individual symbols, each of which deserves contemplation on its own, as well as within the whole context. Again, you are encouraged to begin with seeking your own inner guidance about these symbols before you turn to other sources.

The Rose Croix Jewel

A gold compass is open to 60 degrees and resting on the gold segment of a graduated circle. On one side is a silver or white pelican piercing her breast to feed her seven chicks. In the segment below them is the True Word in Rose Croix cypher. On the other side is a silver or white eagle. Below the eagle is the password in cypher. Between the eagle and pelican is a green sprig of acacia. Above them is a crimson cross bearing a crimson rose on the pelican side. A gold crown sits atop the compasses.

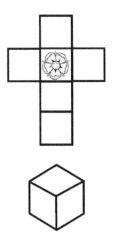

The Cubic Stone and Mystic Rose

Rose Croix Concepts

As with images, there are numerous concepts in the 18th Degree that are worthy of contemplation. Several of them are listed below for you to work with. As always, it is wise to not settle for common understandings of words you recognize from prior experience.

- The Power of Knowledge is Transformative

- Solve et coagula

- Aurum nostrum non est aurum vulgi

- Lux E Tenebris

- Pistis, Elpis, Agape

- Esoteric renderings of INRI (Not all of these are communicated in the degree but are included here because they are used in the work of the next chapter.)

  - Iebeshah, Nour, Ruach, Iam

  - Igne Natura Renovatur Integra

  - Igne Nitrum Roris Invenitur

  - Intra Nobis Regnum Iehova

  - Ieshuah Nascente Rosa Innovatur

Conclusion

Cabala has been of great importance to the Rosicrucian movement from its very inception. Its metaphysical model of creation, illustrated by the Tree of Life and incorporating the Four Worlds, has proven to be a consistently valuable and adaptable guide for the Great Work. Furthermore, Cabala's rich and varied tradition of contemplative practice provides valuable information on the process of shifting consciousness to access different kinds of insight and inspiration and to facilitate personal transformation. Persons who have applied the model and the methods to understanding the manifestos and the Rose Croix Degree have laid a solid foundation for the more involved work of the next two chapters.

CHAPTER 8:
MAGIA

The term *magia* originally referred to the sacerdotal arts practiced among the ancient Persians. All Christians know of it through the magi who followed a sign in the heavens to honor the young Jesus with frankincense, gold, and myrrh. Of course, their skills were not entirely unique, certainly not in the ancient world. The ancient Greeks practiced similar skills in *theurgy*, and in English they fall under the heading of *priestcraft*.[136] However, as the priestly arts and folk religion of many traditions were driven underground, magia became increasingly associated with esoteric, hidden, or even forbidden wisdom of various sorts. Most notably, magia has often been made synonymous with rituals used to invoke and interact with spiritual forces or beings and to effect desired changes like healing. Such practices have been part of the Rosicrucian movement from its onset. In this chapter we first consider the value of ritual in the Great Work, and then provide instructions for how an individual or a group can make intentional use of magia for beneficial psychospiritual purposes.[137]

Ritual is a particular set of behaviors regularly performed. It can be as ordinary and simple as the way you routinely tie your shoelaces or as complex and extraordinary as an initiation ceremony. Ritual is an instinctive aspect of our being and one that we have in common with many other creatures. Nature is filled with examples of ritual performances among a vast number of species, perhaps most obviously in courtship, mating, bonding, and the establishment and maintenance of social structures, such as hierarchies of dominance. Even though humans are not as limited to instinct as other creatures may be, we nonetheless delight in ritual as a means to accomplish important practical objectives and even as an art form capable of producing poignant beauty for its own sake.

Ritual is a ubiquitous part of our lives because it naturally aids with developing familiarity, consistency, and efficiency in many things. Behavioral scientists have found that rituals can improve attention,

136. *Theurgy* means "divine work." It is the practice of ritual and prayer for invocation and evocation of spiritual beings and has been called the "art of effective worship." See Mouni Sadhu, *Theurgy: The Art of Effective Worship* (London: George Allen and Unwin Ldt., 1965), and Jeffery S. Kupperman, *Living Theurgy: A Course in Iamblichus' Philosophy, Theology and Theurgy, Illustrated edition* (London: Avalonia, 2014).

137. Much of this explanation of ritual is adapted from C.R. Dunning, Jr, "Personal Ritual: A Contemplative Tool for Masonry Beyond the Lodge," *The Journal of the Masonic Society*, Fall, no. 46 (2019): 6-7.

confidence, emotional stability, execution, and motivation. Rituals can also strengthen desired behaviors and our sense of self-control, help accomplish lasting change, and enhance the value we place on things.[138] Modern research thus sheds light on why human beings have been intentionally practicing ritual at least as far back as 70,000 years ago.[139] Yet, even without such verification, shamans, priests and priestesses have known through both tradition and their own experience that ritual is efficacious. This truth is patently obvious to everyone who has willingly opened their hearts and minds to the experience of a worship service, wedding, baptism, graduation, initiation, or funeral. A well-executed and sincerely engaged ritual stimulates a shift in consciousness and stirs us to ponder its themes. It changes how we think and feel, at least in the moment, and sometimes brings about effects that continue to flow throughout our lives.

Addressing magia in the same context as Cabala and chymia is wise because the latter two become ritualized simply through routine performance. In fact, even the smallest preparatory acts of entering the place you have chosen for your inner work, turning off your phone, sitting, and closing your eyes constitute a ritual in rudimentary form. Add to these the lighting of a candle or some incense and then starting your inner work with a process of relaxation, focused breathing, and prayer, and you are already performing a ritual that helps you align your attention with your intention. Everything else that might be done in ritual is an extension of the same principles already engaged in these little steps. Ritual becomes more elaborate as we add more symbolic

138. Francesca Gino & Michael Norton, "Why Rituals Work," *Scientific American* (May 14, 2013), *https://scientificamerican.com*. Also see, A.D. Tian, J. Schroeder, G. Häubl, J.L. Risen, M.I Norton, & F. Gino, "Enacting rituals to improve self-control," *Journal of Personality and Social Psychology*, 114, no. 6 (2018), 851-876. Also see, Heidi Grant, "New Research: Rituals Make Us Value Things More," *Harvard Business Review*, *https://hbr.org* (Dec 12, 2013).
139. The Research Council of Norway, "World's Oldest Ritual Discovered – Worshipped The Python 70,000 Years Ago," *ScienceDaily*, *https://www.sciencedaily.com/releases/2006/11/061130081347.htm*.

elements like objects, sounds, words, and movements that help more fully attune our hearts and minds to particular purposes.

USEFUL RITUAL SKILLS

As you proceed, bear in mind that your emotional energies are of great importance to the proper performance and effects of magia. Thus, your emotional state should reflect the intentions and purposes of whatever you are doing in the moment. Just as a good actor calls up genuine feelings befitting the given scene and dialogue, a good ritualist authentically engages the work at an emotional level. In some cases, the intensity of your mood needs to be elevated and strong, while in others it should be subtle and mild. Clear feelings of reverence, respect, awe, wonder, joy, adoration, peace, bright optimism, fierce determination, courage, selfless care and compassion, or hopeful yearning can and should be called upon at different times. Trust your own sense of which feelings are most naturally fitting, but also be willing to experiment!

In addition to emotions, a well-developed visual imagination is also very helpful to a rich, meaningful, and effective experience of ritual. Most of us know how the imagination can be stirred by music, how it can carry our minds away in daydreaming, and how we can slip into the alternate realities of our dreams during sleep. Yet, many forms of Rosicrucian inner work require the intentional use of imagination, and for good reason. The more clearly defined and concrete a mental image is, the more it naturally draws to itself and embodies the energies and qualities it represents. We also tend to recall images better than words.

As with most human abilities, a small percentage of people are naturally gifted with great talents in this area, and a small percentage are severely challenged. However, most of us have the potential to develop considerable imagery skills. It might even be said that we are capable of extraordinary skills, if only because the visual imagination ordinarily remains relatively undeveloped for most people. This section provides you with some very simple, yet powerful exercises to enhance your ability to willfully direct your imagination and focus your consciousness more completely within it. There is no prescribed number of repetitions for each of the 6 phases, but several are advised. You are welcome to work through them at a pace that seems reasonably effective in helping you enhance your imagery skills.

IMAGERY DEVELOPMENT EXERCISES

PHASE 1 - STATIC 2-D IMAGERY

1. Use a bright red marker or cut a piece of red paper to put a triangle on a white sheet of paper. Be sure the triangle is solid red.

2. Lay the sheet of paper on your lap or set it down in front of you, and then take a little time to relax and center yourself with basic meditation.

3. Once you feel relaxed and centered, fix your sight upon the center of the triangle. Try not to blink or move your eyes off the center of the triangle.

4. After staring for some time, you will eventually notice that the triangle and the page seem to glow. This additional light comes from the afterimage that is naturally formed by your nervous system. When you see this glow, inhale while closing your eyes and attend to the afterimage. You will see a green triangle on a dark background, and it may flash back and forth between these new colors and those of the original image.

5. Breathe naturally as you examine the image in your mind, trying to see it as sharply and vividly as possible. You may notice that it changes size or that the shape begins to distort but attempt to hold the image as steadily as possible for as long as possible. Notice the differences between the afterimage and the image that arises while *remembering* the red triangle on the white paper. These are different yet interconnected ways of seeing with the mind's eye.

6. When you are ready, exhale while opening your eyes slowly, and then repeat steps 3 through 5.

As you progress through repeated sessions, feel free to use other colors and shapes, such as a purple cross with a green disk at the crux. In this case, the afterimage is a gold cross with a red disk, or an approximation of a Rose+Cross. The more you practice this exercise, the more your mind responds to your will, and eventually, simply thinking of a triangle, a star, or a Rose+Cross may actually generate the afterimage without having to look at the drawing.

PHASE 2 - STATIC 3-D VISUAL IMAGERY

1. Select a fairly simple object that is small enough to hold in one hand, such as a coin, cup, pen, or cell phone.

2. Hold it in your hand or set it down within reach, and then take a little time to relax and center yourself with basic meditation.

3. Once you feel relaxed and centered, gaze upon the object as you hold it in your hand. Do not turn it around, but instead look at it from this one angle, attending to every little detail.

4. At some point, inhale while closing your eyes slowly, allowing the image to remain in your consciousness.

5. Breathe naturally as you examine the image in your mind, recalling as many details as possible.

6. When you are ready, exhale while opening your eyes slowly, allowing the image in your mind to connect with the image you are receiving through your eyes.

7. Again, attend to the details from this one angle.

8. Repeat steps 3 through 7 until the image is as clear as possible in your imagination, trying to hold the image for a longer and longer period each time.

PHASE 3 - DYNAMIC 3-D VISUAL IMAGERY

Conduct this phase as before, except that you turn the object slowly in your hand, learning how its image changes with the movement, and then recreate the changes and movement using your imagination.

PHASE 4 - DYNAMIC 3-D TACTILE-VISUAL IMAGERY

Building on the previous phases, you now also attend to and try to recreate the feeling as well as the sight of the object moving in your hand.

PHASE 5 - DYNAMIC 3-D AUDIAL-TACTILE-VISUAL IMAGERY

In this phase, use an object that makes a sound, such as a bell, and attend to and recreate the sound, feeling, and sight of the object in your imagination.

PHASE 6 - ADVANCED DYNAMIC IMAGERY

Choose a path to walk in your home that includes several stations at which you can stop and carefully observe something that is not likely to change from one session to another, such as a painting or photograph. After basic meditation, rise and walk slowly along that path, attending to all the sensory details you experience as you walk along it, stopping for a while at each station. When you reach the end of the path, turn around and retrace your steps to return to your original location. Then, sit in meditation as you attempt to sequentially recreate all the sensory experiences of the journey as vividly as possible in your imagination.

SETTING

Various aspects of the Great Work can and should be performed wherever and whenever one feels so moved. Indeed, mindfulness of Rosicrucian principles and virtues practiced throughout the ordinary situations of your daily life helps make your psychospiritual work much more than a retreat or escape. Even sitting on a train, behind the wheel of a car, or in a busy office, you can find many opportunities to make meaningful connections between your external activities, the aspirations of your heart, and the concepts and intentions of your mind. You can help create a mobile setting for such work by the wearing of symbolic jewelry or placing meaningful images or quotations in areas that you frequent. For example, you might use a small Rose+Cross image or one of the traditional Rosicrucian mottos discreetly placed somewhere in your usual place of employment.

Our attempts to live Rosicrucianism in all that we do are significantly enhanced by routinely setting aside time to privately engage the Great Work. It is also very helpful if this can be done in a space dedicated to that purpose in your home, a space traditionally referred to as an *oratory*. Such a location can be as simple as a particular chair or cushion that you would rarely otherwise use. In fact, your own body is an ever-present oratory, which you can mentally adorn with the Tree of Life, as you will be instructed to do later in this chapter. You can make an external space more elaborate by adding symbolic elements, such as a candle or special lamp, an incense burner, or a sacred image or text. To make it even more evocative, you can add an altar or shrine, which can be as basic or intricate as you wish. In a large enough oratory, you might even have stations corresponding to the four quarters of the compass. The simplicity or complexity of your oratory is largely a matter of personal taste and convenience, but it is more important to make use of the barest of accommodations than to wait for something more ornate before actually getting to work with contemplation and ritual.

If your own inclinations and circumstances allow for a more decorative setting, then the act of entering your home oratory and engaging with the various elements becomes a ritual, one which reinforces your awareness and sense of connection with the concepts, energies, or beings those elements represent. It is therefore important to observe symbolic consistency, making use of colors, images, and objects traditionally corresponding to the factors you wish to engage in your work. While there are different approaches within the Rosicrucian movement, in this book, we are using correspondences commonly found in esoteric Christianity and Hermetic adaptations of the four classical elements and the Cabalistic Tree of Life. There are many books and websites addressing such correspondences in great detail, and a basic table is provided in the appendix of this volume.

Incorporating symbolism of all the elements in your oratory has many benefits. Perhaps most importantly, your oratory can serve as an allegorical representation of completeness for both the macrocosm of all creation and the microcosm of your own individual being. Add a Rose+Cross, traditional sacred items like incense and your preferred holy writings, perhaps some emblems from the Rose Croix Degree, and you have an environment in which to enact your aspiration for the most wonderful possibilities of enlightened, harmonious wholeness. Ritually engaging with your oratory thus becomes a portrayal of the Great Work as well as an execution of actual operations in its service.

A basic example for bringing all the elements together in a small space would be to make an altar of a small table or even a special cloth on the floor. If possible, this altar should be to your east because that is the direction of the dawn. Your altar could simply have a Rose+Cross or an image of one. The four arms of the cross serve as reminders of four elements and the rose of their awakened harmonious union with Aether. For a bit more symbolism, in front of the Rose+Cross, you could add four candles in the colors of the elements, situated according to the points of the compass, with a fifth candle for Aether in the middle of your space or in the east beyond that for Air. If you have a large enough space, you might construct a separate altar for each element in its corresponding place around the room. In various rituals, it may also be advantageous to use items and colors corresponding to the sefirot. Note that there are different colors for each sefira in each of the Four Worlds, and those in Briah are standard for most ritual purposes.

No matter what kind of space you have, remember that none of these materials are necessary for you to do good psychospiritual work. Doing the work with no external furnishings at all is much more productive than putting it off until you have all the ideal items in place. In fact, you can and should engage with the symbolism through the use of your imagination, whether or not any items are physically present. Finally, consider that the more items you include in your oratory rituals, the more time you may need to conduct those rituals. Consideration of the time you have available for your psychospiritual work may therefore lead to wise adjustments in how much ritual you do or do not perform.

RITUAL FORMAT

Just like every good story, every good use of your oratory has a beginning, a middle, and an end. In Freemasonry and other esoteric organizations, the beginning and end are typically referred to as the *opening* and *closing*. Between the opening and closing, there might also be an activity of some sort, which may or may not be particularly ritualistic itself. Many things offered in this and the next chapter can serve as activities for your oratory experiences. However, depending on your own preferences and circumstances, opening and closing your oratory, even with a brief contemplative pause in between, can be a fully engaging esoteric experience. On the other hand, it may be that the central activity receives the most time and attention, perhaps with opening and closing reduced to the simplest acts of starting and finishing.

The following outline includes the major steps of most oratory rituals, which you may use in constructing your own. Various parts within the opening and closing can be rearranged, so feel free to try different approaches. In shorter rituals, many steps may be combined or even merely implied rather than actually performed. To increase focus and depth, your own short prayers and/or statements of intention and symbolism can be included with each small action.

1. Opening – The specifics of your opening may be carefully chosen to align with the activity you plan to engage after opening.

    a. Preparations

        i. Cleansing

            1. Personal cleansing might be as elaborate as fully bathing. However, washing the face and hands is entirely appropriate, as is something more symbolic, such as simply rubbing the hands and face. Fanning incense smoke onto one's hands and face is also a common practice. Another meaningful personal cleansing practice is removing shoes and emptying pockets. The symbolism of donning a simple white robe or alb includes cleansing qualities among others.

            2. Cleansing the oratory itself can begin with turning off distracting electronics. More elaborate cleansing can include censing the space and/or sprinkling it with water that has been ritually prepared, such as Holy Water. Movements around the oratory are generally done clockwise to reflect the apparent movement of celestial bodies.

        ii. Set Up – If any elements of your oratory are stored away between sessions, then this is when you bring them out and place them in their proper locations. In some cases, it makes sense for this step to precede cleansing the oratory.

    iii. Illuminating the Lights – Once all the ritual implements are in place, light the candles or lamps. Consider the symbolism of the order of illumination. It may also be that one or more lights are not lit until the very end of the opening process.

    iv. Integration – This act is about personally connecting with each and all of the major symbolic elements of the oratory, recognizing their separate significances and their interconnectedness as parts of the whole.

  b. Relaxation and Centering – After preparations are done, take a moment to still your body and mind, being silent and mindful that you and your oratory have been made ready for work.

  c. Prayer of Invocation – This prayer may be read, memorized, or impromptu. In the broadest sense, it is a welcoming of the Divine Presence, however you conceive it. It is also a humble reminder to yourself of connection with THAT which is most worthy of your awe and reverence.

2. Central activity – Here you perform whatever meditation, experiment, or additional ritual activity you wish; the Prayer of Silence is always a most worthy option. Aside from those described in this book, three excellent options are Centering Prayer, Lectio Divina, and Christian Meditation.[140] At the very least, take a moment to be silently mindful of your presence and actions in your oratory as an expression of the Great Work.

---

140. For more on Centering Prayer and Lectio Divina, visit *https://centeringprayer. com*. For more on Christian Meditation, see *https://wccm.org*.

3. Closing

   a. Prayer of Thanks – The comments made for the prayer of invocation also apply here. It is especially valuable to reflect upon something in the given ritual experience for which you can feel genuine gratitude.

   b. Reconnecting with the Physical Senses – After doing esoteric work, it is often important to carefully reconnect with the material world. Some people refer to this as *grounding*. One of the best ways to do that is by taking a moment to be mindful with each of the five physical senses.

   c. Extinguishing the Lights – This is a good moment to reflect on how you take the invisible esoteric light of your oratory experience with you into the world outside the oratory.

   d. Take down – If you prefer to store away any of your oratory items between sessions, doing so can be helpful in making the shift to your more ordinary activities.

INTRODUCTORY RITUALS

This section provides details for the performance of rituals designed to help you more deeply connect with the Rosicrucian movement and perform the Great Work. First, you are given versions of opening and closing the oratory with different levels of complexity. Then you find a ritual for adoration of the Divine in Nature. Finally, a very short and subtle ritual of focusing on Divine Love is given, one that can be practiced in your home oratory but is also designed to take out of your oratory into other parts of your life.

OPENING & CLOSING

LEVEL ONE

1. Cleanse yourself and your oratory as you wish.

2. Stand facing east with your feet together.

3. Spread your arms horizontally to your sides, and imagine a golden cross within your body, a ruby rose at the crux in your chest. This and the following step constitute the *Internal Rose+Cross*, or *Internal R+C*.

4. Either silently or aloud, intone *"Ars Naturae Ministra, Temporis Natura Filia, Sub Umbra Alarum Tuarum, Jehova"*.

5. Bring your hands to the prayer position in front of your heart, bow your head, and offer a prayer of invocation.

6. Conduct whatever contemplation, meditation, prayer, or additional ritual you wish.

7. To begin closing, perform the Internal R+C.

8. Bring your hands to the prayer position in front of your heart, bow your head, and offer a prayer of thanks.

9. Reconnect with your physical senses.

LEVEL TWO

Perform steps 1 through 4 as in Level One. Steps 5 through 10 in this level are collectively referred to as the *Alchemical Tree*.

5. Visualize a sphere of pure brilliant white light above your head, which is Keter. To the left of your head, at the level of your brow, is a sphere of pearly white light (Hockmah), and to the right is a sphere of radiant blackness (Binah).

6. Take a deep breath and, using a high pitch, intone *INRI*, visualizing and feeling the EE vibrating in Keter. The EE

slides into NN, vibrating in Hockmah, which slides into RR (not a rolled R, but extended) vibrating in Binah, which slides into EE vibrating in Keter again. The intonation of INRI is done through a single long exhalation.

7. With your dominant hand, extend the index and middle fingers, the thumb closed over the other two. This hand position is called the *Sign of the Sword*. Touch your left shoulder, visualize a blue sphere (Hesed) there, and intone *Iam* through a long exhalation as you move to touch above your right hip and visualize the orange sphere of Hod.

8. With the Sign of the Sword, touch your right shoulder to visualize a red sphere (Gevurah) and intone *Nour* as you move to touch above your left hip and visualize a green sphere (Netzach).

9. Touch your brow, remembering the three spheres around your head, then touch your throat and begin intoning *Ruach*. Through the intonation, your hand moves to touch the center of your chest, visualizing a yellow sphere at your heart (Tiferet). Touching your lower abdomen, you visualize a purple sphere (Yesod) and finish the intonation.

10. Point to your feet, visualize a sphere of citrine, olive, russet, and black (Malkut) beneath them, and intone *Iesbeschah*. Bring your hands together in the prayer position at your chest, and then intone *ARARITA* with one breath, followed by *Amen* with another breath. ARARITA is a notarikon acronym for "Achad Rosh Achdotho Rosh Ichudo Temurato Achad," Hebrew words traditionally understood to mean "One is His Beginning; One is His Individuality; His Permutation is One." This ends the Alchemical Tree.

11. Offer a prayer of invocation.

12. Conduct your central activity.

13. Begin closing by again performing the Alchemical Tree.

14. Offer a prayer of thanks.

15. Perform the Internal R+C.

16. Reconnect with your physical senses.

LEVEL THREE

At this level, begin with personal cleansing, then set up your oratory so that you have five candles, one for each of the four elements and Aether placed on an altar or at stations around the oratory. See the table in the appendix for locations, signs, and colors. Then perform the Internal R+C and the Alchemical Tree, followed by these steps:

1. Illuminate the candle for Earth to the north, and then with the Sign of the Sword, trace the alchemical sign for Earth above it, intoning *Iebeshah*. Visualize the sign suspended in the air in the corresponding color of black.

2. Illuminate the candle for Fire to the south, and then trace the alchemical sign for fire above it, intoning *Nour*. Visualize the sign in red.

3. Illuminate the candle for Air to the east, and then trace the sign for air above it, intoning *Ruach*. Visualize the sign in yellow.

4. Illuminate the candle for Water to the west, and then trace the sign for water above it, intoning *Iam*. Visualize the sign in blue.

5. Illuminate the candle for Aether, and then trace the sign for aether above it, intoning *INRI*. Visualize the sign in white.

6. Offer a prayer of invocation.

7. Conduct your central activity.

8. Begin closing by performing the Alchemical Tree.

9.   Offer a prayer of thanks.

10.   Perform the Internal R+C.

11.   Extinguish the candles in the same order as in their illumination (Earth, Fire, Air, Water, Aether), softly speaking the corresponding Power of the Magus for each. As you speak the power, try to feel an attitude befitting it.

12.   Reconnect with your physical senses and end the ritual by conducting any take-down of the oratory that you wish.

Even greater complexity can be developed by finding various ways to add appropriate items, recitations, or mental imagery.

CEREMONIAL CONSECRATION

Consecration is the dedication of a space, an object, an act, or a person to sacred purposes. As noted in the poem at the opening of this part of the book, it can be argued that because all things are already participating in the Divine, no special act of consecration is necessary. Yet, as also noted in various places throughout this book, we easily forget the presence of the Divine in all things. Thus, often by default, we treat things as if they are apart from the Divine, failing to recognize each thing's special relevance to divine purposes. If for no other reason than to serve as a reminder of each thing's inherent divinity, ceremonial consecration is recommended for your oratory and the implements you use within it.

How is ceremonial consecration performed? In some traditions, the very act of using something for a sacred purpose is regarded as itself consecratory. In others, a simple process of prayerfully invoking divine blessing is sufficient. In yet others, consecration is more elaborate, involving various steps such as cleansing, charging, and blessing. A process following those three steps follows, but you are free to choose the complexity of consecration that best suits your own inspirations and understandings.

In keeping with the general trend of this book, this process focuses on the four elements and Aether, but it can easily be adapted to consecrate items corresponding to specific sefirot. See the appendix for useful references. After conducting whichever level of opening you wish, perform these steps, followed by the appropriate closing:

1. Cleansing: Hold the item in your hands or place it on your altar and hold your hands over it. Visualize white light flowing from your hands through the object and say, "In the Ineffable Name and with the aid of the Grand Magus of the Universe, in Whom we live and move and have our being, I cleanse this _____ (name of the item) of all energies unbefitting its sacred purposes. Amen."

2. Charging: Here it is important to have decided if the object has a specific elemental resonance, such as a wand has with Fire or a chalice with Water. A bit of research may help make the decision. If it does not have a specific resonance, then the associations for Aether should be used. With the object in or under your hands, or touched by an appropriate elemental instrument, visualize light in the color of the element streaming from your hands or elemental instrument into the item. Say, "With the _____ (color) light of _____ (element), and the assistance of the archangel _____ (name), I charge this _____ (item). Amen." If you prefer, the charge may be made more explicit by stating the item's specific purpose: "…I charge this _____ (item) for the purpose of _____. Amen."

3. Blessing: With the object in one hand or on the altar, using the Sign of the Sword, make the sign of the Rose+Cross over it. Visualize the formation of a gold cross with a ruby rose at the crux, resting upon the item.

Say, "With the blessings of Divine Life, Light, and Love, I hereby consecrate this _____ (item) to its sacred purposes. Amen."

**Drawing the Sign
of the Rose+Cross**

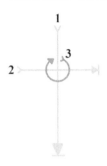

ADORATION OF NATURE

Nature is universally revered in the Rosicrucian movement, and, as in this book, frequently regarded as divine. More specifically, in this tradition and various streams of Christian esotericism and mysticism, Nature is often intimately connected, if not identified, with God's Holy Wisdom by the name *Sofia*, which is Greek for "wisdom." In reflecting on Teilhard de Chardin's essay, "The Soul of the World," Thomas Schipflinger writes:

> *Sophia is nature's contact to God because She was purposefully created to be the Soul of the World. Her mediating function to God is anchored in all of the phenomena of the natural world – in the trees and flowers, the sun by day, the stars by night, and the changing seasons. The miracle of the natural world, itself, allows us to infer the existence of the principle behind nature – Sophia, the Soul of the World created by God.*

[...]

> *On the simplest level of understanding, identifying Sophia as the Soul of the World leads to recognizing that the world and nature are Her body and raiment. A deeper understanding of Her function and dignity leads to knowledge of Her as Yahweh's Amon, God's Beloved Master Builder.*[141]

As boldly declared by Robert Powell, "The divine plan of creation is nothing less than Sofia herself."[142] Nature is the immediate and active presence of Divine Wisdom.

You are therefore encouraged to actively develop a loving relationship with Nature, and this ceremony is designed to facilitate that development. It is based upon the *Canticle of the Sun* (aka *Canticle of the Creatures*) by St. Francis of Assisi, which is perhaps the first known work of literature in the Italian language, composed around 1225 CE. Even though he predated the onset of the Rosicrucian movement by about 400 years, there is much about St. Francis that qualifies him as a fine exemplar for people on a Rosicrucian path. Most notably, he had a great affection and reverence for Nature, which he expressed in the canticle.

For the purposes of this ritual, the Barrett translation has been adapted with imagery and movements to provide a ritual experience that is more resonant with Rosicrucianism. It has also been rearranged so that it relates to INRI in progression through the elements – Iebeshah, Nour, Ruach, Iam. Most of the traditional gender references of the original Italian have been kept. If you prefer different gender references or gender neutrality, then you are welcome to make the necessary adjustments.

---

141. Thomas Schipflinger, *Sophia-Maria: A Holistic Vision of Creation* (York Beach, ME: Weiser, 1998) 295. Note that amon literally means "master worker" in Hebrew. This is a reference to Divine Wisdom identifying Herself as such in Proverbs 8:30.
142. Robert Powell, *The Sophia Teachings: The Emergence of the Divine Feminine in Our Time* (Great Barrier, MA: Lindisfarne, 2001) 11.

Begin with cleansing and setting things up as necessary for whatever level of opening you wish to perform; Level One is perfectly suitable, given the complexity of this particular ritual. If your schedule allows for it, a daily performance of the Adoration of Nature after a Level Two or Three opening can go a long way in aligning you with the Rosicrucian movement and performing the Great Work. A very nice addition is to play appropriate music throughout. Consider meditation music with natural background sounds like birds and water. Gregorian chant is also quite suitable. After completing the opening, take the following steps:

1. In the center of your space, facing east, kneel and read or recite: "Most high, all powerful, all good Lord! All praise is yours, all glory, all honor, and all blessing. To you, alone, Most High, do they belong. No mortal lips are worthy to pronounce your name." Bow your head.

2. Rise and read or recite: "Be praised, my Lord, through all your creatures, especially through my Lord Brother Sun, who brings the day; and you give light through him. And he is beautiful and radiant in all his splendor! Of you, Most High, he bears the likeness." Visualize the Sun half-risen on the horizon, seeing and feeling its warm rays stretching into you.

3. Read or recite, "Be praised, my Lord, through Sister Moon and the stars; in the heavens you have made them, precious and beautiful." Look up and visualize the Moon and stars shining in dark space, radiating their energies down into you.

4. Turn to the north: "Be praised, my Lord, through our Sister Mother Earth, who feeds us and rules us, and produces various fruits with colored flowers and herbs." Visualize a black cow lying in a field of ripe grain, surrounded by overflowing cornucopias and bouquets of flowers and herbs. Imagine a cold dry breeze blowing onto you from the north.

5.   Turn to the south: "Be praised, my Lord, through Brother Fire, through whom you brighten the night. He is beautiful and cheerful, and powerful and strong." Visualize a thickly maned male lion of red flames, grinning and pawing playfully toward you. Imagine a hot dry breeze blowing onto you from the south.

6.   Turn to the east: "Be praised, my Lord, through Brother Wind and Air, and clouds and storms, and all the weather, through which you give your creatures sustenance." Visualize a translucent humanoid angel in a delicate yellow and purple robe, which ripples with the warm humid breeze you feel from the east.

7.   Turn to the west: "Be praised, My Lord, through Sister Water; she is very useful, and humble, and precious, and pure." Visualize a soaring blue eagle reflected in a calm mountain lake of crystal-clear water. Imagine a cool humid breeze flowing onto you.

8.   Turn to the east: "Be praised, my Lord, through those who forgive for love of you; through those who endure sickness and trial. Happy those who endure in peace, for by you, Most High, they will be crowned." Bow your head, humbly and gratefully sensing the weight of a heavy crown upon it.

9.   "Be praised, my Lord, through our Sister Bodily Death, from whose embrace no living person can escape. Woe to those who die in mortal sin! Happy those she finds doing your most holy will. The second death can do no harm to them." Visualize and sense the soil of a freshly filled grave beneath your feet.

10.   Kneel: "Praise and bless my Lord, and give thanks, and serve with great humility." Silently contemplate your interconnectedness with all the works of creation and forces of Nature.

11. This is an excellent opportunity to take a seat for the Prayer of Silence as long as you wish.

12. Perform the appropriate level of closing.

In this context of revering and connecting with the divinity of Nature, we note that it is also a very good idea to spend time in prayer and meditation focused on each of the four classical elements. Two recommended texts in this vein are *Earth, Water, Fire, and Air: Essential Ways of Connecting with Spirit,* by Cait Johnson (2003), and *Water, Wind, Earth, and Fire: The Christian Practice of Praying with the Elements,* by Christine Valters Painter (2010). Many of the practices in these books make excellent central activities in ritual work, and they can also provide enriching experience and insight for practices connected with the elements that are presented further along in this volume.

THE AGAPE CHAPLET

As has been previously noted, love is of utmost importance in the Rosicrucian movement, and for a Knight Rose Croix it is highlighted with devotion to the New Law of Love. This ritual focuses on affirmation of that Law and contemplates love with special reference to 1 Corinthians 13. That chapter is a meditation on the wonders of love in the most encompassing form humans can imagine, addressing it by the Greek term *agape*. It is also the source of the Three Theological Virtues – Faith, Hope, and Love and connects with the sefirot and their correspondences within your body, as previously engaged with the Alchemical Tree. You may also discern its allusions to developing a more refined love through contemplating how the qualities of the sefirot connect with the sayings of the ritual.

The ritual makes use of a chaplet, which is a short string or chain of beads or knots traditionally employed to facilitate prayer and meditation. In this case, it has a cross or crucifix at one end, a medallion at the other, and nine beads between them in three groups of three. You can purchase one, ready-made, from a Catholic supply company or make your own. If you make your own, the beads or knots can be in the Briatic colors of the corresponding sefirot, and the medallion may venerate whatever sacred figure seems fitting to you.

The ritual can be done within your home oratory with whatever level of opening and closing you wish. Additionally, you can carry the chaplet with you at all times to perform the ritual whenever you have a private moment, such as before and/or after meals or during other breaks. In such cases, a ritual opening and closing, as you would do in your oratory, is unnecessary. Here are the steps for the Agape Chaplet:

1. Hold the cross between your thumb and forefinger and perform the Internal R+C.

2. Visualize Malkut beneath your feet or coccyx. Silently or aloud, read or recite, "Love the Lord your God with all your heart and with all your soul and with all your mind. This is the first and greatest commandment. And the second is like it: Love your neighbor as yourself. All the Law and the Prophets depend on these two commandments."

3. Move your grip to the first bead and visualize violet Yesod in your lower abdomen. Read or recite, "If I speak in the tongues of people and of angels, but have not love, I am only a banging gong or a clanging cymbal."

4. At the second bead, visualize orange Hod, saying: "If I have the gift of prophecy and can fathom all mysteries and all knowledge, and if I have a faith that can move mountains, but have not love, I am nothing."

5. At the third bead, visualize green Netzach, saying: "If I give all I possess to the poor and surrender my body to the flames, but have not love, I gain nothing."

6. At the fourth bead, visualize yellow Tiferet, saying: "Love is patient, love is kind. It does not envy, it does not boast, it is not proud."

7. At the fifth bead, visualize red Gevurah, saying: "Love is not rude, it is not self-serving, it is not easily angered, it keeps no record of wrongs."

8. At the sixth bead, visualize blue Hesed, saying: "Love does not delight in evil but rejoices with the truth."

9. At the seventh bead, visualize black Binah, saying: "Love always protects, always trusts, always hopes, always perseveres."

10. At the eighth bead, visualize pearly white Hockmah, saying: "Love never fails. But where there are prophecies, they will cease; where there are tongues, they will be stilled; where there is knowledge, it will pass away."

11. At the ninth bead, visualize brilliant white Keter, saying: "Only these three remain: faith, hope and love, but the greatest of these is love."

12. At the medallion, release the visualization and instead feel your soul reaching infinitely deeper and wider to embrace the Divine and all of creation with warm reverence, affection, and care. The Prayer of Silence is also very fitting here.

13. If you are in your oratory, proceed with the appropriate level of closing. If outside your oratory, offer a brief prayer of thanks and then reconnect with your physical senses.

RITUALS TO ENHANCE CONTEMPLATION

These rituals go further into Rosicrucianism by beginning to work directly with archangels traditionally found in the Abrahamic religions. At this point, it is important to understand that anthropomorphized images of the archangels are to a great extent simply convenient means by which we relate to and interact with intelligences that are beyond our ability to fully conceptualize. Even so, they are useful, and through them, you initially target improvement in the efficacy of your inner work, but they also have other applications.

THE GROUNDING RITUAL

Previously, we spoke of grounding as the effort to return to a more ordinary state of consciousness after having been deeply focused in ritual, prayer, or meditation. In a larger context, grounding has to do with the intention to keep our psychospiritual work relevant to and connected with our existence in the material world. Just as electricity naturally seeks to go to ground, so should our psychospiritual energies participate in the complete current of energy between heaven and earth. Rosicrucianism and the Great Work are not world-renouncing forms of mysticism, nor are they meant to be mere playgrounds or escapes from reality. Rosicrucianism regards creation as essentially good and Nature as divine, and it encourages our involvement in the material world, including its social aspects. Thus, the Great Work is not only about ascending the mystical ladder toward ecstatic union with the Divine, but also about more consciously engaging with manifestation of the Divine Will "on earth as it is in Heaven."

While different traditions relate to the archangels in various and sometimes contradictory ways, the background for this book regards *Uriel* as archangel of the element of Earth and patron of the arts and sciences. The name Uriel, meaning "Light of God," speaks of the presence of Divine Light and Wisdom within even the densest forms of creation. The archangel is visualized as holding stalks of ripened wheat and wearing robes colored by earth tones of black, russet, olive, and citrine. While there are certainly connections in this imagery with the abundance of life nourished by the soil of the earth, there is also an allusion to Uriel being anciently revered as the Angel of Repentance. The stems of wheat remind us that we reap what we sew, that karma (or consequence) is a reality, and that our actions in the World of Assiah are not divorced from the other aspects of our souls. For all these reasons, we contemplate and ritually appeal to Uriel to help ensure the following conditions in our psychospiritual work:

- That it produces beneficial effects in the material world for other creatures as well as ourselves

- That our material and social experiences in Nature help us better understand, relate to, and serve the Divine Light

- That Uriel's influence helps us remain grounded, genuinely humble, and free from delusions

To set the stage for this ritual, it is ideal to typically begin with a Level Three opening as described in the previous chapter, although Level Two can be adequate on occasion. Inclusion of the Adoration of Nature, either immediately after opening or before closing is also recommended, as it serves to integrate and harmonize the elemental forces. When you are ready to begin the Grounding Ritual, perform the following steps:

1.	Turn to face north and extend the Sign of the Sword forward and higher than your head.

2.	Intone *INRI* as you draw the Supernal Triad, starting with Keter, then Hockmah and Binah before returning to Keter. Visualize them projected at least a couple of feet beyond the end of your outstretched hand and a couple of feet higher than your head.

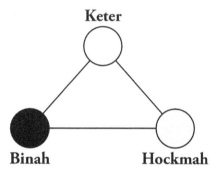

3.	Bring the Sign of the Sword down to point directly in front of you, visualizing the materialization of a white veil hanging between a black column under Binah and a white column under Hockmah.

4.	Intone *Iebeshah* as you draw and visualize the black, downward-pointing and crossed triangle of Earth on the white veil.

5.	Return your hands to the prayer position and begin repeatedly intoning *Uriel*. Through several intonations, visualize the veil gradually fading out to reveal the image of the archangel just beyond the black and white columns. Uriel is a tall, winged, humanoid figure in robes of black, russet, olive, and citrine, holding stalks of ripened wheat.[143]

6. Either spontaneously or with a prepared statement, silently or aloud, communicate your request for Uriel to assist you with grounding your efforts in the Great Work. It is important that you call up and feel strong, sincere, emotions of desire and hope for the fulfillment of your request. You may do so as a general request, or with reference to a specific concern. In either case, your petition should touch on these three points:

    a. That your efforts produce beneficial effects in the material world for other creatures as well as yourself

    b. That your material and social experiences in Nature help you better understand, relate to, and serve the Divine Light and Wisdom

    c. That Uriel's influence helps you remain grounded, genuinely humble, and free from delusions, visualizing that influence as a carpet of freshly tilled, black, fertile soil extending from under Uriel's feet into your oratory, feeling it beneath your feet

7. If you wish, you can also seek guidance and counsel from Uriel about how to more effectively work toward the stated ends, which might be immediately communicated directly to you during the ritual through words or images coming to mind, or outside the ritual in some synchronistic way.

8. When you are ready to finish the ritual, express your heartfelt gratitude to Uriel.

---

143. Different genders may be assigned to the archangels. For congruence and convenience, consider using the same genders you use for the corresponding parts in the Adoration of Nature. For example, if you observe the tradition of addressing "Sister Mother Earth," then Uriel would be visualized and addressed as feminine.

9. Intone *Uriel* a few times as you visualize the archangel's image fading out between the columns. As it fades, the white veil bearing the black sign of Earth reappears between the black and white columns beneath the Supernal Triad.

10. With your hands in the prayer position, intone *INRI* and visualize the columns, veil, and Supernal Triad disappearing.

11. Perform the Adoration of Nature if you wish and then proceed with your closing ritual.

The Grounding Ritual is so closely aligned with the overall spirit of Rosicrucianism and the Great Work that it can be a routine part of your practice. This is especially true when it is done in conjunction with the Adoration of Nature.

THE INSIGHT RITUAL

Many times throughout this book, statements have been made about the importance of opening to the insights, inspirations, and intuitions that can come to us from outside our ordinary conscious thoughts and feelings. Prayerfully making internal space and attending to it is likely to produce useful results, and this ritual can invoke further assistance of that sort. Here we are working with Gabriel, the archangel of Water, traditionally serving as the messenger of God and patron of occupations in communication. Gabriel wears robes of blue and orange and holds a chalice. The connection with water is meaningful in that pools, wells, fountains, falls, and other bodies of water are often regarded as places where the Divine speaks directly to human beings. In fact, one traditional form of divination is to prayerfully gaze upon the still surface of water in a bowl, waiting for revelatory images to arise. Thus, we find meaning in Gabriel's chalice, which represents an open and receptive state of mind as well as a vessel from which we may drink and then share what has been received. The name *Gabriel* means

"Strength of God," with many implications, including the fundamental importance of communication; after all, according to the Book of Genesis, God *spoke* creation into existence. We therefore commune with Gabriel for these purposes:

- Receiving Gabriel's influence to help with opening our hearts and minds to intuition, insight, and inspiration

- More clearly understanding the ideas and feelings coming to us in our reading, discussions, meditations, dreams, and moments of synchronicity

- Improving our ability to make good use of such information and communicate it appropriately and effectively to others

As before, it is best to ordinarily start with a Level Three opening, but Level Two can be used as necessary. The Adoration of Nature is likewise again recommended either just before or just after this ritual. When you are ready to begin the Insight Ritual, perform the following steps:

1. Turn to face west and extend the Sign of the Sword forward and higher than your head.

2. Intone *INRI* as you draw the Supernal Triad, starting with Keter, then Hockmah and Binah before returning to Keter. Visualize them projected at least a couple of feet beyond the end of your outstretched hand and a couple of feet higher than your head.

3. Bring the Sign of the Sword down to point directly in front of you, visualizing the materialization of an orange veil hanging between a black column under Binah and a white column under Hockmah.

4. Intone *Iam* as you draw and visualize the blue, downward-pointing triangle of Water on the orange veil.

5. Return your hands to the prayer position and begin re-peatedly intoning *Gabriel*. Through several intonations, visualize the veil gradually fading out to reveal the image of the archangel just beyond the black and white columns. Gabriel is a tall, winged, humanoid figure in robes of blue and orange, holding a silver chalice.

6. Either spontaneously or with a prepared statement, silently or aloud, communicate your request for Gabriel to assist you with gaining meaningful insights in the Great Work. It is important that you call up and feel strong, sincere, emotions of desire and hope for the fulfillment of your request. You may do so as a general request, or with reference to a specific concern. In either case, your petition should touch on these three points:

    a. Receiving Gabriel's influence to help with open-ing your heart and mind to intuition, insight, and inspiration, which can be visualized as watery blue light streaming from Gabriel's brow into your brain with a gentle electric or magnetic sensation

    b. More clearly understanding the ideas and feelings coming to you in your reading, discussions, medi-tations, dreams, and moments of synchronicity.

    c. Improving your ability to make good use of such information and communicate it appropriately and effectively to others

7. If you wish, you can also seek specific input from Gabri-el, which might be immediately communicated directly to you during the ritual through words or images coming to mind, or outside the ritual in a synchronistic way.

8. When you are ready to finish the ritual, express your heartfelt gratitude to Gabriel.

9. Intone *Gabriel* a few times as you visualize the archangel's image fading out between the columns. As it fades, the

orange veil bearing the blue sign of Water reappears between the black and white columns beneath the Supernal Triad.

10. With your hands in the prayer position, intone *INRI* and visualize the columns, veil, and Supernal Triad disappearing.

11. Perform the Adoration of Nature if you wish and then proceed with your closing ritual.

ADDITIONAL CONSIDERATIONS ON THE GROUNDING AND INSIGHT RITUALS

These two rituals complement each other very well. In fact, a longer operation can be conducted in which you use the Insight Ritual to help receive psychospiritual input, and then turn to the north and move directly into the Grounding Ritual to help anchor that input in your physical and social existence.

As safe and useful as these rituals are, there is a caveat to be observed. Always keep in mind that you are personally responsible for exercising critical thinking and good judgment about insights and inspirations arising from your psychospiritual work. It can be very easy to unwisely take such things too literally or fail to realize that they are only parts of a greater whole that must be carefully and quietly integrated over time. Remember that to keep silent is one of the powers of a magus, yet it is also a hallmark of wisdom to seek the counsel of someone you trust. In any case, special caution is advised about getting caught up in the glamour of feeling specially commissioned by God. Presuming that one has been given marching orders that must be implemented without question has often been the path to hot tempered or cold-blooded fanaticism, with an inflated ego hiding just behind the façade of the humble, devoted servant. Never forget that the New Law of Love is always the best test of our intentions, plans, and actions.

THE DAY C RITUAL

If you feel ready to make a stronger connection with and commitment to the Rosicrucian tradition and other souls following its paths, then this ritual can help you do so. According to the *Fama*, members of the Fraternity of the Rose Cross were expected to meet together in the House of the Holy Spirit on Day C, or explain their absence. However, the actual identity of the day was not given. It has commonly been presumed to be an annual day, and one for which the initial C has special meaning. On the other hand, the C might simply stand for *communio*, the Latin word for "communion," and offer no clue as to where on the calendar it might fall. Nevertheless, many Rosicrucian organizations continue to observe a special annual meeting for their members, the date varying from one organization to another. These meetings may require attendance in person or in spirit through meditation and prayer. In fact, the *Fama's* requirement is widely regarded as being a meeting in spirit.

Because of this book's reference to the Masonic Rose Croix Degree, we turn to it for our guide on choosing an annual day for spiritual communion with others. As noted in Chapter 3, the Rose Croix has a traditional ritual meeting on Maundy Thursday, which is the Thursday before Easter. Thus, Maundy Thursday is the recommended annual Day C for readers of this book, whether or not they are Knights Rose Croix or Masons of any sort. The *Fama* indicates no limitation on more frequent communing in the House of the Holy Spirit, and you are therefore welcome to practice this ritual as often as you wish. Here are the steps:

1. Perform a Level Three opening, preferably followed by the Adoration of Nature.

2. Turn to face west and extend the Sign of the Sword forward and higher than your head.

3. Intone *INRI* as you draw the Supernal Triad, starting with Keter, then Hockmah and Binah before returning to Keter. Visualize them projected at least a couple of feet beyond the end of your outstretched hand and a couple of feet higher than your head.

4. Bring the Sign of the Sword down to point directly in front of you, visualizing the materialization of a black veil hanging between a black column under Binah and a white column under Hockmah.

5. With the Sign of the Sword, trace the sign of the Rose+Cross, visualizing the golden cross and ruby rose appearing on the veil.

6. Sit facing east for meditation, allowing yourself to become more still and calm.

(You may wish to make your own audio recording to guide you through the following steps, being sure to insert pauses long enough to perform the various parts included.)

7. When you are ready, take a deep breath, and with the exhalation, imagine rising out of your body to stand before the black veil. As vividly as possible, visualize the veil, now closer to you, and the image of the Rose+Cross glowing upon it. Feel a warm, healing, harmonizing energy radiating from it into you.

8. Imagine yourself performing the Internal R+C, sensing the words resonating beyond the veil.

9. Imagine bowing your head, taking a short step forward with your dominant foot and, with your hands still in the prayer position, thrusting them into the Rose+Cross.

10. Spread your hands apart to open the veil, revealing a clearing within a beautiful natural landscape, in the darkness before dawn. Step through and look up into a dark indigo sky, filled with twinkling stars, planets, and galaxies.

11. Know that you are not alone, and feel about you the spirits of countless others who have come here by the path of the Rose+Cross. Lovingly recall some of the names and faces of those you regard as exemplars or companions on this path.

12. Mentally speak these words: "Let us join together in highest unity, greatest secrecy, and most kindness, one towards another."

13. Begin silently intoning *Harmonia* from your heart (hhhaaarrrmmmooonnniiiaaa), repeating it several times. Focusing on the intonations, allow the imagery to dissolve into a limitless energetic expanse of formless pure spirit.

14. After several intonations, cease the chant and simply remain in wordless knowledge that your soul is communing with others in the Holy Spirit. If you become distracted, return to a silent intonation of Harmonia as much or as little as needed.

15. Recall the following words and allow the image of the predawn landscape to return around you. "Wisdom, said Solomon, is to us an infinite Treasure, for she is the Breath of the Power of God and a pure Influence that flows from the Glory of the Almighty; she is the Brightness of Eternal Light, an undefiled Mirror of the Majesty of God, and an Image of his Goodness; she teaches us Soberness and Prudence, Righteousness and Strength; she understands the Subtilty of words, and Solution of dark sentences; she foreknows Signs and Wonders, and what shall happen in time to come."

16. Look toward the eastern horizon in front of you and see the light changing as dawn approaches. The soft glow makes visible an altar at the center of the clearing. On the altar rests a large book.

17. Approach the altar, bow, and then kneel facing the dawn. If you wish to receive some particular guidance from the Holy Spirit through this book, then take a moment to formulate your question in a prayerful attitude. If you do not wish to seek an inspiration in this way, then simply wait, communing with Divine Wisdom, knowing that other souls may be seeking guidance at this time and giving them your spiritual support.

18. Take a few moments now to prayerfully form your question or lend your support.

19. If you are seeking guidance, then open the book. Look upon the page to which you have turned, making note of whatever appears in response to your request. It may be something simple or complex, familiar or strange, changing or unchanging. Instead of imagery, you might hear something or simply know what the response is. The response might be nothing noticeable at all. Whatever you might receive, take a moment to attend to it so you can recall and consider it further after this meditation is completed. Then, close the book and offer a prayer of thanks.

20. Whatever your choice at the altar, you now look to the horizon in front of you and see the golden disk of the sun partially risen above the earth. Feel its warmth on your face and chest, reaching into your heart, recalling and feeling the Three Theological Virtues of Faith, Hope, and especially Love.

21. Stand, bow, and then turn around to go back to the portal. See the Supernal Triad and columns from that side, Binah and the black column on your right, Hockmah and the white column on your left. Just beyond them you see your physical body sitting in meditation.

22. Step through, turn around, and reach out toward the columns with your hands. They are once again in their usual positions.

23. Bow as you visualize bringing your hands together in front of you, sealing the veil.

24. Step back and stand with your hands in the prayer position, again visualizing the Rose+Cross glowing on the black veil.

25. Imagine yourself performing the Internal R+C.

26. Allow all the imagery to disappear as you return to your physical body.

27. Sit in meditation on your experience for as long as you wish, and then perform the closing.

CONCLUSION

Ritual is a natural part of our lives, and it has many benefits. It is a powerful tool you can use to enhance your experience of Rosicrucianism and assist your progress in the Great Work. Whether prescribed or self-constructed, an effective ritual facilitates a shift in consciousness. Within ritual, you are reminded of deep truths about yourself, Nature, and the Divine. Such an act objectifies some degree of reformation within the small scale of your personal life, while it also at least alludes to the same for the grand scale of all existence. In all these ways, ritual is vital to Rosicrucian magia.

CHAPTER 9:
CHYMIA

Chymia is an old term for alchemy in general but is here used to specifically reference psychospiritual alchemy. The Rosicrucian manifestos were quite clear in their condemnation of much that was happening in their time under the heading of alchemy. They berated the idea of literal gold-making, and saw much trickery and deceit being used to take advantage of the ignorant and gullible. On the other hand, they openly praised alchemists like Paracelsus, who used alchemy to advance the causes of medicine and as an approach to understanding the mysteries of the macrocosm and the microcosm. Furthermore, the

Chymical Wedding is a tour de force in alchemical imagery and language, allegorically illustrating the possibilities of personal transformation.

Because Rosicrucian chymia is concerned with the healing of the soul and greater actualization of its potentials, it cannot be a merely speculative and symbolic pursuit. Likewise, it also cannot be limited to what we do in the privacy of our own hearts and minds or remain within the oratories, lodges, or temples where we practice contemplation and ritual. As true alchemists have always insisted, chymia is a *practical* pursuit, and some even believe that psychospiritual work should not be referred to as alchemy unless it includes actual operations in a laboratory with chemicals, beakers, distillation equipment, and so forth. In this book's approach, it is enough that chymia requires commitment to disciplined operations intended to engage the entire spectrum of our internal and external being. In other words, chymia is about working toward significant change, not only in our thoughts and feelings, but also changes observable within the laboratories of our bodies and social lives.

The work of study, contemplation, and ritual you have already been considering, if not actually doing, is primarily concerned with making changes in how you think and feel about things. That work obviously requires making behavioral changes, certainly including the actions actually required for meditation and ritual. These practices automatically stimulate some degree of change in your biochemistry. Simply closing your eyes in a wakeful state increases alpha wave activity in your brain, which is associated with relaxation and a sense of calm. Studies have also shown that meditation can reduce cortisol, the so-called "stress hormone" correlated with a plethora of physical and psychological ailments. Sustained, routine practice also produces lasting physical changes in parts of the brain that correlate with greater self-awareness and compassion, and less anxiety and stress. The combination of less anxiety and stress with greater self-awareness and compassion results in different attitudes and reactions to many other things in every part of our lives. The evidence shows that through such practices we can literally become different people, which is to say they can be transformative.

Therefore, to the extent that you have been engaged in contemplative practice and ritual, chymia has already been happening in your life. This chapter is about how you can more intentionally and powerfully engage its processes. While diet and exercise are vital parts of the picture, those matters are left for your own investigation. The present focus is on continuing to engage the subtle energies of mind and body through meditation and ritual, but with greater attention and understanding. *If you have done the work of the previous chapters*, then you are now encouraged to take these steps: (1) do more work with the archangels; (2) purposefully use breath and light imagery to amplify, integrate, and direct subtle energies; (3) more fully incorporate the Tree of Life into your being; (4) open further to your connection with the Divine; and (5) deeply re-examine and reintegrate your personality, realigning it with the deeper intentions, priorities, and essence of your soul.

CONTINUING WITH THE ARCHANGELS

In the previous chapter, you were introduced to archangelic work with Uriel and Gabriel, respectively representing the elements of Earth and Water. In this section, similar rituals are provided for working with the archangels for Fire and Air, which are Mikael and Rafael.

THE PROTECTION RITUAL

This ritual works with the archangel Mikael, who is traditionally viewed as the commanding general of the divine armies that protect and defend the faithful. *Mika-El* is often translated as the question "Who is like God?", which may be understood as a rhetorical assertion of God's unparalleled supremacy. However, the name can also be regarded as alluding to Mikael's authority with the Divine Will and being an epitome of all the virtues together, serving as an exceptional reflection of the Most High. Furthermore, Mikael's association with the sefira Hod highlights the archangel's special relationship with the formation of truth. The association with Fire also brings to mind the burning bush through which God communicated with Moses. For all these reasons, Mikael's name may be interpreted as "Likeness of God," as is practiced in this book.

Now we should take some time to address these questions: (a) If everything is ultimately an expression of Divine Will, then does it make sense to seek or offer protection from anything? (b) If there are real threats to our wellbeing, what are they? These questions are also relevant to health and healing, which is later addressed in greater detail.

Relevant to the first question, in Isaiah 45:7 KJV, God is reported as saying, "I form the light, and create darkness: I make peace, and create evil: I the LORD do all these things." The Hebrew word used for evil in this verse is *ra*. In other places in the Bible, its translations into English also include "adversity," "bad," "calamity," "harm," "hurt," "sad," "sore," "ugly," and "wicked." There are two points to note in these observations, the first of which is that this verse affirms God as the source of everything. The second point is that some of God's sanctioned creation is experienced by us as threatening, offensive, injurious, sickening, and disgusting. Similarly, in the *Book of Job*, we find that even Satan does not act without God's permission. However, despite the bad things in life also being within the dominion of Divine Will, it remains that scripture, common sense, and the survival instinct repeatedly encourage and even command us to protect ourselves and others from the things we call evil. It follows that we must be endowed with a capacity to discern between the good and the bad, and therefore that we have a responsibility to develop this capacity and act in accord with our best judgment. That is not only a strategy for protection, but also the formula for virtue. Mikael is thus the most fitting archangel to help us do those very things.

With regard to the second question, it is abundantly obvious that there are creatures and forces in the natural world that can and do destroy human life. From the tiniest of viruses to hungry mountain lions, not to mention hostile humans, and from poisonous molecules to forest fires, hurricanes, and killer asteroids, the material universe was obviously not designed with human safety as the highest priority. In the psychological and social realm, there are countless forms of mental and emotional suffering that result not only from various physical problems, but also from the ways we think and how we treat each other and ourselves. It is also true that causes for physical suffering are often found in the ways we use our minds or relate to others.

Spiritual traditions the world over tell us that the metaphysical planes of existence also contain creatures and forces that are unconcerned with our safety and can even be hostile. Because they do not reside at the material level, the World of Assiah, such beings' territories are found higher up, such as in Yetzirah. This means that the threats they pose are primarily in the realm of our psyches, and thus some esoteric orders concern themselves with spiritually battling and exorcizing malevolent demons. However, the reality of these issues is distorted by literature, movies, television shows, and individuals who want the ego-aggrandizing glory of being heroic combatants proudly waving their banners and counting coup on their supposed metaphysical foes. Our view is also very skewed if we allow the possibility of metaphysical threats to lead us into constant or recurring feelings of worry, fear, distrust, suspicion, and other forms of negativity. These feelings, along with others like pessimism, resentment, guilt, and shame, when chronically recurring or sustained as character traits, are themselves more destructive and debilitating than the vast majority of metaphysical beings. A clearer view is that such creatures are more subtle and, like parasites, far less interested in destroying us than feeding off of the various energies we generate with our thoughts and feelings. The ordinary contents and operations of our hearts and minds are therefore the most significant factors in our metaphysical safety, which brings our attention back to the matter of virtue.

As was explored in Chapter 3, virtue is not about merely acting in conformity with a list of rules. Instead, virtue begins in how we manage our thoughts and emotions. Virtue is habitually employing our minds to discern the middle way between excesses of various sorts and choosing the actions that we believe facilitate experiences and expressions of truth, beauty, and goodness for ourselves and others. In our time, this ancient approach to wellbeing intertwines with the science of psychology, the craft of psychotherapy, and numerous self-help practices. Most of us secure a vastly safer metaphysical environment though these disciplines than through obsessions with the possibility of noncorporeal beings bent on misleading, possessing, torturing, or annihilating us.

Fiery Mikael always stands ready to boost the flame of your virtue, kindle the warmth of your psychosocial wellbeing, and *help you protect yourself* from threats both physical and metaphysical. That last point bears careful attention, for we cannot expect Mikael to protect us from the natural consequences of either willful ignorance or knowingly acting in ways that invite peril for ourselves or create suffering for others; Mikael is also a keeper and defender of justice.

In the next chapter, attention is given to working with Mikael and the other archangels to benefit others. For now, it is best to develop your rapport with Mikael through addressing these points in your own transformation:

- Identifying and reducing negativity, vices, and other threats to wellbeing relevant to your specific concerns

- Increasing comprehension and implementation of virtues relevant to your specific concerns

- Creating a field of positive energy to provide physical, emotional, intellectual, and spiritual protection

Here are the steps of the ritual to be performed after opening, which should be at Level Three:

1. Turn to face south and extend the Sign of the Sword forward and higher than your head.

2. Intone *INRI* as you draw the Supernal Triad, starting with Keter, then Hockmah and Binah before returning to Keter. Visualize them projected at least a couple of feet beyond the end of your outstretched hand and a couple of feet higher than your head.

3. Bring the Sign of the Sword down to point directly in front of you, visualizing the materialization of a green veil hanging between a black column under Binah and a white column under Hockmah.

4. Intone *Nour* as you draw and visualize the red, upward-pointing triangle of Fire on the green veil.

5. Return your hands to the prayer position and begin repeatedly intoning *Mikael.* Through several intonations, visualize the veil gradually fading out to reveal the image of the archangel just beyond the black and white columns. Mikael is a tall, winged, humanoid figure in robes of red and green, holding a sword.

6. Either spontaneously or with a prepared statement, silently or aloud, communicate your request for Mikael to assist you with protection. It is important that you call up and feel strong, sincere feelings of conviction for the fulfillment of your request. You may do so as a general request or with reference to a specific concern. In either case, your petition should touch on these three points:

   a. Identifying and reducing negativity, vices, and other threats to wellbeing

b.   Increasing your comprehension and implementation of virtues

c.   Creating a field of positive energy for physical, emotional, intellectual, and spiritual protection, which can be visualized as a barrier of bright red light encapsulating your body or oratory, accompanied by feelings of alert confidence, courage, and optimism

7.   If you wish, you can also seek specific input from Mikael, which might be immediately communicated directly to you during the ritual through words or images coming to mind or outside the ritual in a synchronistic way.

8.   When you are ready to finish the ritual, express your heartfelt gratitude to Mikael.

9.   Intone *Mikael* a few times as you visualize the archangel's image fading out between the columns. As it fades, the green veil bearing the red sign of Fire reappears between the black and white columns beneath the Supernal Triad.

10. With your hands in the prayer position, intone *INRI* and visualize the columns, veil, and Supernal Triad disappearing.

11. Perform the Adoration of Nature if you wish and then proceed with your closing ritual.

THE HEALING RITUAL

Rafael is the archangel of healing and patron of health-related occupations. In Hebrew, *Rafa-El* literally means "God has healed." In the deuterocanonical *Book of Tobit*, Rafael is sent by God to cure Tobit's blindness.[144] The apocryphal *Book of Enoch* also has Rafael "set over all the diseases and all the wounds of the children of men."[145]

144. Tobit 3:17.
145. 1 Enoch 40:9.

Rafael's elemental association, Air, is especially relevant to health because actual air is the substance without which we most quickly suffer and die. There are also many physical and psychological maladies that can be alleviated, if not eliminated, by routinely taking deep breaths of clean, fresh air.

Rafael is also associated with the sefira Tiferet, which has an important role in healing. As shown in Chapter 7, Tiferet is the sefira representing the principle of integration and coordination, and we regard the heart as the physiological correlate to that sefira. One of the most anciently recognized and longstanding principles of health is harmony. We are physical, emotional, intellectual, and spiritual beings, and the various systems of our being are meant to work together in coordinated ways. A change in one part naturally results in changes to others. Holism is thus emphasized in psychospiritual healing, and Rafael's connection with Tiferet ideally positions this archangel to be of particular help in this way. This principle of holism indicates our need to integrate psychospiritual healing with other forms of treatment and therapy. In general, it is recommended that psychospiritual healing be part of a balanced approach rather than seen as a substitute for other means of healing. Indeed, if all of Nature is Divine in its essence, then all forms of healing are spiritual in their own ways.

The Cabalistic view of reality holds that the material world is dependent upon the worlds above it for determining its conditions, and ultimately on the Divine Will, which is present right here and now in Nature. It is therefore appropriate that we view all healing as subject to the Divine Will, which includes the laws of Nature. For example, even with Rafael's help, we are not likely to make a broken leg instantaneously transform into a perfectly sound leg, but we can hope to help it heal faster, with fewer complications and less pain. In fact, we may never see any results that we can be certain are from our efforts. A genuine and reasonable humility is therefore an important element in psychospiritual healing. Such an attitude helps prevent our intentions from being twisted into delusions, conceit, arrogance, and foolishness. A key element of that attitude, and one widely affirmed by psychospiritual healers of many different faiths, is acknowledging that healing includes factors beyond our control. Actual physicians, even with all the power of their medicines and machines, know this fact very well. We can see why so many healers assert that God alone is the True Healer, and that the rest of us are God's instruments doing the best we can to facilitate the process.

It is crucial to acknowledge the role of faith, hope, and love in psychospiritual healing. Just as Jesus pointed out that even he could only heal those who believed in him, so too does science point to the power of faith and hope. The placebo effect is a well-documented reality for many ailments, and there is research showing that religious belief and the practice of prayer are correlated with overall better health and longevity. Of course, love in various forms, for oneself as well as between people, is crucial to many kinds of healthy development and wellbeing. The cosmos, like the soul, is an interwoven set of systems, and it too responds to changes in one area with changes in others. That is why the volume and quality of the energy we pour into our healing work is important, and we cannot overemphasize the value of a fervent and zealous combination of faith, hope, and love. A heart that, even for a moment, brightly burns with the humble awe and trust of faith, the positivity and optimism of genuine hope, and the selfless care and affection of love is a heart to which Rafael naturally responds in kind.

Let us return to humility for a moment. While connected with a physical body, the soul is bound to suffer its limitations, illnesses, and injuries. Even so, the greater reality of the soul transcends those limitations, and its particular extension in the form of one person's material life is meant to provide it with unique opportunities to experience and express certain potentials of being. We must therefore accept the possibility that some illnesses and injuries are actually meant to serve greater purposes, and for that reason, physical healing may not be in accord with the higher intentions of the soul. Likewise, we must humbly acknowledge our own inability to always recognize and understand whether or not the healing we desire is actually *called for*. In such cases, spiritual healing may be about better understanding and integrating the experience of illness or injury in a way that can transform the soul at higher levels, but not necessarily the body. For these reasons, the overriding intention of all psychospiritual healing must be for the greater good, whatever it might be, with faith and hope that Rafael guides things according to the archangelic perspective we do not personally have.

Before proceeding to the ritual, note that one should begin practicing this work only upon oneself. The Rosicrucian tradition places high value on serving the health of others, but it is important to make sure the servant's own physical, emotional, mental, and spiritual health are up to the task – "Physician, heal thyself." The work of providing such service to others is addressed in the next chapter. With all these things in mind, we turn to Rafael for assistance with these things:

- Learning more about the craft of psychospiritual healing

- Integrating our healing efforts with mental, emotional, and physical efforts, such as the treatments and guidance provided by actual physicians and therapists

- Directing the energy of your faith, hope, and love in the most beneficial way

Here are the steps of the ritual to be performed after opening, which should be at Level Three:

1. Facing east, extend the Sign of the Sword forward and higher than your head.

2. Intone *INRI* as you draw the Supernal Triad, starting with Keter, then Hockmah and Binah before returning to Keter. Visualize them projected at least a couple of feet beyond the end of your outstretched hand and a couple of feet higher than your head.

3. Bring the Sign of the Sword down to point directly in front of you, visualizing the materialization of a purple veil hanging between a black column under Binah and a white column under Hockmah.

4. Intone *Ruach* as you draw and visualize the yellow, upward-pointing and crossed triangle of Air on the purple veil.

5. Return your hands to the prayer position and begin repeatedly intoning *Rafael*. Through several intonations, visualize the veil gradually fading out to reveal the image of the archangel just beyond the black and white columns. Rafael is a tall, winged, humanoid figure in robes of yellow and purple, holding the Staff of Asclepius, which bears a single entwined serpent.

6. Either spontaneously or with a prepared statement, silently or aloud, communicate your request for Rafael to assist you with healing. It is important that you call up and feel strong, sincere emotions of desire and hope for the fulfillment of your request. You may do so as a general request or with reference to a specific concern. In either case, your petition should touch on these three points:

a. Learning more about the physical, emotional, mental, and spiritual factors relevant to your specific concern

b. Integrating your healing efforts with mental, emotional, and physical efforts, such as the treatments and guidance provided by actual physicians and therapists

c. Directing the energy of your faith, hope, and love in the way most beneficial to the soul, which can be experienced as a warm beam of yellow sunshine connecting your heart with Rafael's and filling your body

7. If you wish, you can also seek specific input from Rafael, which might be immediately communicated directly to you during the ritual through words or images coming to mind, or outside the ritual in a synchronistic way.

8. When you are ready to finish the ritual, express your heartfelt gratitude to Rafael.

9. Intone *Rafael* a few times as you visualize the archangel's image fading out between the columns. As it fades, the purple veil bearing the yellow sign of Air reappears between the black and white columns beneath the Supernal Triad.

10. With your hands in the prayer position, intone *INRI* and visualize the columns, veil, and Supernal Triad disappearing.

11. Perform the Adoration of Nature if you wish and then proceed with your closing ritual.

SUBTLE ENERGY WORK

We begin by reviewing the concept of subtle energies introduced in the *Extraction* section of Chapter 6. Subtle energies are the psycho-physiological energies that move throughout and around the physical body, stimulating and guiding its various processes, certainly including the chemical ones. This kind of energy has been recognized in ancient traditions all around the globe and is known by many names and in various more or less specific forms – *prana, chi, mana, manitou, lung,* etc. Each tradition teaches that we can become more aware of such energy and intentionally use it to improve our psychospiritual wellbeing and to aid in personal transformation. We should not delude ourselves with extreme views like those notoriously involved in fake martial arts, where these energies are supposedly used to perform dazzling feats of physics-defying power, like knocking people down with the slightest touch or without any contact at all. The term *subtle* is used for good reason with such energy, and we should be reasonable about it.

Subtle energy is closely connected with the breath, and the terms used for subtle energy in many traditions actually reference the breath. Such traditions have also developed breathing techniques to intention-ally move this energy in different ways and direct it toward specific pur-poses. Because subtle energy is intertwined with senses, emotions, and thoughts, we also use those faculties to help focus, intensify, and move it. In short, we employ particular ways of breathing combined with several capacities of the imagination to engage subtle energy as best as possible. You have already been doing so if you have been practicing the rituals leading up to this point.

This section provides methods for further amplifying, circulat-ing, and integrating your subtle energies. Each of the following steps should be developed through several sittings before adding the next, so that a number of weeks have passed before you are performing all five steps in a sitting. They should be engaged after at least a Level Two opening and can be done either sitting or standing, although sitting offers the added benefit of greater relaxation.

There are many significant benefits that can come to you from this work. Other kinds of work often provide the satisfaction of immediate insights, interesting internal experiences, or new questions to investigate. The following methods, however, tend to produce effects at deeper levels of one's physiology and psychology, with cumulative benefits that grow with time. For this reason, it is important to make them a sustained, consistent part of one's inner work and not something that is done for a short while and then dropped or only sporadically revisited.

STEP 1: RHYTHMIC BREATHING

Close your eyes, relax your body, and focus on the sensations of your breathing. It is especially helpful to ensure the relaxation of your throat, chest, and belly. Use your fingers to feel for your pulse in either your wrist or neck. Keep time with your pulse by repeatedly counting to four in your mind. After you have the tempo, put your hands back in their original positions. Begin inhaling for a count of four, pausing for two, exhaling for four, and pausing for two. Remember that these breaths are meant to be gentle and quiet. If it is easier to use a six-three or eight-four rhythm, feel free to do so. Maintain whichever rhythm you choose, repeating the process through 10 complete cycles. When the 10 repetitions are complete, cease counting the repetitions and cycles and return to a peaceful natural rhythm.

STEP 2: LATERAL CIRCULATIONS

In this and the following steps, after rhythmic breathing, begin by visualizing the 10 sefirot within your body as in the Alchemical Tree, also adding Daat in the throat. To this imagery, add movement of a ribbon of white light, which is about the width of your hand, flowing down one side of the body and up the other. First, visualize and feel Keter growing a little larger and brighter as you inhale a few breaths of the invisible, pure life energy into it from the atmosphere around you. When you are ready, with your next inhalation, visualize and feel the extra energy descending as a ribbon of light from Keter down the left side of the body. Along the way, its energy radiates into Hockmah, Hesed, and Netzach before it collects in Malkut. Experience Malkut responding by growing a little larger and brighter. Briefly pause, and then exhale while visualizing and feeling the extra energy of Malkut released as a ribbon of light ascending on the right side of the body. Along the way, its energy radiates into Hod, Gevurah, and Binah before it collects in Keter. Experience Keter responding by growing a little larger and brighter. Briefly pause and then inhale to release the extra energy down the left side of the body, beginning to repeat the entire process for 10 complete cycles.

STEP 3: MEDIAL CIRCULATIONS

After the lateral circulations, use the same breathing pattern to inhale as you visualize and feel a ribbon of light descending from Keter down the front of your body and radiating into Daat, Tiferet, and Yesod, then into Malkut. Pause as Malkut responds, and then exhale as you visualize and feel the light ascending your back and again radiating into Yesod, Tiferet, and Daat, then into Keter. Pause as Keter responds, and then repeat the entire cycle 10 times.

STEP 4: THE FOUNTAIN

After the medial circulations, begin with breathing to visualize and feel energy building up within Malkut. When you are ready, with your next inhalation, see the extra energy released as a stream of white light rising up through the core of your body, directly through Yesod, Tiferet, and Daat. When it reaches Keter, pause while you see and feel the brilliant white sphere growing larger and brighter. As you exhale, imagine the extra energy bursting out of Keter as dozens of streams and sparks of white light cascading down, around, and through your body and the sefirot to be drawn back into Malkut. Repeat the process through 10 complete cycles.

STEP 5: THE COCOON

After the Fountain circulations, build energy in Keter. When you are ready, with your next inhalation visualize and feel a ribbon of light spiraling around your body from Keter down to Malkut. As you exhale, another ribbon of light spirals back up, so that you are entirely wrapped within a glowing white cocoon composed of the two ribbons of light. The motion of both spirals is from behind to left to front to right to behind. Complete 10 cycles.

Once you have all five steps working well, you are encouraged to include them as part of your routine practice in some measure. If you do so, you are likely to become more sensitive to their presence and movement in your mind and body. As modern physics has revealed, all energy carries information. Through greater familiarity with the different sensations of subtle energy, when they arise, and how they correlate with different emotions and thoughts, we develop greater understanding of the information carried by them. We are thereby empowered to better recognize the effects of different situations upon us, and to more consciously call upon and intentionally employ different forms of subtle energy toward desired ends.

A CABALISTIC ROSARY

Having engaged with the Tree of Life in combination with the previous subtle energy work, you are better prepared to more fully energize and integrate Rosicrucian principles within your being. This ritual exercise combines devotional prayer, energy work, visualization, and meditation following the Path of Return through the Four Worlds leading to an invocation of union. It includes veneration of Jesus, mottos from the *Fama* and the *Chemical Wedding*, visualizing the Tree of Life, and the recollection of several associations with each sefira. In order to perform it, we make use of the same ancient technology introduced with the Agape Chaplet.

This exercise is an elaborate rosary performed on a standard loop of five decades, with single beads or knots between the decades. A medallion centerpiece connects the two ends of the loop, and from it extends a short string of five beads or knots leading to a cross or crucifix. You are welcomed to purchase such a rosary or make your own.

Because this ritual always begins and ends with the Internal R+C, no other opening or closing is necessary. With the aim of learning the ritual well enough to smoothly complete it entirely from memory, feel free to refer to this text or to your own notes as much as necessary during its repeated performance. Adding any or all of the previous section's energy circulations before the final Internal R+C is encouraged. As with the energy circulations, many of the alchemical benefits of this ritual are not revealed through short-term practice. A commitment to frequent, routine practice is highly advised, as are studies of Cabalistic texts to help improve understanding of its various parts.

1. On the cross, perform the Internal R+C.

2. On the first bead, intone the motto: "Granum Pectori Jesu Insitum."

3. On the next three beads, separately intone: (1) "Ex Deo nascimur, (2) in Jesu morimur, (3) per Spiritum Sanctum reviviscimus."

4. On the bead beneath the centerpiece intone *INRI.*

5. On the centerpiece, intone "Hoc universi, compendium unius, mihi sepulchrum feci." Then intone "Olam Assiah: Legis Jugum," while visualizing a black ox in a white vesica piscis.

6. On the next ten beads, speak the following affirmations, sequentially feeling and visualizing each sefira as vividly as possible (colors in parentheses), beginning at Malkut:

   a. "We return through the virtue of discernment." (black rayed with yellow)

   b. "We return through the virtue of independence." (citrine, flecked with azure)

   c. "We return through the virtue of truthfulness." (yellowish black, flecked with white)

   d. "We return through the virtue of selflessness." (olive, flecked with gold)

   e. "We return through the virtue of devotion to the Great Work." (golden amber)

   f. "We return through the virtue of courage." (red, flecked with black)

   g. "We return through the virtue of obedience." (deep azure, flecked with yellow)

   h. "We return through the virtue of silence." (gray, flecked with pink)

   i. "We return through the virtue of devotion to God." (white, flecked with red, blue, yellow)

j. "We return to the virtue of attainment by the grace of Divine Love." (white, flecked with gold)[146]

7. On the next bead, intone "Olam Yetzirah: Dei Gloria Intacta," visualizing a yellow-robed person in a violet vesica piscis.

8. On the next ten beads, speak the following affirmations, sequentially feeling and visualizing each sefira as vividly as possible, beginning at Malkut:

    a. "We return with a vision of the Holy Guardian Angel." (citrine, olive, russet, black, flecked with gold)

    b. "We return with a vision of the machinery of the universe." (very dark purple)

    c. "We return with a vision of splendor." (russet-red)

    d. "We return with a vision of beauty triumphant." (bright yellowish green)

    e. "We return with a vision of harmony and the Mystery of Crucifixion." (salmon)

    f. "We return with a vision of power." (bright scarlet)

    g. "We return with a vision of love." (deep purple)

    h. "We return with a vision of sorrow." (dark brown)

    i. "We return with a vision of God face to face." (iridescent pearl gray)

    j. "We return with a vision of Unity." (pure white brilliance)

9. On the next bead, intone "Olam Briah: Libertas Evangelii," visualizing a blue eagle in an orange vesica piscis.

---

146. Note the meaningful change of wording from "return through" to "return to".

10. On the next ten beads, silently speak the beginnings of the following affirmations as you inhale, intoning the archangelic names aloud as you exhale. Sequentially feel and visualize each sefira as vividly as possible, beginning at Malkut:

   a. *We return by our Brother,* "Sandalfon." (citrine, olive, russet, black)

   b. *We return by the Strength of God,* "Gabriel." (violet)

   c. *We return by the Likeness of God,* "Mikael." (orange)

   d. *We return by the Grace of God,* "Haniel." (emerald)

   e. *We return by the Healer of God,* "Rafael." (yellow)

   f. *We return by the Seer of God,* "Khamael." (scarlet)

   g. *We return by the Justice of God,* "Tzadkiel." (blue)

   h. *We return by the Contemplation of God,* "Tzaphkiel." (black)

   i. *We return by the Secret of God,* "Ratziel." (pearly white)

   j. *We return by the Prince of Countenances,* "Metatron." (pure white brilliance)

11. On the next bead, intone "Olam Atzilut: Nequaquam Vacuum," visualizing a red lion in a green vesica piscis.

12. On the next ten beads, silently speak the beginnings of the following affirmations as you inhale, intoning the God Names aloud as you exhale. Sequentially feel and visualize each sefira as vividly as possible, beginning with Malkut:

   a. *We return in the Dominion of* "Adonai Ha Aretz" (yellow)

b. *We return in the Foundation of* "Shaddai El Chai" (indigo)

c. *We return in the Splendor of* "Elohim Tzabaot" (violet-purple)

d. *We return in the Victory of* "YHVH Tzabaot" (amber)

e. *We return in the Beauty of* "YHVH Aloa Ve Daat" (clear rose-pink)

f. *We return in the Strength of* "Elohim Gibur" (orange)

g. *We return in the Loving Kindness of* "El" (deep violet)

h. *We return in the Understanding of* "Elohim" (crimson)

i. *We return in the Wisdom of* "YHVH" (pure soft blue)

j. *We return in the Crown of* "Eheyeh" (brilliance)

13. On the next bead, visualize a ruby rose on a gold Latin cross inside a vesica piscis of brilliant white, and intone, "God is love. Whoever lives in love lives in God, and God in them."

14. On each of the next ten beads, whisper "I and My Father are One," sequentially feeling the energy of and visualizing each sephira in your aura as pure white.

15. On the medallion, intone "Hoc universi, compendium unius, mihi sepulchrum feci."

16. On the first bead beneath the medallion, intone *INRI*.

17. On the next three beads, separately intone: (1) "Ayn Sof Aur," (2) "Ayn Sof," (3) "Ayn."

18. On the last bead, intone "Summa Scientia Nihil Scire," and then sit in the Prayer of Silence for a moment.

19. If time permits, perform any or all of the five energy circulations, and/or contemplate something in the ritual.

20. On the cross, perform the Internal R+C.

As a final note on the Cabalistic Rosary, it is worth observing that it, the Agape Chaplet, and the Alchemical Tree are all processes in which the Tree of Life is used to amplify and harmonize the full spectrum of divine energies and principles within one's psychophysiological aura. This condition of integration is one way of understanding the "garment of glory on which were affixed lights of all varieties" mentioned in 3 Enoch 12:1.

INVOCATION OF THE PENTAGRAMMATON

To understand the Pentagrammaton let us first review the Tetragrammaton, the most sacred Divine Name of the Judeo-Christian tradition. That name is spelled, right to left, Yud-Heh-Vav-Heh.

Genesis declares that we are created in the image of God, and so in Cabala we find the human form aligned with the sefirot on the Tree of Life as well as the four letters of the Tetragrammaton.

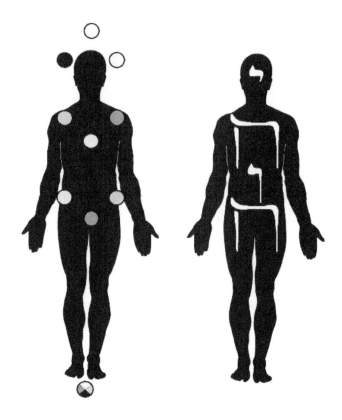

The descending order of the letters reflects the process of emanation in creation with the fourth letter, a repeated Heh, suggesting that the creative process is ever in continuation, and that the lower is a reflection of the higher – *as above, so below.*

The Pentagrammaton is a name derived from the Tetragrammaton. It is formed by placing the Hebrew letter Shin in the middle, between the first Heh and the Vav, which produces Yud-Heh-Shin-Vav-Heh. The name can be pronounced in more than one way, but here we use *Yeshuah.* The Pentagrammaton has been revered as an esoteric name for Christ since at least the late 15th century. It can be seen just beneath the triangle in the following inverted heart diagram from the 17th century mystic Jacob Boehme.

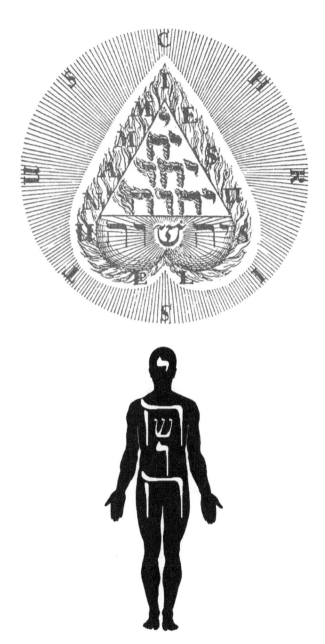

The three-pronged Shin represents the flame of Shekinah, the Divine Glory, blossoming in the heart of one who is awakening to self as an embodiment of the Logos. *Logos* is Greek for "word" or "message" and has other connections with the principle of communication.

When the Gospel of John was written, it was common for philosophers to use *Logos* as a name for the rational animating principle of
the Divine. Likewise, in John 1:1-5 NCV, the author set the tone for
the entire gospel by declaring that the Second Person of the Trinity is
identical with Logos, translated into English as "Word":

> *In the beginning there was the Word. The Word was with God,
> and the Word was God. He was with God in the beginning.
> All things were made by him, and nothing was made without
> him. In him there was life, and that life was the light of all
> people. The Light shines in the darkness, and the darkness has
> not overpowered it.*

In agreement with the philosophers, John asserted that the Logos
is already in *everyone*, no matter how deep in the darkness of ignorance
they may be. Later, in John 17, Jesus offered a prayer for his disciples
and their followers, which included these statements:

> *Holy Father, keep them safe by the power of your name, the
> name you gave me, so that they will be one, just as you and I
> are one. (11c)*

> *I pray for these followers, but I am also praying for all those
> who will believe in me because of their teaching. Father, I pray
> that they can be one. As you are in me and I am in you, I pray
> that they can also be one in us. (20-21b)*

> *Father, I want these people that you gave me to be with me
> where I am. (24a)*

> *Then they will have the same love that you have for me, and I
> will live in them. (26b)*

One's reading does not need to be very esoteric to grasp that
Jesus was praying for his followers to know the same relationship with

the Divine that he knew. Understanding the significance of John's use of the word *Logos* helps us to see that Jesus wanted them to realize that what he intimately knew was also already within them – the very Light, Life, and Love, without which, they would have never existed. This realization is referred to here as *Christ Consciousness*, and many Rosicrucian students and esoteric Christians assert that it is available to sincere aspirants, regardless of their religious identities or beliefs about the historical Jesus.

In the Great Work, the alchemical power of the Pentagrammaton and the realization of Christ Consciousness is that they increasingly dissolve the illusions that create so much confusion, suffering, and ill will in our lives. Our failure to remember our unity with God can lead us to misperceive ourselves as essentially lacking. Trying to fill this misapprehension of a God-sized hollowness amid the give-and-take dualism of the physical world, our natural acquisitiveness can grow distorted into unhealthy extremes of material and social possessiveness. Similarly, ignorance of our interconnectedness with other human be-ings, even all of Nature, allows our innate competitiveness to become twisted into callousness, exploitation, hostility, and brutality. Indeed, these most fundamental illusions of separation from God, Nature, and each other are fertile beds for greed, gluttony, jealousy, envy, angst, despair, escapism, cruelty, injustice, and moral and ecological pollu-tion. We may welcome healing of these existential ailments by em-ploying the Pentagrammaton to willingly open ourselves further to the mysteries of Christ Consciousness. This operation can help coagulate our sense of spiritual union and feelings of gratitude and peace, while also distilling genuine compassion for others suffering the illusions of disconnection. Thus, we are more authentically motivated and empow-ered to lovingly help facilitate spiritual, psychological, social, and envi-ronmental healing and transformation for all.

After conducting at least a Level One opening, perform these steps for the Invocation of the Pentagrammaton:

1. Sit in silent meditation until you feel yourself settled and centered.

2. Silently or aloud, recall from memory these words from the opening of the Book of Genesis: "In the beginning, God created the heavens and the earth, and the earth was without form and void, and darkness was upon the face of the deep."

3. For a moment, imagine yourself as that deep, dark, void.

4. Silently or aloud, continue the words from Genesis: "And the Spirit of God moved upon the face of the waters, and God said, 'Let there be Light,' and there was Light."

5. Visualize a bright white beam of Divine Light shining down from the heavens into you. Try to see and feel its rays penetrating the top of your head and radiating down through your brain and neck, into and through your heart, and down through the rest of your body. Take a moment to more fully experience your communion with the Light of creation.

6. After communing with the Light, silently or aloud, intone each letter in the Pentagrammaton with a separate breath. As you do so, visualize the white light condensing into each letter in turn – Yud in your head, Heh in your upper torso, Shin at your heart, Vav in your belly, and Heh in your lower torso. After the final Heh, return to Yud and repeat the process at least four times. With each repetition of a letter, experience it becoming more vivid and energetic.

7. Stop the intonations and focus for a moment on the images and feelings of the letters within you.

8. Begin intoning the name *Yeshuah* with each breath. Be aware of all five letters, but especially focus on Shin at your heart, pouring out your aspiration to more fully experience and express the presence of Divine Light, Life, and Love in your being. Repeat the intonations at least seven times.

9. After the final intonation of *Yeshuah*, sit in the Prayer of Silence, that silent meditative openness to the Divine in whatever way it may be present, including the silence itself. If you become distracted, use the imagery of the letters within you or occasional intonation of the Pentagrammaton to help return to openness to the Divine Presence.

10. After the Prayer of Silence, begin reflecting on the invocation, recalling what you experienced and what meaning it might have for you. Feel free to open your eyes to read and make notes on any or all of the following points:

    a. Consider the implications of knowing you are an embodiment of Divine Light, Life, and Love.

    b. Consider the implications of everyone else also being an embodiment of Divine Light, Life, and Love, whether they know it or not.

    c. Consider how it might be possible to lose psychological and spiritual balance from contemplating such an intimate connection with Divine Light, Life, and Love.

    d. Consider how this experience might inspire you to think and act in wiser, more harmonious, healthier, and more loving ways toward yourself and others.

11. When you are ready to end the operation, perform the appropriate level of closing.

THE TRANSFORMING CROSS

Many of us have a deeply intuitive sense that there is far more to our being than we are typically encouraged to consider. We may even feel a yearning, if not a compelling drive, to act on that intuition. Like the instinct of a caterpillar, it calls us to enter the chrysalis of transformation so that we might emerge, like butterflies, into the colorful fulfillment of our potentials. Yet, we often find that society at large does little to support us in actually penetrating the veils of ordinary existence or in beginning to explore the mysteries of the soul and our intimate connections with Nature and God. The doctrines, dogmas, and methods of common religion do not entirely meet our needs in this regard and may even be antagonistic. Thus, we may be drawn to learn about things like meditation, contemplation, metaphysics, and theurgy. In the process, some of us have become powerfully attracted to the Rosicrucian tradition and its connection with the Great Work of transforming the soul and the world. If you feel this attraction, then the Transforming Cross can be a powerfully meaningful and productive way of engaging with that tradition.

In keeping with Rosicrucian tradition, the Transforming Cross combines concepts, symbols, and practices from Cabala, magia, and chymia. It recombines and multiplies much of the preceding work in order to take the practitioner through a more intense series of operations corresponding to the alchemical phases of nigredo, albedo, citrinitas, and rubedo. These are the phases of the Great Work, through which the raw fragmented material of the soul is refined and reintegrated into the Universal Medicine represented by a rose and cross conjoined.

This alchemical program of the Transforming Cross is not to be taken lightly, and it is best undertaken after having diligently practiced the previously provided contemplations and rituals. Anyone completing the Transforming Cross will see changes in themself, and will also become more sensitive to and skilled with the elements and phases of the Great Work as repeatedly encountered throughout life. Even so, the fullest possible attainment of the Great Work cannot be guaranteed. Such advancement requires things that are beyond our personal awareness and control. By doing our part, we can make significant progress in preparing ourselves for the tests, trials, boons, and blessings that come from deep within us, the world around us, and, ultimately, from the infinite gracious Love of the Supreme Alchemist and Great Healer. In fact, so long as there is any soul in this world suffering in the Forest of Errors, there should never be a moment at which one would consider the Great Work complete, for all souls are interconnected in the great tapestry of creation.

You are encouraged to read through the entire program before beginning. It is important to have some idea of how it all fits together and what it will demand of you. If proceeding to do the work, then each stage of the program should be completed as prescribed before advancing to the next. Skipping or abbreviating any stage can result in diminished effectiveness of the program and perhaps even more serious consequences. The full operation of each stage should be done at least four days a week, and options from the corresponding supportive practices are ideally practiced every day, with recommended reading done at your own pace. A minimum duration of one month is advised before proceeding from one stage to the next. You are welcome to make adjustments, so that the duration of a particular stage is lengthened if it was not possible to maintain the recommended frequency. Conscientious engagement with the Transforming Cross should therefore require several months to a year or more.

Due to the nature of this program, you might discover a need to consider making changes in your life, such as in your pastimes, relationships, or even your career. It is possible that you could feel a very strong urge to make such changes in order to more fully align your material and social life with changes in your philosophical and spiritual life. In any case, it is suggested that you avoid making any big changes until you have proceeded through all phases of the Transforming Cross, as each phase can bring with it further experiences and insights that modify those of previous phases. Be prudent and patient. *Give yourself time.*

Finally, persons considering this program are cautioned that it can produce psychological stress, and thus it may not be appropriate for anyone struggling with psychosis or significant levels of depression, anxiety, or mania. Persons under the care of physicians or therapists for such issues should consider consulting with them about the program before beginning. Likewise, its operations and meditations are not to be performed while intoxicated with any mind/mood altering substance. Routine consultations with a trusted mentor or friend are strongly advised. Keeping a journal during this program is also highly recommended.

STAGE ONE: THE BLACK CROSS

> *Then Jesus said to his disciples, 'If anyone wants to come after me, they must give themselves up, and pick up their cross, and follow me. Yes: if someone wants to save their life, they must lose it; and if anyone loses their life for my sake, they will find it. What use will it be, otherwise, if you win the whole world but forfeit your true life? What will you give to get your life back?'* [147]

In this stage of the Transforming Cross, you begin the alchemical phase of nigredo, which is here performed as a voluntary penetration of the veils of your assumptions, beliefs, and attitudes about reality, including the Divine, Nature, other beings, and yourself. Just the thought of doing so should raise a sense of caution, which should not be avoided or lightly passed over. This work is the beginning of

147. Matthew 16:24-26, NTE

the metaphorical descent described in Chapter 5 and is largely about welcoming and acknowledging deep layers of doubt, uncertainty, illusion, and ignorance. Most of us are accustomed to glossing over these uncomfortable realities with habits of thought and behavior we have acquired from our own inherent predispositions, our upbringing and cultural experiences, and from calculated decisions we have made. These habits can be so thoroughly entrenched as to happen with little or no conscious awareness on our parts. Our aim is to part the veils of such habits and learn to exist in openness to the doubts, uncertainties, illusions, and ignorance we all naturally have in the face of life's many mysteries. Perhaps chief among these habits is evading the reality of death, especially our own – which could come at any moment. More fully facing that reality, its finality, and the mystery of what lies beyond is therefore central to this stage.

In facing the reality of our doubts, uncertainties, illusions, and ignorance, it may be tempting to berate ourselves for them, for the natural feelings of fear, sadness, and anxiety that go with them, or for the ways we have tried to avoid or deny any of it. However, keep in mind that negativity toward ourselves about such things does no good at all. The greatest good comes with nonjudgmental awareness and acceptance of these very common and perfectly understandable parts of being human. In order to facilitate this process, it is helpful to provide yourself with a starting place by first memorizing the illusions commonly associated with the sefirot, provided in Chapter 7.

RITUAL OPERATION

1. Perform at least a Level Two opening and then sit down.

2. Perform at least 10 cycles of rhythmic breathing.

3. Visualize a black cross within your body. The vertical axis extends between your brow and the coccyx, and the horizontal from shoulder to shoulder.

4. After a deep inhalation, begin to repeatedly intone *In Neci Renascor Integer*. This version of INRI means "In death, one is reborn, intact and pure." This is an invitation for awareness of our mortality and for ego-death, both of which are universally regarded as fundamental to spiritual illumination. With each exhalation, visualize and feel the black cross generating a dense, heavy, cloud of black smoke.

5. After several repetitions, the black smoke should be experienced as penetrating and enveloping your entire body.

6. Cease the repetitions and sit in meditation on the heavy black cloud and the themes of death, impermanence, and your deepest doubts, uncertainties, ignorance, illusions, and fears. Question everything you think you know, believe, or hope. Do not allow yourself to ignore or accept any idea that is a mask or bandage over anything uncomfortable. The natural emotional responses of discomfort, fear, sadness, and uncertainty should be welcomed and embraced. Practice mentally saying, "I don't know," whenever any degree of doubt, ignorance, or uncertainty arises. Weeping should not be resisted. It is vital to allow such thoughts and feelings to arise and be courageously accepted.

7. When you are ready, end the operation with the fitting level of closing.

Supportive Practice

During your ordinary activities and in your dreams, try to be as aware as possible of all instances, signs, symbols, and allusions of death, impermanence, uncertainty, doubt, illusion, ignorance, anxiety, sadness, and fear. Be sensitive to such things within you, and in Nature around you, including the thoughts and feelings of other beings. Practice genuinely saying, "I don't know," "I'm uncertain," or

"I'm not sure" to yourself and others whenever that is the truth. The Grounding Ritual is very appropriate for this stage.

RECOMMENDED READING

- *The Cloud of Unknowing,* by Anonymous

- *Dark Night of the Soul,* by St. John of the Cross

- *The Unknown God: Negative Theology in the Platonic Tradition,* by Deirdre Carabine

OPTIONAL SYMBOLIC ELEMENTS FOR THE ORATORY

- A black candle

- A memento mori, such as an image of a skull

- Myrrh incense, due to its association with embalming (and thus with death), and with Binah and its planetary correspondence of Saturn

STAGE TWO: THE ASHEN CROSS

Here you turn up the psychospiritual and neurophysiological heat, beginning to proceed from nigredo toward albedo. Having rent so many veils between you and your most honest and authentic awareness of being, you are better prepared to face the ways in which you create much suffering for yourself and others. In alchemical terms, you identify and burn away as much psychospiritual dross in your life as you are able. What you confront in yourself at this time is everything you think or do that creates guilt, shame, remorse, regret, disappointment, frustration, or distrust with yourself, or unnecessarily contributes to feelings of pain, anger, disappointment, and distrust in others. While we are not always fully responsible for the feelings of others, it is nonetheless true that we do not always think and act with genuine understanding, compassion, and good faith. Similarly, our own feelings of guilt or shame are not always actually fitting; they may instead be parts of self-defeating patterns in our lives. This stage is not about wallow-ing in the mud of self-loathing and self-punishment, but about bravely confronting our vices, including those wearing the mask of virtue. As with the previous stage, the greatest good comes with nonjudgmental awareness and acceptance of these very common and perfectly under-standable parts of being human. In fact, by carefully integrating these elements of our humanity, we often actually discover talents, gifts, and blessings we would otherwise never know.

A necessary preparatory step for this stage is becoming thorough-ly familiar with the vices corresponding to the sefirot on the Tree of Life, provided in Chapter 7.

RITUAL OPERATION

1. Perform at least a Level Two opening and then sit down.

2. Perform at least 10 cycles of rhythmic breathing.

3. Visualize a black cross within your body.

4. After a deep inhalation, begin to repeatedly intone *Igne Natura Renovatur Integra*. This version of INRI means "Nature is completely renewed by fire." This is an invitation for the raw, primal fire of life itself to rise up from your deepest instinctive reserves and burn away your self-deceptions. Each inhalation should be quick and deep, visualizing a bolt of white lightning striking straight down through the top of your head, down the vertical axis of the black cross in your body, and into the earth. Then, with each long, passionate intonation, visu-alize and feel a tornadic swirl of hot flames spinning up clockwise around the black cross within you, gradually turning its surface to an ashy gray color.

5. After several repetitions, the cross should be experienced as gray and warmer, if not hot, like an ashed-over ember completely concealing the glow within.

6. Cease the repetitions and sit in meditation on the hot ashen cross and the vices of the sefirot on the Tree of Life. Try to identify specific memories and current ways of thinking and acting that have produced or are now leading you to feel guilt, shame, remorse, regret, disappointment, frustration, fear, pain, or anger with yourself. Question all your motives, intentions, and means for everything you have done and are doing. Do not allow yourself to accept any idea that is an excuse or hollow justification for acting in ways that you know were or are less than genuinely virtuous, understanding, compassionate, and honorable. Be especially vigilant for willful ignorance. This vice is the avoidance or denial of information that would make it too hard to wash your hands of responsibility and accountability for the suffering you create or enable. While it is vital to allow all the noted thoughts and feelings to arise and be courageously accepted, it is not advisable to try exaggerating or amplifying them. As with the previous stage, the best benefit comes with nonjudgmental awareness and acceptance of our humanity.

7. When you are ready, end the operation with the fitting level of closing.

Supportive Practices

During your ordinary activities and in your dreams, try to be as aware as possible of all instances, signs, symbols, and allusions of the vices on the Tree of Life and the temptations and self-deceptions that go with them. Be sensitive to the harm such things do within you and in Nature around you, including the thoughts and feelings of other beings. Ongoing performance of all the circulations of subtle energy and working with the archangel Mikael through the Protection Ritual are advised for this stage.

RECOMMENDED READING

- *Owning Your Own Shadow: Understanding the Dark Side of the Psyche*, by Robert A. Johnson

- *Ordinary Vices*, by Judith N. Shklar

- *Meeting the Shadow: The Hidden Power of the Dark Side of Human Nature*, by Connie Zweig, et al

OPTIONAL SYMBOLIC ELEMENTS FOR THE ORATORY

- A gray or silver candle

- An image of a fiery dragon or serpent

- Dragon's Blood incense, due to its association with Gevurah and thus Fire

STAGE THREE: THE WHITE CROSS

Having reduced so many of your self-deceptions to ash, it is now time to wash away that residue and reveal the enduring goodness within you. In this operation, an important focus is to realize that, despite your ignorance, vices, and mixed motives and intentions (and often interwoven with them), there has always been a part of you that genuinely desires and hopes for truth, beauty, and goodness to prevail, and that wants to serve those ends by thinking and acting virtuously, for others as well as yourself. There is a guiding moral sense within you, a spiritual conscience that is not the superego, that Freudian inner critic keeping tally on an inherited list of dos and don'ts. Instead, the deeper and more authentically loving voice is rooted in the mystery of your being itself, a voice wordlessly and intuitively urging you toward virtue. Many of us have learned to ignore that voice to some degree, but this stage includes more fully reawakening to it. Here begins the process of ascent presented in Chapter 5.

Practicing the spiritual discipline of virtue can be very challenging. Both internal and external resistances and temptations are bound to arise, and we are going to miss the mark at times. It is vitally important that you contemplate and recognize that some form of ignorance is always lurking behind every failure to strike the suitable balance that *is* virtue. Perhaps you did not fully recognize or adequately assess all the relevant factors in a given situation. It may be that you did not foresee the possible consequences as well as you might have done, or, as addressed in the previous stage, perhaps it was that sneaky willful ignorance providing you with an excuse to take what seemed to be an easier, more comfortable path. But even willful ignorance itself is based on a deeper ignorance, a failure to more fully discern how much suffering it creates or enables for oneself and others.

Because ignorance is so pervasive, our patience, tolerance, and forgiveness of self and others are essential to this stage of the Transforming Cross. Patience, tolerance, forgiveness, and optimism are indispensable because they keep the door open for learning and growth, for picking up the pieces of a broken opportunity and turning them into another opportunity for insight and the development of virtue. There may be no more moving example of forgiveness than when Jesus, having already experienced betrayal, indignity, injustice, and torture, hanging on the cross and about to die a gruesome death he did not want, prayed to God, "Father, forgive them; for they know not what they do."[148]

Above the head of Jesus was written INRI. In this stage of the work, the acronym represents *Igne Nitrum Roris Invenitur*. These words are traditionally interpreted as "the nitre of dew is found by fire," or "the purifying or cleansing power of dew is revealed by fire." INRI thus becomes a summary for the meaning of the following passage from the *Emerald Tablet of Hermes Trismagistus*:

> *The Sun is its father,*
> *the moon its mother,*
> *the wind hath carried it in its belly,*
> *the earth is its nurse.*

148. Luke 23:34, KJV.

The father of all perfection in the whole world is here.
Its force or power is entire if it be converted into earth.

Separate thou the earth from the fire,
the subtle from the gross
sweetly with great industry.
It ascends from the earth to the heaven
and again it descends to the earth
and receives the force of things superior and inferior.

By this means you shall have the glory of the whole world
and thereby all obscurity shall fly from you.[149]

In the previous operation, you have been refined by fire and deepened awareness of your own innate desire for the mutual good. In Chapter 3, you were equipped with a practical understanding of what virtue is and how it works. You are now prepared to meet ignorance and failure with the grace of patience, tolerance, forgiveness, and optimism. You are ready to engage in the psychospiritual alchemy of albedo by refining and consolidating the virtues of the sefirot in your life. As you do so, keep in mind that science is amassing a growing body of evidence and understanding about how positivity actually produces long-lasting beneficial changes in your neurochemistry and neural pathways, while negativity does the opposite. You are literally doing chemical alchemy in your own body! (as you have been all along.)

A necessary preparatory step for this stage is becoming thoroughly familiar with the virtues corresponding to the sefirot on the Tree of Life, provided in Chapter 7.

Ritual Operation

1.   Perform at least a Level Two opening and then sit down.

2.   Perform at least 10 cycles of rhythmic breathing.

3.   Visualize the ashen cross within your body.

149. Translations of this text can easily be found online.

4. After a deep inhalation, begin to repeatedly intone *Igne Niturm Roris Invenitur.* Each inhalation should be slow, smooth, and full. Visualize a column of white light rising up from your feet to the top of your head. Then, with each long peaceful intonation, visualize and feel the light gushing up and out of your head like a fountain to rain back down, around and through your body. Experience it as a cool refreshing rain, gradually washing away the surface ashes to reveal a spotless solid white cross underneath.

5. After several repetitions, the cross should be experienced as clean and bright white.

6. Cease the repetitions and meditate on the bright white cross and all the virtues of the sefirot on the Tree of Life. Try to identify specific memories and current ways of thinking and acting that are examples of you practicing each of those virtues. Consider how each virtue can serve the mutual good when appropriately applied and imagine yourself exercising them in different scenarios. It is vital to welcome and embrace all the positive feelings that arise from virtuous thought and action.

7. When you are ready, end the operation with the fitting level of closing.

Supportive Practices

During your ordinary activities and in your dreams, try to be as aware as possible of all instances, signs, symbols, and allusions of the virtues on the Tree of Life, and the mutual good resulting from them. Be aware of the need for patience, tolerance, forgiveness, and optimism to encourage the development of greater virtue within you and in others. Address any habits of negativity by patiently noting them and practicing sensitivity to and nurturance of your own deep desire to think and act for the mutual good. Enjoy the positive feelings that go with working for and participating in the mutual good. Use the Insight Ritual to seek Gabriel's assistance for greater inspiration and intuition about serving truth, beauty, and goodness through the virtues. The Cabalistic Rosary is also highly valuable during this phase.

Recommended Reading

- *Bliss Brain: The Neuroscience of Remodeling Your Brain for Resilience, Creativity, and Joy*, by Dawson Church

- *Virtue: An Introduction to Theory and Practice*, by Olli-Pekka Vainio

Optional Symbolic Elements for the Oratory

- A white candle

- An image of a fountain

- Cedar incense, due to its association with Hesed and thus Water

Stage Four: The Golden Cross

In your prior work, you have engaged the sefirot on the Tree of Life in various ways. In this stage, you are challenged to more fully realize that the sefirot represent not only aspects of the natural world, including human qualities and experiences, but also divine attributes that give rise to those things. This is citrinitas, the dawning of a splendor that, in time, might fully illuminate your conscious awareness and actions.

Among Cabalists, all the divine principles, powers, and processes of creation are summarized in the Tetragrammaton, the most sacred four-letter name of God, *I-H-V-H*. Thus, in this stage the application of INRI includes the Tetragrammaton – *Intra Nobis Regnum IHVH*. Because the proper pronunciation of the Tetragrammaton is unknown, and out of reverence for the incomprehensible mystery and majesty of everything it represents, in this application it is not spoken as a single word, but is instead pronounced by its Hebrew letters, Yud-Heh-Vav-Heh.

In this version of INRI, the Tetragrammaton is acknowledged to be the presence of the Living Word of God, the Logos, within each of us, whether we recognize it or not, as was done with the Invocation of the Pentagrammaton and its opening to Christ Consciousness. It is always there, waiting to be rediscovered and more fully known. Unfortunately, many people have been led to believe that the Divine is in some remote heaven, so removed as to be out of reach, if not totally separate from us. In this stage of the Transforming Cross, you may more fully come to know that such separation is an illusion, and one of the biggest barriers to our health, happiness, and wellbeing. You are created in the image of God, and so all the divine powers, principles, and processes are within you, just as they are in Nature around you; they are the framework of your soul. Christ Consciousness is your birthright, and each sefira represents a way in which you are already in direct communion with the Supreme Alchemist and all creation.

Therefore, the Transforming Cross at this stage involves a constancy of opening to, seeking, remembering, and reflecting upon the presence of God within you, around you, in others, in all of Nature. Returning to that presence has been beautifully expressed by the great mystic poet AE (George William Russell) in his poem, "Reconciliation."

> *I begin through the grass once again to be bound to the Lord;*
> *I can see, through a face that has faded, the face full of rest*
> *Of the earth, of the mother, my heart with her heart in accord,*
> *As I lie 'mid the cool green tresses that mantle her breast*
> *I begin with the grass once again to be bound to the Lord.*
>
> *By the hand of a child I am led to the throne of the King*
> *For a touch that now fevers me not is forgotten and far,*

And His infinite sceptred hands that sway us can bring
Me in dreams from the laugh of a child to the song of a star.
On the laugh of a child I am borne to the joy of the King.

In philosophical terms, this perspective on the relationship between God and creation is known as *panentheism*. In practice, it is the enactment of St. Paul the Apostle's exhortations, "Rejoice always, pray without ceasing"[150] and "be transformed by the renewal of your mind, that by testing you may discern what is the will of God, what is good and acceptable and perfect."[151] Furthermore, if we give due regard to God as being the *One* in whom "we live and move and have our being,"[152] then we will come to see how all souls are connected to "form one body, and each member belongs to all the others."[153]

While all of these active ways of relating to God are important and fruitful, you must also know they do not offer the deepest contemplation of the Divine. In Psalm 46:10, God is reported as saying, "Be still and know that I am God." We are therefore called to practice the Prayer of Silence – the contemplative process of releasing all our thoughts, perceptions, and emotions to open ourselves to the vast, still, mysterious silence of the Holy Spirit, the ever-present yet transcendent field through which all thoughts, feelings, and perceptions come and go, from which and within which every dualistic form of consciousness emerges and disappears. In this context, we can appreciate the motto Christian Rosenkreuz chose for himself at the end of the *Chemical Wedding*, which was *Summa Scientia Nihil Scire*, "the highest knowledge is to know nothing."

A necessary preparatory step for this stage is becoming thoroughly familiar with the God Names corresponding to the sefirot on the Tree of Life, provided in Chapter 7.

---

150. 1 Thessalonians 5:16-17, ESV.
151. Romans 12:2, ESV.
152. Acts 17:28, ESV.
153. Romans 12:5, NIV.

RITUAL OPERATION

1. Perform at least a Level Two opening and then sit down.

2. Perform at least 10 cycles of rhythmic breathing.

3. Visualize the white cross within your body.

4. After a deep inhalation, begin to repeatedly intone *Intra Nobis Regnum IHVH*. Each inhalation should be slow, smooth, and full as you visualize drawing golden light into the white cross from the atmosphere around you. Then, with each joyful intonation, visualize and feel the light radiating out into the universe. Experience the golden light as warm, pleasant, and healing, gradually transforming the white cross into gold.

5. After several repetitions, the cross should be experienced as solid, radiant gold.

6. Cease the repetitions and meditate on the glorious golden cross and all the God Names of the sefirot on the Tree of Life. Consider how each sefira represents a way of directly communing with God, healing you both internally and in your interactions with other people and all of Nature. Welcome and embrace the genuine humility and gratitude arising from knowing that you owe everything to the presence of the Divine within and around you, and dwell on the thoughts and feelings of your interconnectedness with everything. At the same time, remember the unfathomable mysteries and meet them with a genuine sense of awe and excitement about the blessing of being a conscious participant and co-creator, in the artistic revelation of God's infinite potentials. Most importantly, practice the Prayer of Silence, sitting in openness to the infinite, ineffable No-Thing that makes all things possible. Extending the minimum meditation time to 20 minutes is recommended in order to allow for more time in the Prayer of Silence.

SUPPORTIVE PRACTICES

During your ordinary activities and in your dreams, try to be as aware as possible of all instances, signs, symbols, and allusions of the sefirot, and thus the God Names and the active healing presence of God within you and in Nature around you. Remind yourself of the mysteries interwoven with all things, responding with wonder and enthusiasm for the gift of having a part in the unfolding of God's unbounded artistry. Allow yourself moments of stillness and silence to simply be present in nonjudgmental acceptance and awareness of what *is*. The Invocation of the Pentagrammaton, Adoration of Nature, and Cabalistic Rosary should all be employed during this stage.

RECOMMENDED READING

- *Nature Mysticism*, by John Edward Mercer

- *Panentheism Across the World's Traditions*, by Loriliai Biernacki and Philip Clayton

- *Mystery Teachings from the Living Earth: An Introduction to Spiritual Ecology*, by John Michael Greer

OPTIONAL SYMBOLIC ELEMENTS FOR THE ORATORY

- A gold or yellow candle

- An image of sunrise

- Frankincense incense, due to its association with the sefira Tiferet, Beauty, where the God Name is *YHVH Aloa Ve Daat*, meaning "God manifest in the mind"

STAGE FIVE: THE ROSE+CROSS

> *[...] divine love does not oppress or lead its servant to the shades below as a captive and a slave, but raises, uplifts, and exalts him above every freedom.*

[...]

Because the heart is enflamed by the divine love, it is finally converted to fire and can enkindle whatever comes in contact with it; for having contracted the divinity to itself it becomes god-like, and consequently its aspect has the power to inspire love, just as in the moon the splendor of the sun can be contemplated and glorified.[154]

The work of this stage is focused on rubedo, the fullest possible conjunction and harmonious integration of the elements of your being with an awareness of God in Nature, including you and all other beings. If your efforts are effective, then the heart of your individuality is more completely filling with the ever-present, eternally-renewing lifeforce and the mysterious, transcendent illumination of Spirit. This union is the meeting of the *Divine Word* and *Divine Wisdom* within you to flower as a unique manifestation of Divine Love. Just as it is the nature of a blooming rose to freely and selflessly share the loveliness of its appearance, fragrance, and nectar, so do you more graciously share the beauties of Love itself, loving the Divine with all that you are and loving others as yourself, just as Jesus directed.

It is important to realize that your love and the Divine Love are intimately linked. "What we are seeking is what is seeking."[155] It is the Divine within us that stirs us to know the Divine. It is your love of the Divine Word that makes a larger place for Christ Consciousness and your love of Divine Wisdom that beckons its inspirations to descend into your heart. Your love brings them together, and their union within you, in turn, magnifies your communion with Divine Love.

Therefore, my friends, let us worship this divine Love which is so kind and favorable to us; let us worship it in such a way

---

154. Giordano Bruno, *The Heroic Frenzies* (1585), Paulo Eugene Memmo, Jr. trans. (1964), Esoteric Archives, *http://esotericarchives.com/bruno/furori.htm.*
155. This quote is attributed to St. Francis of Assisi.

that we come to revere the Wisdom of God and stand in awe and wonder before the Power of God, and thus, through Love, receive the favor of the Godhead in its entirety; and, by loving the Godhead in its entirety by means of Love, we may enjoy it all with everlasting Love.[156]

Divine Love deserves the loftiest concept of it that we can manage. St. Paul tells us it is greater than all other things, even faith and hope, and that without it everything else is meaningless.[157] You are now urged to consider that if there is a divine dimension to human love, or beyond that, if God *is* Love, as attested in the First Epistle of John, then Love must ultimately surpass all the dualistic ways in which we typically relate to it. Divine Love cannot merely be the feelings of attraction and affection that are opposed by feelings of repulsion and dislike, nor is it simply a courageous and compassionate attitude that can be hindered by fear and selfishness. Likewise, Love is not limited to caring ways of thinking and acting that can succumb to hatred or apathy. For the most mystical knowledge of and participation in Love, you must be at least genuinely open to the possibility that Divine Love, and thus the root of human love, is both an ineffably transcendent mystery and an immediately present reality. You are always experiencing and expressing Divine Love in limited forms, within and around you, whether you are aware of it or not.

Given that Divine Love is beyond all opposition, you can begin to see how Love is the Great Reconciler and Redeemer, the quintessence of what Rosicrucian alchemists call the Universal Medicine. On the fifth day of the *Chemical Wedding*, a circle of nymphs sweetly sings of the power of the Universal Medicine with this song:

I

There is nothing better here below,
Than beauteous, noble, Love;

---

156. Marcilio Ficino, *On the Nature of Love: Ficino on Plato's Symposium*, Arthur Farndell, trans. (London: Shepheard-Walwyn, 2016), 160.
157. See 1 Corinthians 13.

Whereby we like to God do grow,
And none to grief do move.
Wherefore let's chant it to the King,
That all the sea thereof may ring.
We question; answer you.

II

What was it that at first us made
It was Love.
And what hath Grace afresh conveyed?
It is Love.
Whence wasn't (pray tell us) we were born?
Of Love
How came we then again forlorn?
Sans Love.

III

Who was it (say) that us conceived?
It was Love.
Who Suckled, Nursed, and Relieved?
It was Love.
What is it we to our parents owe?
It is Love.
What do they us such kindness show?
Of Love.

IV

Who gathers in the Victory?
It is Love.
Can Love by search obtained be?
By Love.
How may a Man good works perform?
Through Love.
Who into one can two transform?
It is Love.

V

Then let our Song sound,
Until it's Echo rebound.
To Loves honor and praise,
Which may ever increase
With our noble Princes, the King,
and the Queen,
The Soul is departed,
Their bodies are within.

VI

And as long as we live,
God graciously give;
That as great love and Amity,
They bear each other mightily;
So we likewise, by Loves own Flame,
May reconjoin them once again.

VII

Then this annoy
Into great Joy
(If many thousand younglings deign)
Shall change, and ever so remain.

The question now is about the extent to which you intentionally seek to be a more aware and active instrument of the Universal Medicine, and thus serve to reconjoin the King of the Divine Word and the Queen of Divine Wisdom in your life and the world around you. Will you more earnestly pursue a love affair with Love?

In the following operation, the Pentagrammaton is incorporated in this version of the INRI acronym, *Ieshuah Nascente Rosa Innovatur*, which means, "Yeshuah ascending renews the rose." You will also make use of the compound name, *Christo-Sofia*, which represents the conscious marriage of the Divine Word and Divine Wisdom in Divine Love. The names Yeshuah and Christo-Sofia help evoke healing and the fullest realization of the Divine at all levels of our being.

RITUAL OPERATION

1. Perform at lease a Level Two opening and then sit down.

2. Perform at least 10 cycles of rhythmic breathing.

3. Visualize the gold cross within your body.

4. With a first slow, smooth, full inhalation, visualize a green leafy stem growing up from the base of the cross and spiraling around it all the way to the top at your brow, where it sprouts three leaves. Then, with the first exhalation, intone *Ieshuah Nascente Rosa Innovatur* and visualize and feel a large, beautiful, dewy red rose blooming around your heart at the crux. With each subsequent inhalation, draw a pulse of green light all the way up the spiraling stem to the three leaves at the level of your brow. With each subsequent intonation, visualize the rose and your heart sparkling with dew and radiating a lovely red glow. After several repetitions, the imagery should be well established, and you may stop the intonations and continue to the next step.

5. Recall Keter above your head. With a first inhalation, visualize a dove of white light descending from Keter straight down the cross to merge with your rose-heart and form a white-winged, dewy, rose-framed heart at the center of the golden cross. Then, intone *Christo-Sofia*, seeing and feeling your winged, dewy rose-heart radiating a pink aura of Divine Love. With each subsequent inhalation, visualize and feel a pulse of white light descending from Keter into your winged, dewy rose-heart. With each subsequent intonation, see and feel your winged, dewy rose-heart glowing with the pink light of Divine Love. After several repetitions, the imagery should be well established.

6. Cease the repetitions and meditate on your beautiful, dewy, winged rose-heart at the center of the golden cross. Reflect on the Divine Names of *Yeshuah* and *Christo-Sofia*. Consider the conjunction of the Divine Word and Divine Wisdom in your communion with God and Nature, including other beings. Welcome and embrace every hint of and reaction to Divine Love within you and others. Contemplate the mysterious healing power of Divine Love, beyond all duality and opposition, as well as the immediately knowable presence of its limited forms in this world.

SUPPORTIVE PRACTICES

During your ordinary activities and in your dreams, try to be as aware as possible of all instances, signs, symbols, and allusions to the Divine Names of *Yeshuah* and *Christo-Sofia*. Strive to be sensitive to the Divine Word, the Divine Wisdom, and their union in Divine Love within you and in Nature. Remind yourself of the healing power of Divine Love, as well as its mysterious transcendence as the essence of all the limited ways beings experience and express love in this world. The Healing Ritual, Agape Chaplet, and the Invocation of the Pentagrammaton are of particular value in this stage.

RECOMMENDED READING

- *The Primacy of Love*, by Ilia Delio

- *Conscious Love: Insights from Mystical Christianity*, by Richard Smoley

- *Sophia: Goddess of Wisdom, Bride of God*, by Caitlin Matthews

OPTIONAL SYMBOLIC ELEMENTS FOR THE ORATORY

- A red candle

- Combined or separate images of a gold cross, red rose, heart, and white dove

- Rose incense

CONCLUSION

If you have conscientiously completed the Transforming Cross, then no matter what the results might have been, you are to be congratulated. Such work is not easy, and it requires deep devotion and perseverance. If nothing else, you have strengthened your own faculties of self-awareness and self-discipline, which are of inestimable value. Hopefully, and to some degree most assuredly, you now have deeper appreciation of the mysteries of your soul, reality, and God. Perhaps along the way you have had moments of true awakening to Christ Consciousness, Divine Love, your oneness with others, with Nature, and with God. In one way or another, you should know that you are not quite the same person who started the Transforming Cross and that you have indeed experienced a meaningful transformation. So, what now?

As was noted in the introduction to the Transforming Cross, this work is never finished. You will find yourself facing future challenges and going through changes that reflect the stages of this program, and now you are better prepared to meet them. The insights and skills you have developed are part of your psychospiritual toolkit, and you are free to continue using them as you see fit. You are also encouraged to remember that others are seeking just as you have done, and you are now better qualified to serve as an understanding companion, a caring servant, perhaps even a worthy mentor. Finally, any actionable answers about your next steps in psychospiritual transformation must come from the deepest voice of your own soul, from the Word and Wisdom united in Love within you.

Chapter 10:
Service

"I desire to know in order to serve." The great 20th century esotericist W.E. Butler said this was the only worthy reason for seeking esoteric knowledge. "Service, true service, is the only key. And that is the reason, service to ourselves, to make of ourselves true sacrifices, to give something worthwhile, to make of ourselves a jewel."[158]

158. W.E. Butler, *Lords of Light: The Path of Initiation in the Western Mysteries, The Teachings of the Ibis Fraternity* (Destiny: Rochester Vermont, 1990), 5-6.

In Rosicrucianism, a constant theme running through explanations of the Great Work is that one does it not only for oneself, but for others and even all of creation. This theme perfectly aligns with the understanding that there is no essential disconnection between individuals, God, and Nature, but that we humans are nonetheless plagued by the illusion of separation, the forgetting of our fundamental interconnectedness. Because of our interconnectedness, everything one does to engage the truth of unity and dispel that illusion of separation within oneself is automatically an act of service to all. Realizing our interconnectedness also means knowing that the confusions, struggles, pains, awakenings, liberations, and joys of others are also one's own, and so one develops greater compassion for others. Many of us are thus naturally moved to do more than practice contemplation and ritual for our own sakes, even knowing that the beneficial effects ripple out through the Cosmos. We increasingly feel driven to act on our compassion by helping others to heal their psychospiritual wounds and dispel the illusions that cause them.

The idea of service in the Great Work often raises thoughts of performing prayers and rituals for the healing and protection of others, teaching, and performing initiations. These are all valuable forms of service, but they are typically not the most immediate and ubiquitous ways to serve. Rather, living a life of loving virtue is at once the way most needed in our world and the most available, most direct manner in which we can practice caring for the wellbeing of everyone we come into contact with, and through them we benefit others we may never know. Let no one on a Rosicrucian path minimize the great restorative and transformative power of virtue and the inner work that supports it. Yet, as we have seen, chief among the virtues of Freemasonry, Knights Rose Croix, and Christianity is the Theological Virtue of Charity, or agape, that universal love of which compassion is a key component.

COMPASSION

Compassion is like a magnetic compass for all the other virtues. The needle of a compass naturally aligns with our planet's magnetic field, which is a constant, stabilizing, protecting, and ever-present force in our physical existence, and thus we may use it for orientation and direction.

The moral compass of compassion likewise naturally aligns with the most constant, stabilizing, protecting, and ever-present force of our spiritual being, which is Divine Love. Therefore, if we are to serve others effectively, it makes sense for us to better understand and practice compassion.

UNDERSTANDING COMPASSION

Compassion's Latin roots, *com* for "with" and *passio* for "suffering," combine to literally mean "suffering with." In the science of compassion, its more precise meaning has two parts: first, to be empathically aware of the suffering of others, and second, to desire for that suffering to be abated. We can further distinguish between *aspirational compassion* and *active compassion*, the latter of which not only wants others to experience relief from suffering but is actually motivated to take helpful action.

Through science, we are learning more truths about compassion, including that it is a natural ability. We are biologically predisposed, or hardwired if you will, to be compassionate. It is an instinct. We naturally recognize and relate to the truth of others' suffering as if it is our own. In fact, there are studies showing that, without any training or extrinsic reward, young children, most primates, and many other animals will take action to help relieve the suffering of others. One erroneous view of compassion is that it cannot be taught, and that you are born with a certain level of compassion and that is simply that. For instance, a defining characteristic of sociopaths is a lack of compassion, but research into the developmental experiences of sociopaths suggests that, rather than being innately incapable of compassion, their capacity for compassion has been impaired in some way, such as through abuse, neglect, or brain injury. We also now know that people can learn more about compassion, how to recognize it in themselves, how to develop it, make it stronger, and more consciously integrate it into their lives, just as with other natural abilities.

The world needs people of virtue guided by compassion. Much of humanity idolizes competitiveness and individualism; indeed, these qualities are often praised as bringing out the best in human beings. They can be valuable qualities; however, it does not take much depth of thought to realize that competitiveness and individualism, unguided by compassion, lead to an extremely divisive existence where the vices of arrogance, greed, and gluttony reign supreme, and the suffering of others is ignored or exploited unless there is some opportunistic profit to be gained by helping them. In such a world, engagement with other human beings is dominated by selfish attitudes, with very little concern for one's fellows. Anyone who has played team sports knows that these attitudes actually undermine a team's effectiveness. Furthermore, teammates who do not genuinely care about each other quickly turn against each other. It should be no surprise that anthropologists and sociologists observe that without compassion, we could not have evolved into highly intelligent creatures capable of building civilizations with intricate systems of interconnecting, interdependent specialties. Consider the implications of this observation for a moment – compassion is more fundamental to our evolutionary progress than other kinds of intelligence! Clearly, compassion is of utmost importance to the Rosicrucian aspiration of reforming the whole wide world. As the 18th century philosopher and Christian esotericist, Louis Claude de Saint-Martin wrote:

> *For our personal advancement in virtue and truth one quality is sufficient, namely, love; to advance our fellows there must be two, love and intelligence; to accomplish the work of man there must be three, love, intelligence, and activity. But love is ever the base and the fount in chief.*[159]

PRACTICING COMPASSION

We find a guide to the practice of compassion in Saint-Martin's conclusion that the "work of man," or the Great Work, requires the integration of love with intelligence and activity. The practice of compassion thus includes cultivation of these abilities:

- emotional awareness to feel another's pain

- identifying and understanding such feelings

- recognizing factors causing or contributing to the suffering

- determining how to effectively relieve some or all of the suffering

- taking action based on the previous points

---

159. Arthur Edward Waite, *The Life of Louis Claude de Saint-Martin, Fellowship Edition* (Jazzybee Verlag, 2015), 182.

Underlying all these abilities are those of being self-aware – intimately familiar and competent with the operations of one's own intuition, thoughts, and feelings – and knowing when and how to exercise self-care. These skills sharpen our mental and emotional clarity in the practice of compassion, and they also help us to maintain resilience, to persevere, and even to abide in peace and joy while being more authentically engaged with the suffering in this world. It is for these reasons that directly addressing service to others has been reserved for the last chapter of the book, reminding readers that each step of instruction and practice should have been conscientiously taken before proceeding to the next.

To more fully develop compassion, we need to refine our abilities of empathic awareness and emotional intelligence. A valuable aid to that process is building an emotional vocabulary that is broader, more precise, and more deeply understood. Precision not only comes with differentiating one type of emotion from another (e.g., mad, sad, glad, etc.), but also the intensities of variants within each type, or how mild or strong an emotion may be (e.g. with mad, ranging from annoyed to enraged). Understanding comes with discerning how specific emotions influence and are influenced by our experiences, thoughts, and actions. There are many charts of emotions available to the public, and you are encouraged to examine a few and then select one for the following steps of connecting that vocabulary with your external and internal experiences. It is strongly recommended that you keep a log or journal in which to record your experiences for each step.

1. Select an emotion and try to recall a time you felt it or imagine a situation that might easily give rise to it. Remember or imagine that feeling as clearly as possible, so that you actually feel it to some degree in the present moment.

2. Notice how that feeling is affecting your body. Attend to the sensations it is creating, such as tension, temperature, pressure, tingling, or pain. Look at yourself in the mirror as you allow yourself to really feel the emotion. What effect does it have on the muscles in various parts of your body, such as your face, neck, chest, belly, or hands? What about your breathing, pulse, or voice? What does it do to your sense of energy?

3. Contemplate the emotion's influence on your thoughts. What kinds of ideas, questions, and images does it naturally stimulate in your imagination? How does it affect your ability to pay attention to things, to think clearly, and make decisions?

4. What expectations, attitudes, or judgments about life, other people or things, or about yourself contribute to the occurrence of this emotion in connection with different experiences? How does this emotion relate with your beliefs about the way things should or should not be, or how you must or must not respond to things?

5. What attitudes about this emotion have been exemplified for you in your family of origin and among your close family and friends? To what extent was this emotion regarded as either a good or bad feeling, one either welcomed, encouraged, resisted, or detested? How can you come to more fully understand the emotion itself as a natural experience, while understanding that what you do with it is a matter of virtue?

6. If you were to act solely in accord with that emotional energy, what might you do? How might it affect the way you interact with other people, interpret their words and actions, and the way you speak and act toward them?

7. Other than trying to deny it or ignore it, how can
    you manage that emotional energy in order to think
    and act in the ways you regard as most virtuous and
    ethical? What mental processes can you use to integrate
    the emotion into your understanding of a situation and
    your decisions about how to respond? What attitudes
    and behaviors can you choose in order to respond in the
    wisest and most loving way?

Challenge yourself to apply these steps to a diverse selection of
emotions and especially those that seem most unfamiliar, uncomfortable, or awkward for you. As you proceed with this work of emotional
self-awareness, you can extend it into everyday life as you learn to more
habitually identify and consciously process the emotions you feel in
any moment.

While you become more thoroughly aware and familiar with
your own emotional being in this way, you can also develop the ability
to better recognize and understand the emotions of others. In other words, you can improve your ability to empathize, picking up on
others' nonverbal cues, like facial expressions and body postures, as
well as words, tones of voice, and inflections. In doing so, you are also
more likely to comprehend how their thoughts and actions might be
affected by their feelings, what initiated or amplified those feelings,
and how your own attitudes and actions might be more or less helpful
to them.

Practicing this empathic aspect of compassion with others means
intentionally attending to such things in an effort to emotionally relate
to people rather than ignoring, discounting, or judging their feelings.
However, it is also vital to avoid assuming that you know exactly what
another person is feeling or what effects the feeling is having. Becoming more comfortable with talking about emotions and welcoming
others to do likewise is therefore necessary for developing our compassion to its fullest. Engaging in such discussion also helps us move
from aspirational compassion to active compassion. In fact, simply

welcoming another human being to speak freely about their suffering can be an immensely touching act of care and concern, providing relief from the burdens of emotional silence and isolation. Further still, through such dialogue, one gains more insight with which to make well-informed choices about how best to help ease the other's pains.

In addition to developing our empathic awareness and practicing it in our connections with others, we can also make use of a contemplative process designed to more directly activate the parts of our psyches and brains that are engaged in compassion. The process advances through four phases.[160] The first phase should be practiced for at least a week, and then each phase can be successively added over a period of several weeks until you are finally practicing all four phases in each sitting. Once a working familiarity has been developed with each phase, then you may place more or less emphasis on various phases, and even rearrange them, as desired. This method is an excellent practice for anyone who wishes to serve in spiritual healing, for it helps in keeping one's soul open to the flow of higher energies and tends to infuse one's healing prayers with the special sweetness of selfless love.

PHASE 1

After at least a Level One opening, call to mind the image of someone you consider to be a great historical embodiment and exemplar of love. For instance, a Christian might think of Jesus, Mary, or one of the saints. Imagine this person standing in front of you with a loving smile. See within this person's chest a flaming heart, radiating love out through the whole body in rich hues of pink, ruby, and golden light, like a splendid sunrise. Feel the warmth on your face and chest. Let yourself respond emotionally to this great figure of love, gratefully returning the smile. Imagine your exemplar reaching into your chest to hold your heart as the flames of love flow into and ignite it. If you feel moved to weep with gratitude or smile or laugh with joy, allow

160. From C.R. Dunning, Jr., *Contemplative Masonry*, (Stone Guild: 2016), 203-210.

that to happen as you continue to meditate upon this person as an embodiment of Divine Love, a living vessel through which God loves the world, including you. To accept this love is itself an act of love for God, for the exemplar, and for yourself. You may speak with your exemplar if you wish.

In your meditation, consider that to ancient people the heart was not merely symbolic of emotions but was also the seat of intuition, inspiration, beauty, peace, and harmony. There is much to encounter here about the nature of love, which includes far more than our feelings of affection and sympathy, and actually subsumes and transcends all dimensions of our being. When you are ready to end the meditation, simply let the image fade. Offer a final prayer of thanks in proceeding with the appropriate level of closing, and return your consciousness to the external world, though now infused with an elevated awareness of love.

PHASE 2

Proceed through the previous exercise and, just past the point where your heart is ignited by the exemplar, allow the image of the exemplar to fade. In the exemplar's place, imagine someone among your friends and family with whom you share a deep bond of love. Perhaps this is someone you know to be in extra need of receiving love at this time. See the individual smiling in the warmth of the pink, ruby, and golden light radiating out through your body. Imagine yourself reaching forward to hold that person's heart in your hands. See and feel the flames of your heart flowing through your arms to ignite the other person's heart with love. Speak your love to this person if you wish. Meditate upon the love you have shared, how it has been expressed between you, and how it might grow.

When you are ready, allow that person's image to fade. If you feel moved to do so, allow the image of another cherished friend or family member to arise, and then repeat the entire process. You can continue through as many loved ones as you wish, eventually ending the meditation as before.

As with the previous phase, this can be a very touching and joyful exercise, and yet it can also prove challenging. In focusing on your love for another, you might discover areas of uncertainty or sense something lacking. For example, you might realize that in some way you have not been as expressive of your love and affection as you might be. This could be due to various fears or inhibitions for either or both of you. You might also discover you have resentments, frustrations, or other negative feelings about the individual that seem to prevent you from more fully and freely loving. As you practice the exercise with different people in mind, you may become more aware of how your love differs from one person to another. With some people, your sentiments might be more affectionate, with others, more appreciative or admiring, while for others, you may feel more compassionate or sympathetic. In any case, this phase of spreading the cement can help you learn more about how you feel, think, and behave in your relationships with loved ones, and thus provide you with many opportunities to refine your ability to love each person in your life in a way as unique and meaningful as each one is.

PHASE 3

Work through the first two phases, and then begin extending your love toward someone you feel has mistreated or offended you in some way, or someone you have difficulty trusting. Let go of your judgment of this person and regard the individual as human being who is suffering with struggles in life, many of which you surely no nothing about. Give just as freely and energetically to this soul as you did in the second phase. Meditate upon the many pearls of wisdom in loving those we may not find easy to love. Reflect on what it means to love someone you do not necessarily like. Ponder how you might manifest love for this person more outwardly. As before, repeat the process until you are ready to end the meditation.

After working through all the previous phases, meditate upon the universe as existing within the Flaming Heart of the Divine. Recall that your heart is aflame with that same Divine Fire and think of it as a spark of that Divine Fire, as are all the hearts of God's children. Pour out feelings and thoughts of love for all of creation. Allow all the implications of meaning, virtue, and action to flow freely through your heart and mind, with neither resistance nor attachment but with awareness, acceptance and love.

Routine practice of this meditation with all four phases helps make compassionate awareness and action more habitual, flow more smoothly, and resonate with greater joy and peace. However, as we have been considering, we can also meet with challenges in striving to think and act with greater compassion. We will misunderstand, make mistakes, and sometimes grow weary from the effort required to intentionally practice compassion. After all, we are only human. We need to exercise self-compassion too, and to welcome others' compassion for us. That kind of self-love helps us to sustain our compassion for others and to refine it, and thus, to better perform the Great Work of Rosicrucianism.

TO CURE THE SICK, AND THAT GRATIS

According to the *Fama*, when acting as members of their Order, the original Rosicrucians professed only one form of service to others, which was to offer healing at no cost. Healing has therefore been a vital part of Rosicrucianism ever since, whether in the actual practice of physical medicine or psychospiritual healing. Yet, not all acts of Rosicrucian service may be acts of healing for what we might typically view as illness or injury. Indeed, in its broadest sense, any form of service which seeks to ease the burdens and benefit the wellbeing of others can be considered psychospiritual healing. Each of us, simply because we are human, suffers from various *dis-eases* or conditions in which one is, to some extent, out of harmony within oneself, with other people, the natural world, or the Divine.

ETHICS IN PSYCHOSPIRITUAL SERVICE

Before beginning such work, one should give careful consideration to the ethics of psychospiritual service. There are various perspectives on this matter, and it is suggested that you compose and write down your own code of ethics, returning to it from time to time for further contemplation and perhaps amendment. In addition to relying on the moral compass of compassion, the following principles are strongly recommended for your consideration in developing your own ethical orientation for Rosicrucian service.

1. Beneficence: This principle is about the commitment to do what is in the best interest of the individuals or groups we serve. It also includes the intention to do no harm and, therefore, to be diligent about considering unintended affects from one's efforts. This is the foundation of the other principles, which further elaborate on acting in beneficence.

2. Truthfulness: With this principle we acknowledge that we have a duty to be honest with ourselves and those we serve. We accurately communicate what we do and do not have to offer, making no claims or promises for things that are beyond our abilities and control. We clearly delineate between fact, opinion, and belief.

3. Respectfulness: Our work includes an integration of respect for God, respect for other beings, and self-respect.

    a. Respect for God means acknowledging to God, others, and ourselves that truth and the Divine Will are very often mysterious and that faith, hope, and especially love are our guiding virtues.

    b. Respect for others also entails revering and upholding their autonomy, which includes:

        i. Honoring their right to be informed about what kind of psychospiritual care would be provided;

        ii. Not acting without their prior consent;

        iii. Maintaining their confidentiality.

    c. Respect for ourselves requires us to ensure that we care for our own wellbeing and that we act with integrity and authenticity.

Finally, when performing psychospiritual service for others, it is strongly urged that one does so without asking for, seeking, or expecting compensation, as is the Rosicrucian custom. For those of us employed in helping professions, when we are acting in a professional capacity, we should carefully follow our own profession's ethical guidelines and laws regarding compensation. It is further incumbent upon us to clearly distinguish the line between our professions and our Rosicrucian service, avoiding unethical dual relationships.

PERFORMING THE WORK

There are numerous methods of psychospiritual service that readers may investigate elsewhere, but here we focus on using the archangelic rituals previously provided in this book. In essence, these rituals are used as forms of intercessory prayer or refined means of seeking and facilitating spiritual assistance for someone else as an act of compassionate service. This kind of psychospiritual work emphasizes and relies upon the wisdom and power of the Divine over the insight and control of the practitioner. Other systems require more specific training in such things as metaphysical diagnostics and the practitioner's focused generation and application of subtle energies. Careful and well-informed engagement in such systems is not discouraged, but they are best regarded as fields of expertise where one learns under the guidance of one or more genuinely qualified teachers. The present intention is to provide an approach that can be adequately learned and ethically practiced without formal training, and it is a system very similar to those employed by other Rosicrucian students and esoteric Christians.

While the present approach does not go far into diagnostics, it is helpful to consider which archangel or archangels best suit the needs of the person or group you wish to help, herein identified as the *subject*, which may even be all of humanity, planet Earth, or all of creation. Clarification is best achieved by discussing the nature of the need with the subject, if that is possible. By practicing empathic communication in keeping with the previously noted ethical principles, we avoid acting upon our own assumptions about what the subject wants or upon our own beliefs about what *should* be wanted.

Rafael is almost always the most suitable primary agent for any act of healing an illness or injury, whether physical, psychological, or spiritual. However, one or more of the other archangels can play an important supporting role, depending on the specific needs of the subject. Any of the archangels may be primary in cases where the issue or relevant factors are related to their elemental or sefirotic roles or traditional patronages.[161]

In practice, this work entails performing the archangelic rituals just as before, except that you visualize the subject positioned in the portal between you and the archangel (and the archangel's energies) going to the subject instead of to you. In cases where you cannot discover what an individual subject looks like, you can imagine a human form in white light without specific physical details. If you are trying to assist a group, you can visualize one or two leaders or a symbol of the group.

---

161. There are many online resources identifying the powers and patronages of the archangels in Roman Catholicism, Orthodox Christianity, and various esoteric perspectives.

In any case, do your best to use the subject's actual name, and it also helps to recall where the individual or group resides.

THE THEOLOGICAL VIRTUES IN ROSICRUCIAN SERVICE

Here we take an opportunity for further consideration of the significance of faith, hope, and charity in the context of service. In doing so, let us realize that, when genuine, these are far more than garments of piety. They are indeed virtues, practical means of aligning with and serving as a channel for divine attributes.

FAITH

It is apparent that this virtue is a deeply spiritual response to the fact of mystery, not to be confused with merely subscribing to the particular beliefs, doctrines, or customs of a given religious community. Hebrews 11:1 points to this relationship between faith and mystery when faith is explained as "the evidence of things unseen." Thus, the fact that we intuit and trust in the reality of something good, true, and beautiful, beyond the veils of our physical senses and personal self, is regarded as *evidence of* that enigmatic something. In 1 Corinthians 12:9, Christians are encouraged to regard faith as a gift from the Holy Spirit, something that wells up within us from beyond our ordinary conscious faculties. What is a gift if not evidence of a giver, even if the giver is unseen, and a testimony of the importance of the giver's relationship with the receiver?

Acknowledging and accepting the mystery of things is vital for Rosicrucian service to others. It is the foundation of our ability to humbly admit the limitations of our understanding about what is best for anyone, including ourselves. From this position, instead of serving with an attitude of masterful power and control over unseen forces and entities, we make sacrificial offerings of our own energies with faith that they are then directed according to the higher wisdom and understanding of the Divine. More specifically, the force of our own lovingly passionate desire to help others is delivered to the archangels, trusting that it is employed by them in the most appropriate way, and perhaps even contradicting our own best understanding of what is needed and how things should work out. In short, it is a heartfelt expression of the same humble and wise submission voiced by Jesus when his prayer to be spared from betrayal, torture, and execution ended with "Nevertheless, not my will but Yours be done."[162] Our service to others must always be thoroughly infused with this virtue.

HOPE

Faith naturally inspires hope. Hebrews 11:1 says that faith is the *hypostasis* of hope, which means it is the essence, fundamental substance, or underlying reality of hope. Faith begets hope; hope is a development of faith. Yet, virtuous hope is not only optimism in faithfully awaiting the good, beautiful, and true. It also includes a vision for how the good, beautiful, and true would appear, and that vision, in turn, urges action to assist its manifestation. For example, compassion is hopeful, because it naturally imagines relief from a particular kind of suffering and then encourages relevant efforts.

In Rosicrucian service, despite how disturbing we may find the circumstances of those we serve, we act with the virtue of hope by performing our ritual work with the most positive, spiritually affirming, optimistic, caring emotions we can generate. Our energies are ours to freely give or withhold as we so choose, and we build up and pour out those feelings in our rituals, faithfully sacrificing their energy to the Divine Will through the particular archangels we believe are most fitting. While doing so, we carefully visualize the souls of our subjects benefitting from our efforts, seeing them joyfully bathed in and

162. Luke 22:42.

glowing with light, confident in their eventual spiritual gain no matter how things may develop in the short term.

CHARITY

Charity, caritas, or agape, has already received extensive attention in this book. At this point, it may be especially meaningful to consider how Paul could declare charity to be the greatest of virtues, greater even than faith and hope, especially when it is so often asserted that faith is the key to salvation. For deeper insight, let us consider the intersection of two previous observations – first, that the virtue of faith is a gift from the Holy Spirit, and second, that a virtue is a human reflection of a divine attribute. What is it that moves the Holy Spirit to give the gift of faith? It is Divine Love. Love begets faith, which begets hope. Thus, we see the primacy of charity, that virtue through which we most align with and participate in the very Heart of God. All the compassionate acts of service we perform in faith and hope are earthly transformations that, like burning incense, return the fragrance of love to its Heavenly Source.

A CLOSING WORD

At the closing of this chapter, we return to the idea of psychospiritual chivalry introduced in Chapter 4. One of the most positive qualities of knightly virtue is being a person of courageous action in the world, not only one of noble ideas and sentiments or profound meditations and prayers. The knight of old was willing to take mortal risks, offering the body in service to a cause, and so should anyone do who aspires to more fully embody the Rose+Cross.

As we have seen, the cause of Rosicrucianism is two-fold – transformation of self and reformation of the world. To the extent that one realizes interconnectedness of self with all, then neither aspect of the Rosicrucian cause can be done justice without the other. The essence and the whole of one's being is not limited within one's skin. It is also with everyone and everything else, and it is so at all times. Therefore, those of us on a Rosicrucian path should not devalue the importance of our involvement in the material world, of very directly serving our fellow creatures, humanity, and Nature – and God within them – with our hands, feet, back, and material resources.

> *Come, you who are blessed by my Father; take your inheritance, the kingdom prepared for you since the creation of the world. For I was hungry and you gave me something to eat, I was thirsty and you gave me something to drink, I was a stranger and you invited me in, I needed clothes and you clothed me, I was sick and you looked after me, I was in prison and you came to visit me. ... Truly I tell you, whatever you did for one of the least of these brothers and sisters of mine, you did for me.*[163]

Despite the genuine importance of our private work in Cabala, magia, and chymia, we must be wary of allowing it to become an escape from physical efforts for the betterment of life in this world. Inner work and metaphysical forms of service are woefully incomplete if one is not being a lovingly virtuous presence to others, compassionately helping people in managing the burdens of their material, social, and political lives, and humbly tending to the environment we are parts of and upon which we all depend. In your pursuit of the Great Work, how do your faith, hope, and charity move you to serve a more active role in life around you? How will you voluntarily invest your time, energy, body, and other material resources for manifesting the good, the true, and the beautiful, now and for future generations?

---

163. Matthew 25:34-36, 40, NIV.

You are the light of the world. A town built on a hill cannot be hidden.
Neither do people light a lamp and put it under a bowl.
Instead, they put it on its stand, and it gives light to everyone in the house.
In the same way, let your light shine before others,
that they may see your good deeds and glorify your Father in heaven.[164]

164. Matthew 5:14-16 NIV.

AFTERWORD

AFTERWORD

Dear Reader,

  Having started this book with such a personal tone, it seems fitting to end it in a similar manner, and I want to thank my editors for suggesting it. So, I've decided to use this afterword to reflect with you on a few different ways of "keeping it real." This topic is important because, if you're like me, at various times in your psychospiritual journey, you have been or will be challenged to discern the practicality, realism, genuineness, and authenticity of your thoughts and actions. In the process, you might discover a singularly potent, all-encompassing, and ever-resilient guiding light, one that can intimately illuminate your personal self while also transcending it.

  Through my own experiences, listening to the accounts of others, and observing others, I know how very easy it is to play con games with ourselves and create all sorts of illusions without consciously realizing that we are doing so. That's easy enough to do in an ordinary life with no interest at all in esotericism and mysticism, but it can be magnified in these fields by their tendency to engage the imagination in trying to relate to the vast mysteries of the unseen and ineffable. In fact, it seems to be a common part of the developmental process that esotericists and mystics go through the experience of unconsciously building up towers of psychospiritual illusion that must eventually collapse to bring us back down to the essential truths and aspirations that were at their foundations. This process may even be somewhat necessary, because a greater number, complexity, and depth of factors involved in our illusions often can only be recognized and grasped experientially.

  Such toppling can be painful, disappointing, frustrating, angering, and even depressing, not only to oneself but to one's friends, family, and other associates. I've been through the cycle many times. I've witnessed others go through it, and some of them were so disappointed that they gave up on whatever path they were following, if not psychospiritual pursuits in general. It helps to understand that such events aren't all that unique to oneself and that there are things to learn from them that, in time, can carry us further into the mysteries and toward the ideals that call to us, further than we otherwise would have gone. With time and effort, we can get better at being mindful of the illusoriness in our work and thus become less likely to bring ourselves and others to serious pain; the process can become more consciously engaged in a proactive way and suffered less severely in a reactive way.

It's undeniably true that the biggest challenges I have faced in Christian mysticism, Rosicrucianism, Freemasonry, and, well, life, have been fueled, if not created, by my own ego. In this context, *ego* means the notion that each of us has of being a separate, self-contained, stable entity that needs to assert, protect, and defend itself. The basic issue with having an ego is overidentifying with it and assuming it is supposed to be the star of the show in one's life. Tower-toppling is always a reminder that the ego functions best as a servant of the greater self and not the master. Even so, the awareness of oneself as a somewhat unique identity is important, if for no other reason than it's a fact, but also because the ego plays a vital managerial role for one's presence in this world.

One of the ego challenges I've repeatedly needed to face is the spiritual pride spoken of in Chapter 4. It recurs because most of us don't get much of anything done in this world of Assiah without our personalities being involved in some way. For example, psychospiritual development normally requires the engagement of our personal desires, decision-making, physical actions, and social relationships. Thus, it has been easy for me to feel good about the conscious active role I take in aligning these elements of my being with the deeper inspirations and aspirations of my soul. That natural sense of satisfaction is harmless enough, perhaps even helpful, but the problems start when the ego uses it to counterattack one's own deep-seated feelings of insecurity or inadequacy, which most of us have to some extent. When those feelings are compounded by comparing self with others, then the accomplishment can suddenly become justification for arrogance and condescension toward those I would foolishly judge as lesser in some way, all with the unconscious intention of making me feel even better about myself. On the other hand, I've also caught my ego sometimes recognizing a moment of genuine humility and then seizing it and playing it up into the saccharine of false humility.

At another extreme of the ego's games are self-berating and self-flagellation, with which I also have first-hand familiarity. Yes, these too can indeed be about the ego, but now despising itself for failing to fulfill its own expectations or its inability to make the desired illusions into reality. For Christian aspirants, and others, this is often where our energy goes when we get a good honest reflection of the truth of ourselves, and the ego then overcompensates by wallowing in the mud of exaggerated guilt and shame. Here again is the ego trying to be the star of the show, this time a tragic melodrama, in which we may even be paradoxically trying to "merit" grace through our performance of self-loathing.

Then there is the whole matter of attempting to conceptualize things that ultimately transcend our conceptual minds. Intellectual types (I'm looking in the mirror here) can revel in the process of constructing models for explaining everything. We may then get so pleased with the results that the models begin to be taken too seriously, even literally. Sometimes I chuckle from reflecting on all the time and energy I've spent trying to learn or devise the finer details of things like the planes of manifestation, the particular natures of various spiritual beings and their hierarchies, the exact demarcations between one type of subtle energy and another, the most accurate correspondences between things physical and metaphysical, the ideal structure and performance of rituals, and the precise meanings of words. I'm hesitant to say that such time and energy has been wasted, if for no other reason than in hindsight, I have gained a greater appreciation for how often towers such as these have also been illusory monuments to my ego.

Moderating the ego can be tricky business, and in far more ways than presented here. I'm not aware of any quick and easy cure for egoic ills (by some accounts they can continue even beyond physical death), but I do find esoteric views about the structure of the soul to be helpful. They point toward a reality in which what one commonly knows of oneself is only a relatively tiny and fragile part of the mysterious whole. Accepting that truth can help us release some of the unrealistic expectations that become self-inflicted snares; the entire proposition of improving oneself can be rife with them. With all the talk of "annihilating" the ego in some circles, and setting aside the transcendent moments in which the ego simply disappears, in the context of everyday life, it can be more useful to consider what it might mean to depose the ego from the throne of the self, a throne that the average ego tends to enshrine within a tower of illusions. In this context, I have to say that truly welcoming and enjoying the mystery of existence, having an appreciation for the complexity and limitations of human nature, the capacity for self-compassion, a healthy sense of humor, and supportive friends and cherished mentors, are all genuine blessings from Heaven for keeping it real. I hope you know these blessings too.

Bearing these egoic reflections in mind, let's make a bit of a shift here into deeper waters. A truly mystical spirit flows throughout this book, a spirit of honoring and seeking to more fully realize our oneness with the Great Mystery that is God and all creation. Despite that spirit having been invoked from the beginning, recalled at various times, and directly engaged at other times, it may have become clouded by my giving so much attention to the work of examining, exercising, and developing the various faculties of one's personal being. I invite you to join me in trying to ensure that these matters are kept in context and not turned into another tower of egoic illusion.

In our time, religion, esotericism, and psychology are filled with authorities stressing the refinement of the personal self in one way or another, which has even been central to my career as a counselor and psychotherapist. Freemasonry has a similar focus with its work of perfecting the allegorical ashlar and polishing and adorning the mind, as does Rosicrucianism with its psychospiritual alchemical transformations. In this atmosphere, it can be easy to get the idea, and in fact it is sometimes actually taught, that the personality is the core concern of our being, if not the very point of all the cosmos. Some esotericists seem to further teach that their followers should aspire to elevate their personal selves to the status of gods, even recalling that Jesus himself echoed Psalm 82:6 when he said, "Is it not written in your Law, 'I have said you are gods'?" (Ego bait, anyone?)

As previously noted, the ego is in an important position, and the uniqueness of the personal self's fleeting appearance in creation – like a meteor, a sunrise, or a performance of improvisational art – deserves to be witnessed with respect, wonder, and joy. Yet, even at a purely ordinary psychological level, it must be admitted that one's conscious self is very small and limited. In the worldview presented by this book, the personal self is regarded as something like a temporary and constantly changing mask for the immortal soul within a staggeringly immense physical and metaphysical context. In another sense, it is like a collection of instruments – a toolkit – manifested for the purposes of higher levels of the soul, which itself is a divine emanation of God. However, our personal selves and their egos also appear to be endowed with some degree of choice about learning and embracing their potentials, aligning and harmonizing with the other aspects of self, welcoming mystery and disillusionment, and preparing for realization of the Divine through mystical devotion. It is to these ends that much of Rosicrucianism is aimed, and that is certainly true of this volume.

Some of the exercises here are obviously directed to these purposes, but they all can be. Indeed, every prescribed moment of silence in all the practices of this book can be an opportunity for the personal self to simply sit in the Prayer of Silence, open to the Divine Presence, without any expectations or conditions. We do so not to magnify ourselves; that motive is ultimately counterproductive. In such a state, we may or may not be conscious of an infusion of transpersonal wisdom, strength, and beauty, but in any case, our intention is to be more available to these principles than we would otherwise be. Progress in this work requires the willingness of the ego to not be the point of everything and the genuine humility and surrender of authentic servanthood to That which is most worthy. It may seem ironic to some, but in this way of relating to the mystery of being there is much freedom, joy, and peace to be found for ourselves and others.

Relating to the mystery of being: In many ways that phrase encompasses everything this book is about – indeed all my writings and my whole life. Really, what does it not encompass? If there is one word with which I would sum it all up, maybe by now you know that it's *Love*. Love is why all of creation came into being, why each of us was born, why we continue to be, and why we continue to beget being. Love is not only the fundamental *why* of everything, but also the essential *what* and the ever-present *how*. Nothing keeps it real better than Love; yet, nothing is more enigmatic than Love. Even in its profound mysteriousness, it is the most indispensable element of the Great Work of Rosicrucianism – healing our ills, transforming our lives, and reforming the whole wide world.

My first esoteric teacher, John Miller, communicated these views of Love to me on many occasions, and for years I had something of an intellectual understanding of his words while not really knowing or *becoming one with* their underlying truth, even after some significant spiritual experiences. Then, in the early 2000s, there came several moments that produced a mystical awakening by which the previously unrealized theme of my life was revealed, and the rightful occupant of my life's throne was recognized. In the terms of the theologian Paul Tillich, it was an ecstatic surrender to my *ultimate concern* (*Dynamics of Faith*, 1957). In the language of esotericism, it was an initiation that produced a psychospiritual regeneration and reintegration that continues unfolding to this day.

I'm not inclined to confine that awakening within conceptual boxes more specific than those, but it has certainly illuminated many of my musings. In that new light, in 2006 I wrote a kind of manifesto, which I share with you now.

> *After all these years in the study and practice of philosophy, psychology, and other crystallizations of human knowledge, after thousands of meditations and prayers, and countless dreams in both night and day, I have fallen in love with Love. After so long lightly kissing Her hand with the lip service of sophistication, I find myself reeling head over heels into the grand romance, to be seduced by the sacred Lover that is Love and Light and Life Herself. For long enough now, I have been coy with Love and settled for fascination with Her many adornments – the jewels of science that rest upon Her flawless breast, the silky rainbow of arts that are the garments veiling Her blinding perfection. I long to no longer fear being a fool for Love, and I wish to abandon myself in Her, for She is the essence of all wisdom. All the most precious sentiments and noble passions stirring in our hearts, all the most illuminating ideas within our minds, are these not the echoes of Her holy voice?*

> *The great virtues of body, mind, and spirit are nothing more than reflections of Love's transcendent beauty. No mortal can hope to cultivate or command Her, for She is the Supreme Virtue to whom we can only surrender and serve. No mystic realizes union with the Divine but through Love's unfathomable grace. St. Paul was right that faith, hope, and*

even miraculous works are nothing without Her. Yet, few of us are able to keep the eyes of our souls upon Her at all times, with all people, in all things. In our moments of failing vision, faith and hope are means by which we open ourselves to once again fall into the immediacy of Love's embrace. To have faith in each other, to trust, to give our fidelity, to have hope for our mutual benefit, to cultivate optimism and confidence that together we can give birth to peace and joy, are these not the caresses of Her fingertips?

Join me and let us be lovers of Love. Let us find Her even in those we might hate for their ignorance and fear of Her. Let us sacrifice our own ignorance and fear that we might see Love's singular light even in the distorted reflections we call evil. In Love, we need not conquer or destroy, but nurse all harm into healing and nurture all suffering as the pains of rebirth. Join me, and let us be lovers of Love.

More recently, during a contemplative retreat with the Academy of Reflection, while meditating upon the image of the Rose+Cross as a symbol of the Great Mystery, I was inspired to write a poem that I offer for your contemplation. It was obviously influenced by the song of the nymphs in the *Chemical Wedding*, which I have since learned is much like an earlier poem by Raymond Lully.

Throw Open the Gate

Christos,
Logos+Sophia,
Verbum+Sapientia,
Risen from Unthinkable Truth,
Formed by Undoable Good,
Wedded in Unbearable Beauty,
You are the Divine Word and Wisdom conjoined.
You are also your own dying god and divine child,
The ever-present becoming and passing away
Of the ineffable word of Wisdom
And the inscrutable wisdom of the Word.

O Thou Most Undeniable Absurdity,
In foolish necessity and necessary folly
We blindly seek your overtly hidden door,
Silently knocking and mutely asking
That you reveal the unrevealable.

Then seek, knock, and ask with your hearts!
Whence comes our conception of you?
From love!
By what intelligence do we know you?
By love!
With what power may we serve you?
With love!
To what end do we follow you?
To love!
How shall we be one with you
and be where you are?
I am the Rose of Love!
Behind the gate of each of yourselves,
Your willing welcoming heart is the fertile garden
Where I am born, crucified, and reborn
Upon the crux of space and time.
The light of your contemplation
Is the sunshine upon my leaves.
The tears of your sacrifices
Form the dew upon my petals.
The sighs of your joy
Carry the fragrance of my blossoming.
The acts of your compassion
Are the honey made from my nectar.
Throw open the gate
And be one with me where I Am!
Maranatha!

If you get nothing else from this volume, then I hope you feel
moved to further plumb the mysteries of Love in your own meditations, readings, conversations, and every other aspect of your life.

Perhaps you too will discover Love as the standard for keeping it real. So, now, I warmly thank you for your attention, wish you well, and leave you with a short list of recommended books on Love, some of which have been previously mentioned in this text.

- *Conscious Love: Insights from Mystical Christianity*, by Richard Smoley

- *I Want You to Be: On the God of Love*, by Tomas Halik

- *Pluriform Love: An Open and Relational Theology of Well-Being*, by Thomas Jay Oord

- *The Primacy of Love*, by Ilia Delio

- *The Work of Love: Creation as Kenosis*, by John Polkingholm

By the Cross and the Rose,
C.R. "Chuck" Dunning, Jr.

APPENDIX

Correspondences of the Four Classical Elements & Aether					
	Earth	**Water**	**Fire**	**Air**	**Aether**
INRI Term	Iebeshah	Iam	Nour	Ruach	N/A
Primary & Secondary Colors	Black & White	Blue & Orange	Red & Green	Yellow & Violet	Brilliant White & Rainbow
Archangel	Uriel	Gabriel	Mikael	Rafael	Metatron
Holy Creature	Ox	Eagle	Lion	Humanoid Angel	N/A
Direction	North	West	South	East	Up or Center
Season	Winter	Autumn	Summer	Spring	N/A
Atmosphere	Cold & Dry	Cool & Humid	Hot & Dry	Warm & Humid	Electric or Magnetic
Alchemical Sign	▽	▽	△	△	⊛
Ritual Implement	Pentacle	Chalice	Wand	Sword	N/A
Psychological Aspect[165]	Physical	Emotional	Volitional	Intellectual	Spiritual
Powers of the Magus	Tacere "To Keep Silent"	Audere "To Dare"	Velle "To Will"	Noscere "To Know"	Esse "To Be"[166]

165. It should be understood that the psychological aspects are useful generalizations, and that each element can sometimes be used to represent a different aspect than what is assigned here.

166. While it is not one of the four traditional powers of the magus, Esse, "To Be," is here suggested as a fitting correspondence for Aether.

						Color & Symbol Correspondences of the Sefirot		
Sefira	**Atzilut Color**	**Briah Color**	**Yetzirah Color**	**Assiah Color**	**Theurgic Images**	**Symbols**
Keter	Brilliance	Brilliant white	White	White flecked with gold	An ancient face in profile	Crown, point, All-seeing Eye
Hockmah	Soft blue	Pearly white	Pearly gray	White flecked with blue, red, and yellow	A bearded mature man	Wand, tower, line, Celestial Globe of Jachin
Binah	Crimson	Black	Dark brown	Gray flecked with pink	A mature woman	Vesica piscis, chalice, triangle, Saturn, lead, Terrestrial Globe of Boaz
Daat	Lavender	Silvery gray	Violet	Gray flecked with gold	A head with two faces looking in opposite directions	Empty room, an open window to black starless space, prism
Hesed	Deep violet	Blue	Deep purple	Deep azure flecked with yellow	A mighty crowned and throned king	Tetrahedron, pyramid, equal-armed cross, square, Jupiter, tin
Gevurah	Orange	Red	Bright scarlet	Red flecked with black	A mighty charioteer	Sword, spear, pentagram, pentagon, Mars, iron

Color & Symbol Correspondences of the Sefirot						
Sefira	Atzilut Color	Briah Color	Yetzirah Color	Assiah Color	Theurgic Images	Symbols
Tiferet	Rose pink	Golden Yellow	Salmon	Golden amber	A majestic king, child, sacrificed god	Rose+Cross, Calvary Cross, perfect ashlar, hexagram, hexagon, Sun, gold
Netzach	Amber	Green	Yellow green	Olive flecked with gold	A beautiful naked woman	Lamp, rose, heptagram, heptagon, Venus, copper
Hod	Violet-purple	Orange	Russet	Yellowish black flecked with white	An intersex person	Octagram, octagon, Mercury, quicksilver
Yesod	Indigo	Violet	Dark purple	Citrine flecked with azure	A beautiful naked man	Crescent, nonagram, nonagon, Moon, silver
Malkut	Yellow	Citrine, Olive, Russet, Black	Citrine, Olive, Russet, Black flecked with gold	Black rayed with yellow	A young woman, crowned and throned	Pentacle, decagram, decagon, globe, rough ashlar, stone

GLOSSARY

GLOSSARY

This glossary focuses primarily on the Hebrew, Latin, and Greek terms used in this book. Readers should understand that exact pronunciations and meanings can vary from one authority to another and that those provided here are suggestions. In general, the meaning and intent of words is more important than their pronunciations, although respect for the nuanced sounds of a language is always advised. Furthermore, when *intoning* words during ritual and meditation, some pronunciations are more conducive than others to the desired effects. So, it can be reasonable to experiment with different pronunciations, so long as they do not become different words with other meanings. Regarding intonations or chanting, while in normal speech a particular syllable is often emphasized, intoning more often gives equal stress to each syllable, including extension the vowel sounds and perhaps also those "soft" consonants such as F, H, L, M, N, R, S, etc. The bracketed pronunciations follow this guide:

Pronunciation Guide													
Phonetic Representation	A	Ay	Ah	E	Ee	i	Iy	o	u	Uh	ch	g	kh
Pronounced as in the English Word	at	ate	calm	egg	see	it	sight	go	true	up	chat	gag	•
• The kh sound is a fricative pharyngeal h, produced by constricting exhalation with the back of the tongue, as in the Scottish Gaelic word *loch*.													

Adonai Ha Aretz [ah-do-NIY hah AH-rets] Hebrew for "Lord of the Earth," a God name associated with Malkut

Agape [ah-GAH-pay] Greek word for universal unconditional love, sometimes described as spiritual love or selfless love

Albedo [ahl-BE-do] Latin for "whitening;" name of the second phase in alchemical production of the Philosopher's Stone

Amo [AH-mo] Latin for "I love"

ARARITA [ah-rah-ree-tah] acronym for the Hebrew "Achad Rosh Achdotho Rosh Ichudo Temurato Achad," which means "One is His Beginning; One is His Individuality; His Permutation is One"

Ars Naturae Ministra [ahrs nah-TU-ray mee-NEE-strah] one of two mottos found on the medal presented to Knights of the Golden Stone in the *Chemical Wedding of Christian Rosenkreuz*; Latin for "Art is the Priestess of Nature" or "Art is the Handmaiden of Nature;" also see *Temporis Natura Filia*

Assiah [AH-see-ah] Hebrew for "action," denoting the World of Action, the fourth of the Four Worlds of Emanation in Cabala

Atzilut [at-SEE-lut] Hebrew for "emanation," denoting the World of Emanation, the first of the Four Worlds of Emanation in Cabala

Aurum Nostrum Non Est Aurum Vulgi [OR-um NO-strum nohn est OR-um WUL-gee] Latin motto meaning "our gold is not the common gold," clarifying that psychospiritual alchemy is concerned with production of a metaphorical gold

Ayn [iyn] Hebrew for "nothingness" or "formlessness;" name for the first of the three Cabalistic Veils of Negative Existence, which describe the Godhead in its mysterious transcendence of the Tree of Life by primarily asserting what God is not, honoring the ineffable and incomprehensible nature of the Divine; Ayn is most transcendent and may begin to be understood as expressing how God beyond creation is ultimately not a thing, and thus is *No-Thing*

Ayn Sof [iyn-SOF] Hebrew for "infinite nothingness" or "limitless nothingness;" name for the second Veil of Negative Existence, expressing that God's transcendence is not limited by space or time

Ayn Sof Aur [iyn-sof-OR] Hebrew for "infinite light of nothingness;" name for the third Veil of Negative Existence, closest to the Tree of Life, expressing that the Divine Light is one with its Divine Source and not limited to anything literally or mentally perceptible

Azoth [AH-zoth] from the Latin *azoc*, derived from the Arabic *al-za-buq* for "mercury;" alchemists and esotericists have used this term variously for the Universal Medicine, the primary facilitator of transformation, the animating spirit secluded within all matter, the element of mercury, the god Mercury, and the astral light

Binah [bee-NAH] Hebrew for "understanding" or "intelligence," denoting the third sefira on the Cabalistic Tree of Life

Briah [bree-AH] Hebrew for "creation," denoting the second of the Four Worlds of Emanation in Cabala

Cabala [kah-bah-LAH] from the Hebrew for "reception," denoting a tradition of esoteric teachings and practices originating in Jewish mysticism, but which have also been adapted by persons of other faiths; one of the three general categories of Rosicrucian study and practice, along with chymia and magia; also commonly spelled with an initial *K* (especially to denote the Jewish tradition) or *Q* (especially to denote its use in Hermeticism), sometimes with two *B*s and/or two *L*s, and often with an *H* at the end; the present spelling with *C* is used because that is how it appeared in the earliest Rosicrucian texts, and is generally regarded as representing Christianized Cabala

Caritas [KAH-ree-tahs] Latin for "love;" often used as a translation for the Greek *agape*, and translated into English as either *love* or *charity*

Christos [KREE-stos] Greek for "anointed;" popularly used as a title for Jesus of Nazareth; sometimes used in esoteric Christianity as a title for anyone who has realized unity with the Divine

Chymia [KEE-mee-ah] Latin for "chemistry;" this spelling is here especially associated with psychospiritual alchemy, which aims at the transformation of the psyche or soul and thus one's presence in the world; one of the three general categories of Rosicrucian study and practice, along with Cabala and magia

Citrinitas [see-TREE-nee-tahs] Latin for "yellowing;" name of an intermediate step in transition from the alchemical phase of albedo to rubedo in production of the Philosopher's Stone

Cresco [KRES-ko] Latin for "I grow," "I thrive," or "I multiply"

Dat Rosa Mel Apibus [daht RO-sah mel AH-pee-bus] Latin for "a rose gives honey to the bees;" a motto from an engraving in *Summum Bonum*, a defense of the Rosicrucians by Robert Fludd

Daat [daht] Hebrew for "knowledge," denoting the pseudo-sefira between Binah and Hesed on the Cabalistic Tree of Life; akin in meaning to Greek *gnosis*

Dei Gloria Intacta [DAY-ee GLO-ree-ah een-TAHK-tah] one of several Latin mottos found on the altar in the tomb of C.R.C. in the *Fama Fraternitatis*, meaning "God's glory is inviolable"

Eheyeh [eh-he-YEH] Hebrew for "I am;" God Name associated with Keter; the full answer to Moses' question to the burning bush about God's name was *Eheyeh Asher Eheyeh*, "I am that I am"

El [el] Hebrew for "God;" the God Name associated with Hesed

Elohim [el-o-HEEM] from Hebrew, traditionally translated in the Bible simply as "God;" the root *eloh* is feminine for "god," and the masculine *-im* suffix indicates the plural; some Christian theologians see an allusion to the Holy Trinity in this name; God Name associated with Binah

Elohim Gibur [el-o-HEEM GEE-bur] Hebrew for "Powerful God" or "God of Power;" God Name associated with Gevurah

Elohim Tzabaot [el-o-HEEM tzah-bah-OT] Hebrew for "God of Hosts;" God Name associated with Hod

Emigrandum [e-mee-GRAHN-dum] Latin for "migrating"

Eros [E-ros] Greek for "love," especially used by Socrates and Plato to refer to the innate desire for and attraction to beauty in all its forms; Plotinus regarded it as the human response to or reflection of Logos

Etz Chaim [aytz KHIYM] Hebrew for "Tree of Life;" the most common Cabalistic diagram for the powers and processes of creation and consciousness

Eudiamonia [yu-diy-MO-nee-a] Greek for "well-being," especially emphasizing a positive or happy spirit

Ex Deo Nascimur, In Jesu Morimur, Per Spiritum Sanctum Reviviscimus [eks DAY-o NAH-skee-mur, een YAY-su MOR-ee-mur, per SPEE-ree-tum SAHNK-tum, RAY-wee-wee-skee-mus] Latin motto meaning "We are born in God, we die in Jesus, we live again in the Holy Spirit;" found at the end of C.R.C's eulogy in *Book T*, as described in the *Fama Fraternitatis*

Ex Fructibus [eks fruk-TEE-bus] Latin for "from the fruits"

Fidelis Sum [fee-DAY-lees sum] Latin for "I am faithful"

Fidens Non Videns [FEE-dens non WEE-dens] Latin for "trusting, not seeing" or "trusting, not understanding"

Gabriel [gah-bree-EL] Hebrew for "Strength of God," name of the archangel of the element Water and also associated with Yesod

Gevurah [ge-VU-rah] Hebrew for "strength" or "power," denoting the fifth sefira on the Cabalistic Tree of Life

Gnosis [NO-sees] Greek for "knowledge," especially referring to spiritual or mystical knowledge attained through profound insight or received through revelation

Granum Pectori Jesu Insitum [GRAH-num PEK-to-ree Ye-su een-SEE-tum] Latin motto meaning "A grain, buried in the heart of Jesus," found at the beginning of C.R.C's eulogy in *Book T*, as described in the *Fama Fraternitatis*

Haniel [hah-nee-EL] Hebrew for "Grace of God;" name of the archangel associated with Netzach

Hesed [KHE-sed] Hebrew for "loving kindness" or "mercy," denoting the fourth sefira on the Cabalistic Tree of Life

Hoc Universi Compendium Unius Mihi Sepulcrum Feci [hok u-nee-WER-see kom-PEN-dee-um U-nee-us MEE-hee se-PUL-krum FE-chee] one of several Latin mottos found on the altar in the tomb of C.R.C. as described in the *Fama Fraternitatis*, meaning "This compendium of the one Universe I made as a tomb for myself;" sometimes given as Hoc Universi Compendium *Vivus* Mihi Sepulcum Feci, meaning "This compendium of the Universe I made during my lifetime as a tomb for myself"

Hockmah [khok-MAH] Hebrew for "wisdom," denoting the second sefira on the Cabalistic Tree of Life

Hod [hod] Hebrew for "splendor," denoting the eighth sefira on the Cabalistic Tree of Life

Illuminor [ee-LU-mee-nor] Latin for "I illuminate," "I adorn," or "I make conspicuous"

INRI [EEN-ree, or by the individual letters] Latin acronym originally representing *Iesu Nazarenus Rex Ieudaeorum*, meaning "Jesus of Nazareth, King of the Jews;" also has many esoteric meanings, including these:

- *Iebeshah, Nour, Ruach, Iam* [ye-be-SHAH nor ru-AHKH yahm] Hebrew words respectively suggesting the elements Earth, Fire, Air, and Water

- *Ieshua Nascente Rosa Innovatur* [ye-SHU-ah nah-SKEN-tay RO-sah een-no-WAH-tur] Latin for "Yeshua Ascending Renews the Rose"

- *Igne Natura Renovatur Integra* [EEG-nay nah-TU-rah ray-no-WAH-tur een-TE-grah] Latin for "All of Nature is Renovated by Fire"

- *Igne Nitrum Roris Invenitur* [EEG-nay NEE-trum RO-rees een-WEN-ee-tur] Latin for "By Fire the Nitre of Dew is Revealed"

- *Intra Nobis Regnum Iehova* [EEN-trah NO-bees RAYG-num yay-HO-wah] Latin for "Within us Reigns Jehova"

Jesus Mihi Omnia [YAY-sus MEE-hee OM-nee-ah] One of several Latin mottos found on the altar in the tomb of C.R.C. as described in the *Fama Fraternitatis*, meaning "Jesus, my all" or "Jesus is everything to me"

Khamael [khah-mah-EL] Hebrew for "Seer of God;" name of the archangel associated with Gevurah

Keter [KE-ter] Hebrew for "crown," denoting the first sefira on the Cabalistic Tree of Life

Legis Iugum [LE-gees YU-gum] one of several Latin mottos found on the altar in the tomb of C.R.C. as described in the *Fama Fraternitatis*, meaning "Yoke of the law"

Libertas Evangelii [lee-BER-tahs e-wahn-je-LEE-ee] one of several Latin mottos found on the altar in the tomb of C.R.C. as described in the *Fama Fraternitatis*, meaning "Liberty of the Gospel"

Logos [LO-gos] Greek for "word," "speech," "narrative," "language," "reason," "consideration," or "causation;" variously used by Stoics, Neoplatonists, Hellenistic Jews, and Christian theologians for the self-unifying aspect of the Divine, the inherent formative principle of existence, rational animating intelligence in creation, or an intermediary divine being; equated with the Second Person of the Trinity in the *Gospel of John*

Lux E Tenebris [luks e te-NE-brees] Latin motto meaning "Light out of Darkness;" from the Knight Rose Croix Degree of Scottish Rite Freemasonry, expressing both the mystery of creation and of psychospiritual illumination

Magia [MAH-jee-ah] from the Latin and ancient Greek for "magic," especially referencing the performance of rites and rituals by which priests of ancient religions engaged with divine beings to seek wisdom and effect desired change; one of the three general categories of Rosicrucian study and practice, along with Cabala and chymia

Malkut [mahl-KHUT] Hebrew for "Dominion" or "Kingdom," denoting the tenth sefira on the Cabalistic Tree of Life

Maranatha [mah-rah-NAH-thah] Aramaic expression that may be translated as either the affirmation "the Lord has come" or the invitation "come Lord"

Mellifico [me-LEE-fee-co] Latin for "I make honey"

Metatron [ME-tah-tron] name of the archangel for Keter; chief of the archangels; the exact origin and meaning of the name is unclear, but Metatron is also called the Prince of Countenances, the Prince of the Presence, and the Lesser YHVH.

Mikael [mee-kah-EL] Hebrew for "Who is Like God" or "Likeness of God;" name of the archangel of the element of Fire, also associated with Hod

Mollesco [mo-LES-ko] Latin for "I soften" or "I become mild"

Nec Citra Nec Ultra [nek SEE-trah nek UL-trah] Latin for "neither this side nor the other side"

Nequaquam Vacuum [ne-KWAH-kwahm wah-KU-um] one of several Latin mottos found on the altar in the tomb of C.R.C. as described in the *Fama Fraternitatis*, meaning "Nowhere exists a Void"

Netzach [NET-zahkh] Hebrew for "Victory," denoting the seventh sefira on the Cabalistic Tree of Life

Nigredo [nee-GRE-do] Latin for "blackening;" name of the first alchemical phase in producing the Philosopher's Stone

Paroket [pah-RO-khet] Hebrew for "veil," "curtain," or "screen," referring to the veil in the Tabernacle (and then to the Temple of Solomon) that concealed the Holy of Holies; name of a psychospiritual boundary on the Tree of Life between Tiferet and the Astral Triad of Netzach, Hod, and Yesod

Phila [FEE-lee-ah] Greek for "brotherly love"

Pistis, Elpis, Agape [PEE-stees, EL-pees, ah-GAH-pay] Greek for "faith, hope, love," the Three Theological Virtues first presented in 1 Corinthians 13:13 and central to the ethos of Freemasonry

Probor [PRO-bor] Latin for "I test" or "I prove"

Qui Sitit, Bibet [kwee SEE-teet BEE-bet] Latin for "who thirsts, drink"

Radicabor [rah-DEE-kah-bor] Latin for "I take root"

Rafael [rah-fah-EL] Hebrew for "Healer of God;" name of the archangel of the element Air and also of the sefira Tiferet

Ratziel [rah-tzee-EL] Hebrew for "Secret of God;" name of the archangel of Hockmah

Revivisco [re-wee-WEE-sko] Latin for "I revive" or "I am restored to life"

Rose Croix [roz kwah] French for "rose cross;" often pronounced "roz kroy" by English speakers; refers to the rose cross symbol; as a color, *rose* refers to pink in French, however the range of tints and shades is broad, and images of the Rose+Croix most often bear a dark pink, ruby, or blood red rose

Rubedo [ru-BE-do] Latin "reddening;" name of the final phase in the alchemical production of the Philosopher's Stone; red and gold were often equated in alchemical texts

Sandalfon [SAHN-dahl-fon] no exact translation but can be interpreted from Greek as "Co-Brother;" name of the archangel of Malkut

Sefira [se-fee-RAH] Hebrew for "emanation" or "expression," denoting one of the ten fundamental principles of creation and consciousness represented on the Cabalistic Tree of Life; *sefirot* [se-fee-ROT] is plural

Sermo [SER-mo] Latin for "a discussion," "a discourse," or "a manner of speaking"

Shaddai El Chai [shah-DIY el KHIY] Hebrew for "Almighty Living God;" God name associated with Yesod

Shekinah [she-khee-NAH] Hebrew for "dwelling" of "settling," indicating the Divine Presence personified as a feminine spirit sometimes visible as a glorious flame or pillar of fire; associated with the Holy Spirit and Sofia

Sofia [so-FEE-ah] Greek for "Wisdom;" name of the Greek goddess of wisdom, also associated with the feminine personification of Divine Wisdom in the book of Proverbs and other texts; sometimes also associated with the Holy Spirit, the Third Person of the Trinity, and Shekinah

Solve Et Coagula [SOL-way et co-AH-gu-lah] Latin motto meaning "dissolve and coagulate," expressing a purification and refinement process in alchemy

Sub Umbra Alarum Tuarum, Jehova [sub UM-brah ah-LAH-rum tu-AH-rum ye-HO-wah] Latin for "Under the shadow of thy wings, Jehova;" the closing statement of the *Fama Fraternitatis*

Summa Scientia Nihil Scire [SU-mah skee-EN-tee-ah NEE-heel SKEE-re] Latin for "The highest knowledge is to know nothing;" the motto chosen by Christian Rosenkreuz when he became a Knight of the Golden Stone in the *Chemical Wedding of Christian Rosenkreuz*

Superaedificor [su-per-ay-DEE-fee-cor] Latin for "I build upon"

Temporis Natura Filia [tem-PO-rees nah-TU-rah fee-LEE-ah] Latin for "Nature is the Daughter of Time;" one of two mottos found on the medal presented to Knights of the Golden Stone in the *Chemical Wedding of Christian Rosenkreuz*; also see **Ars Naturae Ministra**

Tiferet [tee-FER-et] Hebrew for "beauty," denoting the sixth sefira on the Cabalistic Tree of Life

Tzadkiel [tzahd-kee-EL] Hebrew for "Justice of God;" name of the archangel for Hesed

Tzafkiel [tzahf-kee-EL] Hebrew for "Contemplation of God;" name of the archangel for Binah

Uriel [u-ree-EL] Hebrew for "Light of God;" name of the archangel of the element of Earth

Virtus Junxit Mors Non Separabit [WEER-tus yunx-eet mors non se-pah-RAH-beet] Latin for "virtue joins, death does not separate;" the motto engraved within the ring worn by Scottish Freemasons of the 14th Degree, declaring that the practice of virtue forms a bond between the human soul and the Divine and also with other souls that death cannot break

VITRIOL [WEE-tree-ol] a Latin name for sulfuric acid; it serves as an acronym in psychospiritual alchemy for the internal part of the Great Work – *Visita interiora terrae rectificando invenies occultum lapidum*, which means "visit the interior of the earth and by rectification (of yourself) find the hidden stone"

Yeshuah [ye-SHU-ah] Hebrew for "Jesus;" one pronunciation for the Pentagrammaton, the five-lettered esoteric name for Christ, represented by YHVH plus the Hebrew letter Shin, resulting in YHShVH, which is not the actual Hebrew spelling for "Jesus"

Yesod [ye-SOD] Hebrew for "foundation," denoting the ninth sefira on the Cabalistic Tree of Life

Yetzirah [yet-see-RAH] Hebrew for "formation;" the third of the Four Worlds of Emanation

YHVH [pronounced by each letter, yuhd-hay-vahv-hay] the most sacred Hebrew name for God, which in Jewish tradition is spoken by its letters, but by Christian convention may be rendered as *Jehova* [ye-HO-wah] as was done by the first Rosicrucians; "Yahweh" or "Lord" is often used in its place; the tradition of pronouncing by each letter is observed in this book when YHVH is used in God Names connected with the Tree of Life, where is it used alone specifically with the sefira Hockmah; etymologically, YHVH may be understood to suggest "Ever Becoming;" also called the *Tetragrammaton*, Greek for "four-lettered name"

YHVH Aloa Ve Daat [yuhd-hay-vahv-hay ah-LOH-ah vay daht] Hebrew for "YHVH Manifest in Knowledge;" God Name associated with Tiferet

YHVH Elohim [yuhd-hay-vahv-hay el-o-HEEM] Hebrew for "YHVH God;" God Name associated with Daat

YHVH Tzabaot [yuhd-hay-vahv-hay tzah-bah-OT] Hebrew for "YHVH of Hosts;" God Name associated with Netzach

ABOUT THE AUTHOR

C.R. Dunning, Jr. with J. Augustus Knapp's original
painting, *The Jewel of the Rose Croix*, in the library
of the Philosophical Research Society

C.R. "Chuck" Dunning, Jr. is an author, advocate, consultant,
and facilitator in contemplation and esotericism, with special interest in traditions like Rosicrucianism, esoteric Christianity, and Freemasonry. With over 30 years of experience in esoteric studies and
practice, he is a lineage holder in two different Rosicrucian systems, a
co-founder and trainer in the Masonic Legacy Society, and the founding superintendent of the Academy of Reflection. Chuck's other books

include *Contemplative Masonry: Basic Applications of Mindfulness, Meditation, and Imagery for the Craft* (2016), and *The Contemplative Lodge: A Manual for Masons Doing Inner Work Together* (2021). He was also a contributor to *The Art and Science of Initiation* (2019). In 2018, the readers of *Fraternal Review* ranked him among the top ten esoteric Masonic authors, and in 2021 they chose *Contemplative Masonry* as third among the top Masonic books since the turn of the millennium. Chuck is a popular guest speaker for both in-person and virtual events and a leader of workshops and retreats. He can be contacted through his online presence, which includes ChuckDunning.com, the Contemplative Builder YouTube Channel, and the Contemplative Builder Facebook page.

Printed in France by Amazon
Brétigny-sur-Orge, FR

13381876R00208